Get organ-ised for Biology with CGP...

There's a lot to learn in GCSE Biology, that's for sure. Luckily, this CGP book explains all the facts, theory and practical skills you'll need — with practice questions on each page to test you on what you've learned.

How to access your free Online Edition

This book includes a free Online Edition to read on your PC, Mac or tablet.
To access it, just go to **cgpbooks.co.uk/extras** and enter this code...

1779 3848 1967 8192

By the way, this code only works for one person. If somebody else has used this book before you, they might have already claimed the Online Edition.

CGP — still the best! ☺

Our sole aim here at CGP is to produce the highest quality books — carefully written, immaculately presented and dangerously close to being funny.

Then we work our socks off to get them out to you
— at the cheapest possible prices.

Contents

Working Scientifically

The Scientific Method 2

Communication & Issues Created by Science 3

Risk 4

Designing Investigations 5

Collecting Data 6

Processing and Presenting Data 7

Units and Equations 9

Drawing Conclusions 10

Uncertainties and Evaluations 11

↳ Both papers

Topic 1 — Key Concepts in Biology

Cells 12

Specialised Cells 13

Microscopy 14

More Microscopy 15

Enzymes 16

More on Enzymes 17

Enzymes in Breakdown and Synthesis 18

Testing for Biological Molecules 19

Energy in Food 20

Diffusion, Osmosis and Active Transport 21

Investigating Osmosis 22

Revision Questions for Topic 1 23

↳ PAPER 1

Topic 2 — Cells and Control

Mitosis 24

Cell Division and Growth 25

Stem Cells 26

The Brain and Spinal Cord 27

The Nervous System 28

Synapses and Reflexes 29

The Eye 30

Revision Questions for Topic 2 31

↳ PAPER 1

Topic 3 — Genetics

Sexual Reproduction and Meiosis 32

Asexual and Sexual Reproduction 33

DNA 34

Protein Synthesis 35

More on Protein Synthesis 36

The Work of Mendel 37

Genetic Diagrams 38

More Genetic Diagrams 39

Sex-Linked Genetic Disorders 40

Inheritance of Blood Groups 41

Variation 42

The Human Genome Project 43

Revision Questions for Topic 3 44

↳ PAPER 1

Topic 4 — Natural Selection and Genetic Modification

Natural Selection and Evidence for Evolution 45

Darwin and Wallace 46

Fossil Evidence for Human Evolution 47

More Evidence for Evolution 48

Classification 49

Selective Breeding 50

Tissue Culture 51

Genetic Engineering 52

GMOs and Human Population Growth 53

Revision Questions for Topic 4 54

↳ PAPER 1

Topic 5 — Health, Disease and the Development of Medicines

Health and Disease 55

Viruses and STIs 56

Plant Diseases 57

Fighting Disease 58

Memory Lymphocytes and Immunisation 59

Monoclonal Antibodies 60

More on Monoclonal Antibodies 61

Antibiotics and Other Medicines 62

Investigating Antibiotics and Antiseptics 63

Non-Communicable Diseases 65

Measures of Obesity 66

Treatments for Cardiovascular Disease 67

Revision Questions for Topic 5 68

↳ PAPER 2

Topic 6 — Plant Structures and Their Functions

Photosynthesis 69

Limiting Factors in Photosynthesis 70

Transport in Plants 71

Stomata and Transpiration 72

Adaptations of Leaves and Plants 73

Plant Hormones 74

Commercial Uses of Plant Hormones 75

Revision Questions for Topic 6 76

→ PAPER 2

◢◢◢ Topic 7 — Animal Coordination, Control and Homeostasis

Hormones...77
Adrenaline and Thyroxine..............................78
The Menstrual Cycle......................................79
Controlling Fertility.......................................80
Homeostasis — Control of Blood Glucose........81
Diabetes..82
Thermoregulation..83
Osmoregulation and The Kidneys...................84
More on The Kidneys.....................................85
Revision Questions for Topic 7.......................86

→ PAPER 2

◢◢◢ Topic 8 — Exchange and Transport in Animals

Exchange of Materials....................................87
Diffusion and the Alveoli...............................88
Circulatory System — Blood..........................89
Circulatory System — Blood Vessels...............90
Circulatory System — The Heart.....................91
Respiration..92
Investigating Respiration................................93
Revision Questions for Topic 8.......................94

→ PAPER 2

◢◢◢ Topic 9 — Ecosystems and Material Cycles

Ecosystems and Interactions Between Organisms........95
Investigating Ecosystems................................96
Ecosystems and Energy Transfers...................97
More on Ecosystems and Energy Transfers.......98
Human Impacts on Biodiversity......................99
Conservation and Biodiversity.......................100
Food Security...101
The Carbon Cycle...102
The Water Cycle...103
The Nitrogen Cycle.......................................104
Indicator Species..105
Decomposition..106
Revision Questions for Topic 9......................107

Practical Skills

Safety, Ethics and Heating............................108
Measuring Substances..................................109

Answers..111
Index..113

Published by CGP
From original material by Richard Parsons

Editors: Chris McGarry, Ciara McGlade, Rachael Rogers and Hayley Thompson
Contributor: Paddy Gannon

ISBN: 978 1 78294 571 0

With thanks to Susan Alexander and Katherine Faudemer for the proofreading.
With thanks to Jan Greenway for the copyright research.

Percentile growth chart on page 25 copyright © 2009 Royal College of Paediatrics and Child Health.

With thanks to Getty Images for permission to reproduce the image on page 48.

Definition of health on page 55 from: Preamble to the Constitution of the World Health Organization as adopted by the International Health Conference, New York, 19 June – 22 July 1946; signed on 22 July 1946 by the representatives of 61 States (Official Records of the World Health Organization, no. 2, p. 100) and entered into force on 7 April 1948.

Every effort has been made to locate copyright holders and obtain permission to reproduce sources. For those sources where it has been difficult to trace the originator of the work, we would be grateful for information. If any copyright holder would like us to make an amendment to the acknowledgements, please notify us and we will gladly update the book at the next reprint. Thank you.

Printed by Elanders Ltd, Newcastle upon Tyne.
Clipart from Corel®

The Scientific Method

This section isn't about how to 'do' science — but it does show you the way most scientists work.

Scientists Come Up With Hypotheses — Then Test Them

1) Scientists try to explain things. They start by observing something they don't understand.

2) They then come up with a hypothesis — a possible explanation for what they've observed.

3) The next step is to test whether the hypothesis might be right or not. This involves making a prediction based on the hypothesis and testing it by gathering evidence (i.e. data) from investigations. If evidence from experiments backs up a prediction, you're a step closer to figuring out if the hypothesis is true.

Hundreds of years ago, we thought demons caused illness.

Several Scientists Will Test a Hypothesis

1) Normally, scientists share their findings in peer-reviewed journals, or at conferences.

2) Peer-review is where other scientists check results and scientific explanations to make sure they're 'scientific' (e.g. that experiments have been done in a sensible way) before they're published. It helps to detect false claims, but it doesn't mean that findings are correct — just that they're not wrong in any obvious way.

3) Once other scientists have found out about a hypothesis, they'll start basing their own predictions on it and carry out their own experiments. They'll also try to reproduce the original experiments to check the results — and if all the experiments in the world back up the hypothesis, then scientists start to think the hypothesis is true.

4) However, if a scientist does an experiment that doesn't fit with the hypothesis (and other scientists can reproduce the results) then the hypothesis may need to be modified or scrapped altogether.

Then we thought it was caused by 'bad blood' (and treated it with leeches).

If All the Evidence Supports a Hypothesis, It's Accepted — For Now

1) Accepted hypotheses are often referred to as theories. Our currently accepted theories are the ones that have survived this 'trial by evidence' — they've been tested many times over the years and survived.

2) However, theories never become totally indisputable fact. If new evidence comes along that can't be explained using the existing theory, then the hypothesising and testing is likely to start all over again.

Now we've collected more evidence, we know that illnesses that can be spread between people are due to microorganisms.

Theories Can Involve Different Types of Models

1) A representational model is a simplified description or picture of what's going on in real life. Like all models, it can be used to explain observations and make predictions. E.g. the lock and key model of enzyme action is a simplified way of showing how enzymes work (see p.16). It can be used to explain why enzymes only catalyse particular reactions.

Scientists test models by carrying out experiments to check that the predictions made by the model happen as expected.

2) Computational models use computers to make simulations of complex real-life processes, such as climate change. They're used when there are a lot of different variables (factors that change) to consider, and because you can easily change their design to take into account new data.

3) All models have limitations on what they can explain or predict. Climate change models have several limitations — for example, it's hard to take into account all the biological and chemical processes that influence climate. It can also be difficult to include regional variations in climate.

I'm off to the zoo to test my hippo-thesis...

The scientific method has developed over time, and many people have helped to develop it. From Aristotle to modern day scientists, lots of people have contributed. And many more are likely to contribute in the future.

Communication & Issues Created by Science

Scientific developments can be great, but they can sometimes <u>raise more questions</u> than they answer...

It's Important to Communicate Scientific Discoveries to the General Public

Some scientific discoveries show that people should <u>change their habits</u>, or they might provide ideas that could be <u>developed</u> into new <u>technology</u>. So scientists need to <u>tell the world</u> about their discoveries.

<u>Gene technologies</u> are used in <u>genetic engineering</u> to produce <u>genetically modified crops</u>. Information about these crops needs to be communicated to <u>farmers</u> who might <u>benefit</u> from growing them and to the <u>general public</u>, so they can make <u>informed decisions</u> about the food they buy and eat.

Scientific Evidence can be Presented in a Biased Way

1) <u>Reports</u> about scientific discoveries in the <u>media</u> (e.g. newspapers or television) <u>aren't</u> peer-reviewed.

2) This means that, even though news stories are often <u>based</u> on data that has been peer-reviewed, the data might be <u>presented</u> in a way that is <u>over-simplified</u> or <u>inaccurate</u>, making it open to <u>misinterpretation</u>.

3) People who want to make a point can sometimes <u>present data</u> in a <u>biased way</u>. (Sometimes <u>without knowing</u> they're doing it.) For example, a scientist might overemphasise a relationship in the data, or a newspaper article might describe details of data <u>supporting</u> an idea without giving any evidence <u>against</u> it.

Scientific Developments are Great, but they can Raise Issues

Scientific <u>knowledge is increased</u> by doing experiments. And this knowledge leads to <u>scientific developments</u>, e.g. new technologies or new advice. These developments can create <u>issues</u> though. For example:

<u>Economic issues:</u> Society <u>can't</u> always <u>afford</u> to do things scientists recommend (e.g. investing in alternative energy sources) without <u>cutting back elsewhere</u>.

<u>Social issues:</u> Decisions based on scientific evidence affect <u>people</u> — e.g. should alcohol be banned (to prevent health problems)? Would the <u>effect on people's lifestyles be acceptable</u>...?

<u>Personal issues:</u> Some decisions will affect <u>individuals</u>. For example, someone might support <u>alternative energy</u>, but object if a <u>wind farm</u> is built next to their house.

<u>Environmental issues:</u> <u>Human activity</u> often affects the <u>natural environment</u> — e.g. <u>genetically modified crops</u> may help us to produce <u>more food</u> — but some people think they could cause <u>environmental problems</u> (see p.52).

Science Can't Answer Every Question — Especially Ethical Ones

1) We don't <u>understand everything</u>. We're always finding out <u>more</u>, but we'll never know <u>all</u> the answers.

2) In order to answer scientific questions, scientists need <u>data</u> to provide <u>evidence</u> for their hypotheses.

3) Some questions can't be answered <u>yet</u> because the data <u>can't</u> currently be <u>collected</u>, or because there's <u>not enough</u> data to <u>support</u> a theory.

4) <u>Eventually</u>, as we get <u>more evidence</u>, we'll answer some of the questions that <u>currently</u> can't be answered, e.g. what the impact of global warming on sea levels will be. But there will always be the "<u>Should we be doing this at all?</u>"-type questions that experiments <u>can't</u> help us to answer...

Think about <u>new drugs which can be taken to boost your 'brain power'</u>.

- Some people think they're <u>good</u> as they could improve concentration or memory. New drugs could let people think in ways beyond the powers of normal brains.

- Other people say they're <u>bad</u> — they could give you an <u>unfair advantage</u> in exams. And people might be <u>pressured</u> into taking them so that they could work more <u>effectively</u>, and for <u>longer hours</u>.

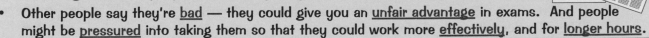

THE GAZETTE
BRAIN-BOOSTING DRUGS MAKE A MOCKERY OF EXAMS

THE POST
GENIUS PILLS TO BECOME THE NEW COFFEE

Tea to milk or milk to tea? — Totally unanswerable by science...

Science can't tell you whether or not you should do something. That's for you and society to decide. But there are tons of questions science might be able to answer, like where life came from and where my superhero socks are.

Risk

By reading this page you are agreeing to the risk of a paper cut or severe drowsiness...

Nothing is Completely Risk-Free

1) A hazard is something that could potentially cause harm.

2) All hazards have a risk attached to them — this is the chance that the hazard will cause harm.

3) The risks of some things seem pretty obvious, or we've known about them for a while, like the risk of causing acid rain by polluting the atmosphere, or of having a car accident when you're travelling in a car.

4) New technology arising from scientific advances can bring new risks, e.g. scientists are unsure whether nanoparticles that are being used in cosmetics and suncream might be harming the cells in our bodies. These risks need to be considered alongside the benefits of the technology, e.g. improved sun protection.

5) You can estimate the size of a risk based on how many times something happens in a big sample (e.g. 100 000 people) over a given period (e.g. a year). For example, you could assess the risk of a driver crashing by recording how many people in a group of 100 000 drivers crashed their cars over a year.

6) To make decisions about activities that involve hazards, we need to take into account the chance of the hazard causing harm, and how serious the consequences would be if it did. If an activity involves a hazard that's very likely to cause harm, with serious consequences if it does, it's considered high risk.

People Make Their Own Decisions About Risk

1) Not all risks have the same consequences, e.g. if you chop veg with a sharp knife you risk cutting your finger, but if you go scuba-diving you risk death. You're much more likely to cut your finger during half an hour of chopping than to die during half an hour of scuba-diving. But most people are happier to accept a higher probability of an accident if the consequences are short-lived and fairly minor.

2) People tend to be more willing to accept a risk if they choose to do something (e.g. go scuba diving), compared to having the risk imposed on them (e.g. having a nuclear power station built next door).

3) People's perception of risk (how risky they think something is) isn't always accurate. They tend to view familiar activities as low-risk and unfamiliar activities as high-risk — even if that's not the case. For example, cycling on roads is often high-risk, but many people are happy to do it because it's a familiar activity. Air travel is actually pretty safe, but a lot of people perceive it as high-risk.

4) People may over-estimate the risk of things with long-term or invisible effects, e.g. ionising radiation.

Investigations Can be Hazardous

1) Hazards from science experiments might include:

    - Microorganisms, e.g. some bacteria can make you ill.
    - Chemicals, e.g. sulfuric acid can burn your skin and alcohols catch fire easily.
    - Fire, e.g. an unattended Bunsen burner is a fire hazard.
    - Electricity, e.g. faulty electrical equipment could give you a shock.

Hmm... Where did my bacteria sample go?

2) Part of planning an investigation is making sure that it's safe.

3) You should always make sure that you identify all the hazards that you might encounter. Then you should think of ways of reducing the risks from the hazards you've identified. For example:

    - If you're working with sulfuric acid, always wear gloves and safety goggles. This will reduce the risk of the acid coming into contact with your skin and eyes.
    - If you're using a Bunsen burner, stand it on a heat proof mat. This will reduce the risk of starting a fire.

You can find out about potential hazards by looking in textbooks, doing some internet research, or asking your teacher.

Not revising — an unacceptable exam hazard...

The world's a dangerous place, but if you can recognise hazards, decide how to reduce their risks, and be happy to accept some risks, you can still have fun. Just maybe don't go skydiving with a great white shark on Friday 13th.

Designing Investigations

Dig out your lab coat and dust down your badly-scratched safety goggles... it's <u>investigation time</u>.

Investigations Produce Evidence to Support or Disprove a Hypothesis

1) Scientists <u>observe</u> things and come up with <u>hypotheses</u> to explain them (see p.2). You need to be able to do the same. For example:

> <u>Observation</u>: People have big feet and spots. <u>Hypothesis</u>: Having big feet causes spots.

2) To <u>determine</u> whether or not a hypothesis is <u>right</u>, you need to do an <u>investigation</u> to gather evidence. To do this, you need to use your hypothesis to make a <u>prediction</u> — something you think <u>will happen</u> that you can <u>test</u>. E.g. people who have bigger feet will have more spots.

3) Investigations are used to see if there are <u>patterns</u> or <u>relationships</u> between <u>two variables</u>, e.g. to see if there's a pattern or relationship between the variables 'number of spots' and 'size of feet'.

Evidence Needs to be Repeatable, Reproducible and Valid

1) <u>Repeatable</u> means that if the <u>same person</u> does an experiment again using the <u>same methods</u> and equipment, they'll get <u>similar results</u>.

2) <u>Reproducible</u> means that if <u>someone else</u> does the experiment, or a <u>different</u> method or piece of equipment is used, the results will still be <u>similar</u>.

Investigations include experiments and studies.

3) If data is <u>repeatable</u> and <u>reproducible</u>, it's <u>reliable</u> and scientists are more likely to <u>have confidence</u> in it.

4) <u>Valid results</u> are both repeatable and reproducible AND they <u>answer the original question</u>. They come from experiments that were designed to be a FAIR TEST...

To Make an Investigation a Fair Test You Have to Control the Variables

1) In a lab experiment you usually <u>change one variable</u> and <u>measure</u> how it affects <u>another variable</u>.

2) To make it a fair test, <u>everything else</u> that could affect the results should <u>stay the same</u> — otherwise you can't tell if the thing you're changing is causing the results or not.

3) The variable you CHANGE is called the INDEPENDENT variable.

4) The variable you MEASURE when you change the independent variable is the DEPENDENT variable.

5) The variables that you KEEP THE SAME are called CONTROL variables.

> You could find how <u>temperature</u> affects the rate of an <u>enzyme-controlled reaction</u>. The <u>independent variable</u> is the <u>temperature</u>. The <u>dependent variable</u> is the <u>rate of reaction</u>. <u>Control variables</u> include the <u>concentration</u> and <u>amounts</u> of reactants, <u>pH</u>, the <u>time period</u> you measure, etc.

6) Because you can't always control all the variables, you often need to use a <u>control experiment</u>. This is an experiment that's kept under the <u>same conditions</u> as the rest of the investigation, but <u>doesn't</u> have anything <u>done</u> to it. This is so that you can see what happens when you don't change anything at all.

The Bigger the Sample Size the Better

1) Data based on <u>small samples</u> isn't as good as data based on large samples. A sample should <u>represent</u> the <u>whole population</u> (i.e. it should share as many of the characteristics in the population as possible) — a small sample can't do that as well. It's also harder to spot <u>anomalies</u> if your sample size is too small.

2) The <u>bigger</u> the sample size the <u>better</u>, but scientists have to be <u>realistic</u> when choosing how big. For example, if you were studying how lifestyle affects people's weight it'd be great to study everyone in the UK (a huge sample), but it'd take ages and cost a bomb. It's more realistic to study a thousand people, with a mixture of ages, gender and race.

This is no high street survey — it's a designer investigation...

Not only do you need to be able to plan your own investigations, you should also be able to look at someone else's plan and decide whether or not it needs improving. Those examiners aren't half demanding.

Collecting Data

You've designed the perfect investigation — now it's time to get your hands mucky and <u>collect some data</u>.

Your Data Should be Repeatable, Reproducible, Accurate and Precise

1) To <u>check repeatability</u> you need to <u>repeat</u> the readings and check that the results are similar. You need to repeat each reading at least <u>three times</u>.

2) To make sure your results are <u>reproducible</u> you can cross check them by taking a <u>second set of readings</u> with <u>another instrument</u> (or a <u>different observer</u>).

3) Your data also needs to be ACCURATE. Really accurate results are those that are <u>really close</u> to the <u>true answer</u>. The accuracy of your results usually depends on your <u>method</u> — you need to make sure you're measuring the right thing and that you don't <u>miss anything</u> that should be included in the measurements. E.g. estimating the <u>amount of gas</u> released from a reaction by <u>counting the bubbles</u> isn't very accurate because you might <u>miss</u> some of the bubbles and they might have different <u>volumes</u>. It's <u>more accurate</u> to measure the volume of gas released using a <u>gas syringe</u> (see p.110).

Brian's result was a curate.

Repeat	Data set 1	Data set 2
1	12	11
2	14	17
3	13	14
Mean	13	14

Data set 1 is more precise than data set 2.

4) Your data also needs to be PRECISE. Precise results are ones where the data is <u>all</u> <u>really close</u> to the <u>mean</u> (average) of your repeated results (i.e. not spread out).

Your Equipment has to be Right for the Job

1) The measuring equipment you use has to be <u>sensitive enough</u> to measure the changes you're looking for. For example, if you need to measure changes of 1 cm^3 you need to use a measuring cylinder that can measure in 1 cm^3 steps — it'd be no good trying with one that only measures in 10 cm^3 steps.

2) The <u>smallest change</u> a measuring instrument can <u>detect</u> is called its RESOLUTION. E.g. some mass balances have a resolution of 1 g, some have a resolution of 0.1 g, and some are even more sensitive.

3) Also, equipment needs to be <u>calibrated</u> by measuring a known value. If there's a <u>difference</u> between the <u>measured</u> and <u>known value</u>, you can use this to <u>correct</u> the inaccuracy of the equipment.

You Need to Look out for Errors and Anomalous Results

1) The results of your experiment will always <u>vary a bit</u> because of RANDOM ERRORS — unpredictable differences caused by things like <u>human errors</u> in <u>measuring</u>. E.g. the errors you make when reading from a measuring cylinder are random. You have to estimate or round the level when it's between two marks — so sometimes your figure will be a bit above the real one, and sometimes it will be a bit below.

2) You can <u>reduce</u> the effect of random errors by taking <u>repeat readings</u> and finding the <u>mean</u>. This will make your results <u>more precise</u>.

If there's no systematic error, then doing repeats and calculating a mean can make your results more accurate.

3) If a measurement is wrong by the <u>same amount every time</u>, it's called a SYSTEMATIC ERROR. For example, if you measured from the very end of your ruler instead of from the 0 cm mark every time, all your measurements would be a bit small. Repeating the experiment in the exact same way and calculating a mean <u>won't</u> correct a systematic error.

4) Just to make things more complicated, if a systematic error is caused by using <u>equipment</u> that <u>isn't zeroed properly</u>, it's called a ZERO ERROR. For example, if a mass balance always reads 1 gram before you put anything on it, all your measurements will be 1 gram too heavy.

5) You can <u>compensate</u> for some systematic errors if you know about them though, e.g. if your mass balance always reads 1 gram before you put anything on it you can subtract 1 gram from all your results.

6) Sometimes you get a result that <u>doesn't fit in</u> with the rest at all. This is called an ANOMALOUS RESULT. You should investigate it and try to <u>work out what happened</u>. If you can work out what happened (e.g. you measured something totally wrong) you can <u>ignore</u> it when processing your results.

Watch what you say to that mass balance — it's very sensitive...

Weirdly, data can be really precise but not very accurate. For example, a fancy piece of lab equipment might give results that are really precise, but if it's not been calibrated properly those results won't be accurate.

Processing and Presenting Data

Processing your data means doing some <u>calculations</u> with it to make it <u>more useful</u>. Once you've done that, you can present your results in a nice <u>chart</u> or <u>graph</u> to help you <u>spot any patterns</u> in your data.

Data Needs to be Organised

Tables are dead useful for <u>organising data</u>. When you draw a table <u>use a ruler</u> and make sure <u>each column</u> has a <u>heading</u> (including the <u>units</u>).

You Might Have to Process Your Data

1) When you've done repeats of an experiment you should always calculate the <u>mean</u> (a type of average). To do this <u>add together</u> all the data values and <u>divide</u> by the total number of values in the sample.

2) You might also need to calculate the <u>range</u> (how spread out the data is). To do this find the <u>largest</u> number and <u>subtract</u> the <u>smallest</u> number from it.

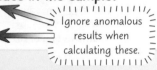
Ignore anomalous results when calculating these.

> **EXAMPLE:** The results of an experiment to find the volume of gas produced in an enzyme-controlled reaction are shown below. Calculate the mean volume and the range.
>
> | Repeat 1 (cm³) | Repeat 2 (cm³) | Repeat 3 (cm³) | Mean (cm³) | Range (cm³) |
> |---|---|---|---|---|
> | 28 | 37 | 32 | (28 + 37 + 32) ÷ 3 = 32 | 37 − 28 = 9 |

3) You might also need to calculate the <u>median</u> or <u>mode</u> (two more types of average). To calculate the <u>median</u>, put all your data in <u>numerical order</u> — the median is the <u>middle value</u>. The number that appears <u>most often</u> in a data set is the <u>mode</u>.

> E.g. If you have the data set: 1 2 1 1 3 4 2
> The <u>median</u> is: 1 1 1 <u>2</u> 2 3 4. The <u>mode</u> is <u>1</u> because 1 appears most often.

If you have an even number of values, the median is halfway between the middle two values.

Round to the Lowest Number of Significant Figures

The <u>first significant figure</u> of a number is the first digit that's <u>not zero</u>. The second and third significant figures come <u>straight after</u> (even if they're zeros). You should be aware of significant figures in calculations.

1) In <u>any</u> calculation, you should round the answer to the <u>lowest number of significant figures</u> (s.f.) given.

2) Remember to write down <u>how many</u> significant figures you've rounded to after your answer.

3) If your calculation has multiple steps, <u>only</u> round the <u>final</u> answer, or it won't be as accurate.

> **EXAMPLE:** A plant produces 10.2 cm³ of oxygen in 6.5 minutes whilst photosynthesising. Calculate the rate of photosynthesis.
> rate = 10.2 cm³ ÷ 6.5 min = 1.5692... = 1.6 cm³/min (2 s.f.)
> 3 s.f.   2 s.f.
> Final answer should be rounded to 2 s.f.

If Your Data Comes in Categories, Present It in a Bar Chart

1) If the independent variable is <u>categoric</u> (comes in distinct categories, e.g. flower colour, blood group) you should use a <u>bar chart</u> to display the data.

2) You also use them if the independent variable is <u>discrete</u> (the data can be counted in chunks, where there's no in-between value, e.g. number of bacteria is discrete because you can't have half a bacterium).

3) There are some <u>golden rules</u> you need to follow for <u>drawing</u> bar charts:

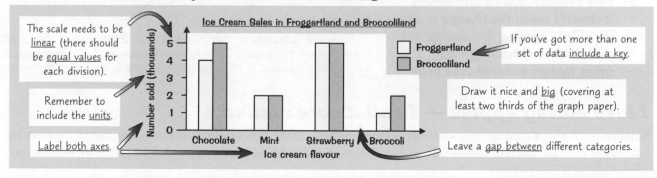

The scale needs to be <u>linear</u> (there should be <u>equal values</u> for each division).

Remember to include the <u>units</u>.

<u>Label both axes.</u>

If you've got more than one set of data <u>include a key</u>.

Draw it nice and <u>big</u> (covering at least two thirds of the graph paper).

Leave a <u>gap between</u> different categories.

If Your Data is Continuous, Plot a Graph

If both variables are <u>continuous</u> (numerical data that can have any value within a range, e.g. length, volume, temperature) you should use a <u>graph</u> to display the data.

Here are the rules for plotting points on a graph:

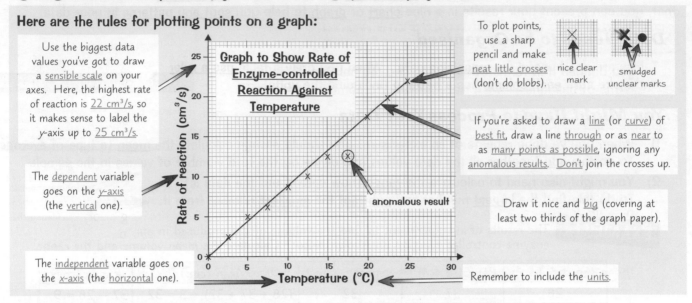

Use the biggest data values you've got to draw a <u>sensible scale</u> on your axes. Here, the highest rate of reaction is <u>22 cm³/s</u>, so it makes sense to label the y-axis up to <u>25 cm³/s</u>.

The <u>dependent</u> variable goes on the <u>y-axis</u> (the <u>vertical</u> one).

The <u>independent</u> variable goes on the <u>x-axis</u> (the <u>horizontal</u> one).

Graph to Show Rate of Enzyme-controlled Reaction Against Temperature

anomalous result

To plot points, use a sharp pencil and make <u>neat little crosses</u> (don't do blobs).

nice clear mark

smudged unclear marks

If you're asked to draw a <u>line</u> (or <u>curve</u>) of <u>best fit</u>, draw a line <u>through</u> or as <u>near</u> to as <u>many points as possible</u>, ignoring any <u>anomalous results</u>. <u>Don't</u> join the crosses up.

Draw it nice and <u>big</u> (covering at least two thirds of the graph paper).

Remember to include the <u>units</u>.

Graphs Can Give You a Lot of Information About Your Data

1) The <u>gradient</u> (slope) of a graph tells you how quickly the <u>dependent variable</u> changes if you change the <u>independent variable</u>.

$$\text{gradient} = \frac{\text{change in } y}{\text{change in } x}$$

This <u>graph</u> shows the <u>volume of gas</u> produced in a reaction against <u>time</u>. The graph is <u>linear</u> (it's a straight line graph), so you can simply calculate the <u>gradient</u> of the line to find out the <u>rate of reaction</u>.

1) To calculate the gradient, pick <u>two points</u> on the line that are easy to read and a <u>good distance</u> apart.

2) <u>Draw a line down</u> from one of the points and a <u>line across</u> from the other to make a <u>triangle</u>. The line drawn down the side of the triangle is the <u>change in y</u> and the line across the bottom is the <u>change in x</u>.

Change in y = 6.8 − 2.0 = 4.8 cm³   Change in x = 5.2 − 1.6 = 3.6 s

Rate = gradient = $\frac{\text{change in } y}{\text{change in } x}$ = $\frac{4.8 \text{ cm}^3}{3.6 \text{ s}}$ = <u>1.3 cm³/s</u> or <u>1.3 cm³s⁻¹</u>

You can use this method to calculate other rates from a graph, not just the rate of a reaction. Just remember that a rate is how much something changes over time, so x needs to be the time.

The units of the gradient are (units of y)/(units of x). cm³/s can also be written as cm³s⁻¹.

2) The <u>intercept</u> of a graph is where the line of best fit crosses one of the <u>axes</u>. The <u>x-intercept</u> is where the line of best fit crosses the x-axis and the <u>y-intercept</u> is where it crosses the y-axis.

Graphs Show the Relationship Between Two Variables

1) You can get <u>three</u> types of <u>correlation</u> (relationship) between variables:

2) Just because there's correlation, it doesn't mean the change in one variable is <u>causing</u> the change in the other — there might be <u>other factors</u> involved (see page 10).

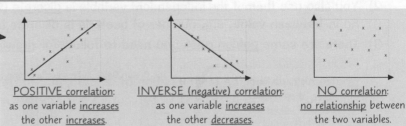

<u>POSITIVE</u> correlation: as one variable <u>increases</u> the other <u>increases</u>.

<u>INVERSE</u> (negative) correlation: as one variable <u>increases</u> the other <u>decreases</u>.

<u>NO</u> correlation: <u>no relationship</u> between the two variables.

I love eating apples — I call it core elation...

Science is all about finding relationships between things. And I don't mean that biologists gather together in corners to discuss whether or not Devini and Sebastian might be a couple... though they probably do that too.

Units and Equations

Graphs and maths skills are all very well, but the numbers don't mean much if you can't get the <u>units</u> right.

S.I. Units Are Used All Round the World

1) It wouldn't be all that useful if I defined volume in terms of <u>bath tubs</u>, you defined it in terms of <u>egg-cups</u> and my pal Sarwat defined it in terms of <u>balloons</u> — we'd never be able to compare our data.

2) To stop this happening, scientists have come up with a set of <u>standard units</u>, called S.I. units, that all scientists use to measure their data. Here are some S.I. units you'll see in biology:

Quantity	S.I. Base Unit
mass	kilogram, kg
length	metre, m
time	second, s

Scaling Prefixes Can Be Used for Large and Small Quantities

1) Quantities come in a huge <u>range</u> of sizes. For example, the volume of a swimming pool might be around 2 000 000 000 cm³, while the volume of a cup is around 250 cm³.

2) To make the size of numbers more <u>manageable</u>, larger or smaller units are used. These are the <u>S.I. base unit</u> (e.g. metres) with a <u>prefix</u> in front:

prefix	tera (T)	giga (G)	mega (M)	kilo (k)	deci (d)	centi (c)	milli (m)	micro (μ)	nano (n)
multiple of unit	10^{12}	10^{9}	1 000 000 (10^{6})	1000	0.1	0.01	0.001	0.000001 (10^{-6})	10^{-9}

3) These <u>prefixes</u> tell you <u>how much bigger</u> or <u>smaller</u> a unit is than the base unit. So one <u>kilometre</u> is <u>one thousand</u> metres.

The conversion factor is the number of times the smaller unit goes into the larger unit.

4) To <u>swap</u> from one unit to another, all you need to know is what number you have to divide or multiply by to get from the original unit to the new unit — this is called the <u>conversion factor</u>.

- To go from a <u>bigger unit</u> (like m) to a <u>smaller unit</u> (like cm), you <u>multiply</u> by the conversion factor.
- To go from a <u>smaller unit</u> (like g) to a <u>bigger unit</u> (like kg), you <u>divide</u> by the conversion factor.

5) Here are some conversions that'll be useful for GCSE biology:

Mass can have units of kg and g.

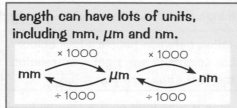

Length can have lots of units, including mm, μm and nm.

Time can have units of min and s.

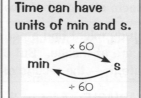

Volume can have units of m³, dm³ and cm³.

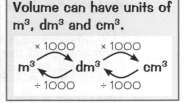

Always Check The Values Used in Equations Have the Right Units

1) Formulas and equations show <u>relationships</u> between <u>variables</u>.

2) To <u>rearrange</u> an equation, make sure that whatever you do to <u>one side</u> of the equation you also do to the <u>other side</u>.

> You can find the <u>magnification</u> of something using the equation: magnification = image size ÷ real size (see p.15). You can <u>rearrange</u> this equation to find the <u>image size</u> by <u>multiplying each side</u> by the real size: image size = magnification × real size.

3) To use a formula, you need to know the values of <u>all but one</u> of the variables. <u>Substitute</u> the values you do know into the formula, and do the calculation to work out the final variable.

4) Always make sure the values you put into an equation or formula have the <u>right units</u>. For example, if you're calculating the magnification of something, but your image size is in mm and the real size is in μm, you'll have to <u>convert</u> both measurements into the same unit (either mm or μm) before you start.

5) To make sure your units are <u>correct</u>, it can help to write down the <u>units</u> on each line of your <u>calculation</u>.

I wasn't sure I liked units, but now I'm converted...

It's easy to get in a muddle when converting between units, but there's a handy way to check you've done it right. If you're moving from a smaller unit to a larger unit (e.g. g to kg) the number should get smaller, and vice versa.

Drawing Conclusions

Congratulations — you're nearly at the end of a gruelling investigation, time to draw conclusions.

You Can Only Conclude What the Data Shows and NO MORE

1) Drawing conclusions might seem pretty straightforward — you just look at your data and say what pattern or relationship you see between the dependent and independent variables.

The table on the right shows the heights of pea plant seedlings grown for three weeks with different fertilisers.	Fertiliser	Mean growth / mm	CONCLUSION: Fertiliser B makes pea plant seedlings grow taller over a three week period than fertiliser A.
	A	13.5	
	B	19.5	
	No fertiliser	5.5	

2) But you've got to be really careful that your conclusion matches the data you've got and doesn't go any further. → You can't conclude that fertiliser B makes any other type of plant grow taller than fertiliser A — the results could be totally different.

3) You also need to be able to use your results to justify your conclusion (i.e. back up your conclusion with some specific data). → Over the three week period, fertiliser B made the pea plants grow 6 mm more on average than fertiliser A.

4) When writing a conclusion you need to refer back to the original hypothesis and say whether the data supports it or not: → The hypothesis for this experiment might have been that adding fertiliser would increase the growth of plants and that different types of fertiliser would affect growth by different amounts. If so, the data supports the hypothesis.

Correlation DOES NOT Mean Cause

If two things are correlated (i.e. there's a relationship between them) it doesn't necessarily mean a change in one variable is causing the change in the other — this is REALLY IMPORTANT — DON'T FORGET IT. There are three possible reasons for a correlation:

1) CHANCE: It might seem strange, but two things can show a correlation purely due to chance.

> For example, one study might find a correlation between people's hair colour and how good they are at frisbee. But other scientists don't get a correlation when they investigate it — the results of the first study are just a fluke.

2) LINKED BY A 3RD VARIABLE: A lot of the time it may look as if a change in one variable is causing a change in the other, but it isn't — a third variable links the two things.

> For example, there's a correlation between water temperature and shark attacks. This isn't because warmer water makes sharks crazy. Instead, they're linked by a third variable — the number of people swimming (more people swim when the water's hotter, and with more people in the water you get more shark attacks).

3) CAUSE: Sometimes a change in one variable does cause a change in the other. You can only conclude that a correlation is due to cause when you've controlled all the variables that could, just could, be affecting the result.

> For example, there's a correlation between smoking and lung cancer. This is because chemicals in tobacco smoke cause lung cancer. This conclusion was only made once other variables (such as age and exposure to other things that cause cancer) had been controlled and shown not to affect people's risk of getting lung cancer.

I conclude that this page is a bit dull...

...although, just because I find it dull doesn't mean that I can conclude it's dull (you might think it's the most interesting thing since that kid got his head stuck in the railings near school). In the exams you could be given a conclusion and asked whether some data supports it — so make sure you understand how far conclusions can go.

Uncertainties and Evaluations

Hurrah! The end of another investigation. Well, now you have to work out all the things you did <u>wrong</u>.

Uncertainty is the Amount of Error Your Measurements Might Have

1) When you <u>repeat</u> a measurement, you often get a <u>slightly different</u> figure each time you do it due to <u>random error</u>. This means that <u>each result</u> has some <u>uncertainty</u> to it.

2) The measurements you make will also have some uncertainty in them due to <u>limits</u> in the <u>resolution</u> of the equipment you use (see page 6).

The range is the largest value minus the smallest value (p.7).

3) This all means that the <u>mean</u> of a set of results will also have some uncertainty to it. You can calculate the uncertainty of a <u>mean result</u> using the equation:

$$\text{uncertainty} = \frac{\text{range}}{2}$$

4) The <u>larger</u> the range, the <u>less precise</u> your results are and the <u>more uncertainty</u> there will be in your results. Uncertainties are shown using the '±' symbol.

 **EXAMPLE:** The table below shows the results of a respiration experiment to determine the volume of carbon dioxide produced. Calculate the uncertainty of the mean.

Repeat	1	2	3	mean
Volume of CO_2 produced (cm^3)	20.2	19.8	20.0	20.0

1) First work out the range:
Range = 20.2 − 19.8
= 0.4 cm^3

2) Use the range to find the uncertainty:
Uncertainty = range ÷ 2 = 0.4 ÷ 2 = 0.2 cm^3. So the uncertainty of the mean = 20.0 ± 0.2 cm^3

5) Measuring a <u>greater amount</u> of something helps to <u>reduce uncertainty</u>. For example, in a rate of reaction experiment, measuring the amount of product formed over a <u>longer period</u> compared to a shorter period will <u>reduce</u> the <u>percentage uncertainty</u> in your results.

Evaluations — Describe How it Could be Improved

An evaluation is a <u>critical analysis</u> of the whole investigation.

1) You should comment on the <u>method</u> — was it <u>valid</u>? Did you control all the other variables to make it a <u>fair test</u>?

2) Comment on the <u>quality</u> of the <u>results</u> — was there <u>enough evidence</u> to reach a valid <u>conclusion</u>? Were the results <u>repeatable</u>, <u>reproducible</u>, <u>accurate</u> and <u>precise</u>?

3) Were there any <u>anomalous</u> results? If there were <u>none</u> then <u>say so</u>. If there were any, try to <u>explain</u> them — were they caused by <u>errors</u> in measurement? Were there any other <u>variables</u> that could have <u>affected</u> the results? You should comment on the level of <u>uncertainty</u> in your results too.

4) All this analysis will allow you to say how <u>confident</u> you are that your conclusion is <u>right</u>.

5) Then you can suggest any <u>changes</u> to the <u>method</u> that would <u>improve</u> the quality of the results, so that you could have <u>more confidence</u> in your conclusion. For example, you might suggest <u>changing</u> the way you controlled a variable, or <u>increasing</u> the number of <u>measurements</u> you took. Taking more measurements at <u>narrower intervals</u> could give you a <u>more accurate result</u>. For example:

<u>Enzymes</u> have an <u>optimum temperature</u> (a temperature at which they <u>work best</u>). Say you do an experiment to find an enzyme's optimum temperature and take measurements at 10 °C, 20 °C, 30 °C, 40 °C and 50 °C. The results of this experiment tell you the optimum is <u>40 °C</u>. You could then <u>repeat</u> the experiment, taking <u>more measurements around 40 °C</u> to a get a <u>more accurate</u> value for the optimum.

6) You could also make more <u>predictions</u> based on your conclusion, then <u>further experiments</u> could be carried out to test them.

When suggesting improvements to the investigation, always make sure that you say why you think this would make the results better.

Evaluation — next time, I'll make sure I don't burn the lab down...

So there you have it — Working Scientifically. Make sure you know this stuff like the back of your hand. It's not just in the lab that you'll need to know how to work scientifically. You can be asked about it in the exams as well.

Cells

When someone first peered down a microscope at a slice of cork and drew the boxes they saw, little did they know that they'd seen the <u>building blocks</u> of <u>every organism on the planet</u>...

Organisms Can be Eukaryotes or Prokaryotes

1) <u>All living things</u> are made of <u>cells</u>.

2) Cells can be either <u>eukaryotic</u> or <u>prokaryotic</u>. Eukaryotic cells are <u>complex</u> and include all <u>animal</u> and <u>plant</u> cells. Prokaryotic cells are <u>smaller</u> and <u>simpler</u>, e.g. bacteria (see below).

3) <u>Eukaryotes</u> are organisms that are made up of <u>eukaryotic cells</u>.

4) A <u>prokaryote</u> is a <u>prokaryotic cell</u> (it's a single-celled organism).

Plant and Animal Cells Have Similarities and Differences

The different parts of a cell are called <u>subcellular structures</u>.
Most <u>animal</u> cells have the following subcellular structures:

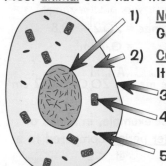

1) <u>Nucleus</u> — contains <u>genetic material</u> that controls the activities of the cell. Genetic material is arranged into <u>chromosomes</u> (see page 34).

2) <u>Cytoplasm</u> — gel-like substance where most of the <u>chemical reactions</u> happen. It contains <u>enzymes</u> (see page 16) that control these chemical reactions.

3) <u>Cell membrane</u> — holds the cell together and controls what goes <u>in</u> and <u>out</u>.

4) <u>Mitochondria</u> — these are where most of the reactions for <u>respiration</u> take place (see page 92). Respiration transfers <u>energy</u> that the cell needs to work.

5) <u>Ribosomes</u> — these are involved in <u>translation of genetic material</u> in the <u>synthesis of proteins</u>.

Plant cells usually have <u>all the bits</u> that <u>animal</u> cells have, plus a few <u>extra</u> things that animal cells <u>don't</u> have:

1) Rigid <u>cell wall</u> — made of <u>cellulose</u>. It <u>supports</u> the cell and strengthens it.

2) <u>Large vacuole</u> — contains <u>cell sap</u>, a weak solution of sugar and salts. It maintains the <u>internal pressure</u> to support the cell.

3) <u>Chloroplasts</u> — these are where <u>photosynthesis</u> occurs, which makes food for the plant (see page 69). They contain a <u>green</u> substance called <u>chlorophyll</u>.

Bacterial Cells Have No Nucleus

<u>Bacterial cells</u> are a lot <u>smaller</u> than plant or animal cells and have these <u>subcellular structures</u>:

1) <u>Chromosomal DNA</u> (<u>one</u> long circular chromosome) — controls the cell's <u>activities</u> and <u>replication</u>. It <u>floats free</u> in the <u>cytoplasm</u> (not in a nucleus).

2) <u>Ribosomes</u>

3) <u>Cell membrane</u>

4) <u>Plasmid DNA</u> — <u>small loops</u> of <u>extra DNA</u> that aren't part of the chromosome. Plasmids contain genes for things like <u>drug resistance</u>, and can be <u>passed</u> between bacteria.

5) <u>Flagellum</u> (plural <u>flagella</u>) — a long, hair-like structure that <u>rotates</u> to make the bacterium <u>move</u>. It can be used to move the bacteria <u>away from</u> harmful substances like <u>toxins</u> and <u>towards</u> beneficial things like <u>nutrients or oxygen</u>.

Cell structures — become a property developer...

On this page are typical cells with all the typical bits you need to know. But cells aren't all the same — they have different structures depending on the job they do. There's more about this on the next page.

Q1   Describe the function of these subcellular structures: a) nucleus, b) mitochondria, c) ribosomes. [3 marks]

Specialised Cells

The previous page shows the structure of some <u>typical cells</u>. However, most cells are <u>specialised</u> for a particular function, so their <u>structure</u> can vary...

Different Cells Have Different Functions

1) <u>Multicellular organisms</u> contain lots of different <u>types</u> of cells (i.e. cells with different <u>structures</u>).
2) Cells that have a structure which makes them <u>adapted</u> to their function are called <u>specialised cells</u>.
3) You need to know how <u>egg</u>, <u>sperm</u> and <u>ciliated epithelial cells</u> are <u>adapted</u> to their functions:

Egg Cells and Sperm Cells Are Specialised for Reproduction

1) In <u>sexual reproduction</u>, the <u>nucleus</u> of an egg cell <u>fuses</u> with the nucleus of a sperm cell to create a <u>fertilised egg</u>, which then develops into an <u>embryo</u>. Both the nucleus of an egg cell and of a sperm cell only contain <u>half</u> the number of chromosomes that's in a <u>normal</u> body cell — so they are called 'haploid'.

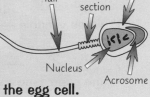
There's more about sexual reproduction on page 32.

2) This is important as it means that when an egg and sperm nucleus <u>combine</u> at <u>fertilisation</u>, the resulting cell will have the <u>right number</u> of chromosomes.

Egg cell

Nucleus

The main functions of an <u>egg</u> are to carry the female DNA and to <u>nourish</u> the developing embryo in the early stages. This is how it's adapted to its function:
1) It contains <u>nutrients</u> in the <u>cytoplasm</u> to feed the embryo.
2) It has a <u>haploid nucleus</u>.
3) Straight after <u>fertilisation</u>, its <u>membrane</u> changes <u>structure</u> to stop any more sperm getting in. This makes sure the offspring end up with the <u>right amount</u> of DNA.

Sperm cell

The <u>function</u> of a sperm is to <u>transport</u> the <u>male's DNA</u> to the <u>female's egg</u>.
1) A sperm cell has a <u>long tail</u> so it can <u>swim</u> to the egg.
2) It has lots of <u>mitochondria</u> in the middle section to provide the <u>energy</u> (from respiration) needed to <u>swim</u> this distance.
3) It also has an <u>acrosome</u> at the front of the 'head', where it stores <u>enzymes</u> needed to <u>digest</u> its way through the <u>membrane</u> of the egg cell.
4) It also contains a <u>haploid nucleus</u>.

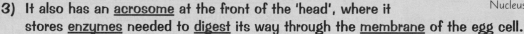
Tail   Middle section   Head   Nucleus   Acrosome

Ciliated Epithelial Cells Are Specialised for Moving Materials

1) Epithelial cells <u>line the surfaces</u> of organs.
2) Some of them have <u>cilia</u> (hair-like structures) on the <u>top surface</u> of the cell.
3) The function of these <u>ciliated epithelial cells</u> is to <u>move substances</u> — the cilia beat to <u>move</u> substances in <u>one direction</u>, <u>along the surface</u> of the tissue.
4) For example, the <u>lining of the airways</u> contains <u>lots</u> of ciliated epithelial cells. These help to move <u>mucus</u> (and all of the particles from the air that it has trapped) up to the <u>throat</u> so it can be <u>swallowed</u> and <u>doesn't reach</u> the lungs.

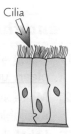
Cilia

Everyone knows eggs are specialised — fried, boiled, scrambled...

Nearly every cell in your body is specialised to carry out some kind of function, but the ones on this page are the examples you need to learn for your exams. Right, now have a go at this question to see what you remember.

Q1   a) What is the function of sperm cells?   [1 mark]
      b) Explain two ways in which sperm cells are adapted for this function.   [4 marks]

Microscopy

Without <u>microscopes</u> we would never have discovered cells. We can even use them to look <u>inside</u> cells.

Cells are Studied Using Microscopes

1) Microscopes use lenses to <u>magnify</u> images (make them look bigger). They also increase the <u>resolution</u> of an image. <u>Resolution</u> means how well a microscope distinguishes between <u>two points</u> that are <u>close together</u>. A <u>higher resolution</u> means that the image can be seen <u>more clearly</u> and in <u>more detail</u>.

2) <u>Light microscopes</u> were invented in the 1590s. They work by passing <u>light</u> through the specimen. They let us see things like <u>nuclei</u> and <u>chloroplasts</u> and we can also use them to study <u>living cells</u>.

3) <u>Electron microscopes</u> were invented in the 1930s. They use <u>electrons</u> rather than <u>light</u>. Electron microscopes have a higher <u>magnification</u> and <u>resolution</u> than light microscopes, so they let us see much <u>smaller things</u> in <u>more detail</u> like the <u>internal structure</u> of mitochondria and chloroplasts. This has allowed us to have a much <u>greater understanding</u> of <u>how cells work</u> and the <u>role of subcellular structures</u> (although they can't be used to view living cells).

This is How to View a Specimen Using a Light Microscope... 〔PRACTICAL〕

1) Your specimen needs to <u>let light through it</u> so you'll need to take a <u>thin slice</u> of it to start with.

2) Next, take a clean <u>slide</u> and use a <u>pipette</u> to put one drop of water in the middle of it — this will <u>secure</u> the specimen in place. Then use <u>tweezers</u> to place your specimen on the slide.

3) Add a drop of <u>stain</u> if your <u>specimen</u> is completely <u>transparent</u> or <u>colourless</u> — this makes the specimen <u>easier to see</u> (different stains highlight different structures within cells, e.g. methylene blue stains DNA).

4) Place a <u>cover slip</u> at one end of the specimen, holding it at an <u>angle</u> with a <u>mounted needle</u> and carefully <u>lower</u> it onto the slide. Press it down <u>gently</u> so that no <u>air bubbles</u> are trapped under it. Then <u>clip</u> the slide onto the <u>stage</u>.

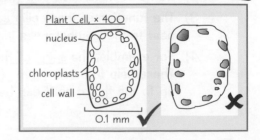

Eyepiece lens

High and low power objective lenses

Coarse adjustment knob

Clip

Stage

Fine adjustment knob

Lamp

5) Select the <u>lowest-powered objective lens</u>.

6) Use the <u>coarse adjustment knob</u> to move the stage <u>up</u> so that the slide is <u>just underneath</u> the objective lens. Then, <u>looking</u> down the <u>eyepiece</u>, move the stage <u>downwards</u> (so you don't accidently crash it into the lens) until the specimen is <u>nearly in focus</u>.

7) Then <u>adjust the focus</u> with the <u>fine adjustment knob</u>, until you get a <u>clear image</u>. Position a <u>clear ruler</u> on the stage and use it to measure the <u>diameter</u> of the circular area visible — your <u>field of view</u> (<u>FOV</u>).

8) If you need to see your specimen with <u>greater magnification</u>, swap to a <u>higher-powered objective lens</u>, <u>refocus</u> and <u>recalculate</u> your <u>FOV</u> accordingly (e.g. if your FOV was 5 mm then you swap to a lens that is 10 times more powerful, your FOV will now be 5 mm ÷ 10 = 0.5 mm).

Measuring your field of view allows you to estimate the size of your specimen.

...and this is How to Create a Scientific Drawing of a Specimen 〔PRACTICAL〕

1) Using a <u>sharp</u> pencil, draw <u>outlines</u> of the <u>main features</u> using <u>clear, unbroken lines</u>. Don't include any <u>colouring</u> or <u>shading</u>.

2) Make sure that your drawing takes up <u>at least half</u> of the space available and remember to keep all the parts <u>in proportion</u>.

3) <u>Label</u> the <u>important features</u> of your diagram with <u>straight lines</u> which <u>don't cross over</u> each other, and include the <u>magnification</u> used and a <u>scale</u>.

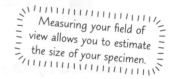

Plant Cell, × 400

nucleus

chloroplasts

cell wall

0.1 mm ✓   ✗

Gather your microscopes, comrades — it's the bio resolution...

There's lots of important stuff here about how you use a light microscope to view specimens — so get learning.

Q1 A student prepares a slide with a sample of onion cells and places it on the stage of a light microscope. Describe the steps she should take to get a focused image of the cells. [4 marks]

More Microscopy

Sometimes you need to do a bit of <u>maths</u> with microscope images. It's time to get your <u>numbers head on</u>...

Magnification is How Many Times Bigger the Image is

1) If you know the <u>power</u> of the lenses used by a microscope to view an image, you can work out the <u>total magnification</u> of the image using this simple formula:

total magnification = eyepiece lens magnification × objective lens magnification

2) For example, the <u>total magnification</u> of an image viewed with an <u>eyepiece lens</u> magnification of <u>× 10</u> and an <u>objective lens</u> magnification of <u>× 40</u> would be 10 × 40 = <u>× 400</u>.

3) If you don't know which lenses were used, you can still work out the magnification of an image as long as you can <u>measure the image</u> and know the <u>real size of the specimen</u>. This is the <u>formula</u> you need:

$$\text{magnification} = \frac{\text{image size}}{\text{real size}}$$

Both measurements should have the same units. If they don't, you'll need to convert them first (see below).

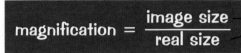

image size / magnification × real size

4) If you're working out the <u>image size</u> or the <u>real size</u> of the object, you can rearrange the equation using the <u>formula triangle</u>. <u>Cover up</u> the thing you're trying to find. The parts you can <u>still see</u> are the formula you need to use.

<u>Estimating</u> can help you to <u>check</u> that your answer is <u>correct</u>. To estimate an answer, <u>round</u> the numbers so you can do the maths in your <u>head</u>. E.g. say you know the real size of a specimen is <u>21.5 μm</u> and the image size is <u>9800 μm</u>. To get an estimate of the <u>magnification used</u>, round both numbers to <u>1 significant figure</u> (see p.7) and do <u>10000 ÷ 20 = × 500</u>.

You Might Need to Work With Numbers in Standard Form and Convert Units

1) Because microscopes can see such <u>tiny objects</u>, sometimes it's useful to write figures in <u>standard form</u>.

2) This is where you change <u>very big</u> or <u>small</u> numbers with <u>lots of zeros</u> into something more manageable, e.g. 0.017 can be written 1.7×10^{-2}. To do this you just need to <u>move</u> the <u>decimal point</u> left or right.

3) The number of places the decimal point moves is then represented by a <u>power of 10</u> — this is <u>positive</u> if the decimal point's moved to the <u>left</u>, and <u>negative</u> if it's moved to the <u>right</u>.

4) You can also use <u>different units</u> to express very big or very small numbers. E.g. <u>0.0007 m</u> could be written as <u>0.7 mm</u>. The <u>table</u> shows you how to <u>convert between different units</u>. The right hand column of the table shows you how each unit can be expressed as a <u>metre</u> in <u>standard form</u>.

Unit		In standard form:
To convert ×1000	Millimetre (mm) ÷1000	$\times 10^{-3}$ m
×1000	Micrometre (μm) ÷1000	$\times 10^{-6}$ m
×1000	Nanometre (nm) ÷1000	$\times 10^{-9}$ m
	Picometre (pm)	$\times 10^{-12}$ m

So 1 pm = 0.000000000001 m. (That's tiny!)

5) Here's an example of a <u>calculation</u> in standard form:

EXAMPLE:

A specimen is 5×10^{-6} m wide. Calculate the width of the image of the specimen under a magnification of × 100. Give your answer in standard form.

1) <u>Rearrange</u> the magnification formula. image size = magnification × real size
2) Fill in the <u>values</u> you know. image size = 100 × (5×10^{-6} m)
3) Write out the values <u>in full</u> (i.e. don't use standard form). = 100 × 0.000005 m
4) Carry out the calculation and then <u>convert back</u> into standard form. = 0.0005 m
= 5×10^{-4} m

Note: 0.0005 m could also be written as 0.5 mm or 500 μm.

Mi-cros-copy — when my twin gets annoyed...

If you've got a scientific calculator, you can put standard form numbers into your calculator using the 'EXP' or the '×10ˣ' button. For example, enter 2.67×10^{15} by pressing 2.67 then 'EXP' or '10ˣ', then 15. Easy.

Q1 Calculate the length of a cell which has an image size of 7×10^{-1} mm under a magnification of × 400. Write your answer in μm. [3 marks]

Enzymes

Chemical reactions are what make you work. And enzymes are what make them work.

Enzymes Are Catalysts Produced by Living Things

1) Living things have thousands of different chemical reactions going on inside them all the time.

2) These reactions need to be carefully controlled — to get the right amounts of substances.

3) You can usually make a reaction happen more quickly by raising the temperature. This would speed up the useful reactions but also the unwanted ones too... not good.

4) So... living things produce enzymes which act as biological catalysts. Enzymes reduce the need for high temperatures and we only have enzymes to speed up the useful chemical reactions in the body.

A catalyst is a substance which increases the speed of a reaction, without being changed or used up in the reaction.

Enzymes Have Special Shapes So They Can Catalyse Reactions

1) Chemical reactions usually involve things either being split apart or joined together.

2) The substrate is the molecule changed in the reaction.

3) Every enzyme has an active site — the part where it joins on to its substrate to catalyse the reaction.

4) Enzymes usually only work with one substrate. They are said to have a high specificity for their substrate.

5) This is because, for the enzyme to work, the substrate has to fit into the active site. If the substrate's shape doesn't match the active site's shape, then the reaction won't be catalysed. This is called the 'lock and key' mechanism, because the substrate fits into the enzyme just like a key fits into a lock.

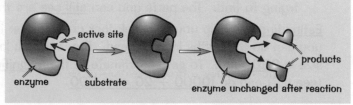

Temperature, pH and Substrate Concentration Affect the Rate of Reaction

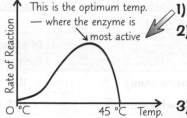

This is the optimum temp. — where the enzyme is most active

1) Changing the temperature changes the rate of an enzyme-catalysed reaction.

2) Like with any reaction, a higher temperature increases the rate at first. But if it gets too hot, some of the bonds holding the enzyme together break. This changes the shape of the enzyme's active site, so the substrate won't fit any more. The enzyme is said to be denatured.

3) All enzymes have an optimum temperature that they work best at.

4) The pH also affects enzymes. If it's too high or too low, the pH interferes with the bonds holding the enzyme together. This changes the shape of the active site and denatures the enzyme.

5) All enzymes have an optimum pH that they work best at. It's often neutral pH 7, but not always — e.g. pepsin is an enzyme used to break down proteins in the stomach. It works best at pH 2, which means it's well-suited to the acidic conditions there.

Optimum pH

6) Substrate concentration also affects the rate of reaction — the higher the substrate concentration, the faster the reaction. This is because it's more likely that the enzyme will meet up and react with a substrate molecule.

7) This is only true up to a point though. After that, there are so many substrate molecules that the enzymes have about as much as they can cope with (all the active sites are full), and adding more makes no difference.

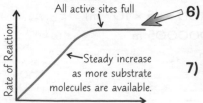

All active sites full

Steady increase as more substrate molecules are available.

If the lock and key mechanism fails, get in through a window...

Make sure you use the special terms like 'active site' and 'denatured' — the examiners will love it.

Q1   Explain why enzymes have an optimum pH.   [2 marks]

More on Enzymes

You'll soon know how to investigate the effect of pH on the rate of enzyme activity... I bet you're thrilled.

You Can Investigate the Effect of pH on Enzyme Activity | PRACTICAL

The enzyme amylase catalyses the breakdown of starch to maltose. It's easy to detect starch using iodine solution — if starch is present, the iodine solution will change from browny-orange to blue-black. This is how you can investigate how pH affects amylase activity:

1) Put a drop of iodine solution into every well of a spotting tile.

2) Place a Bunsen burner on a heat-proof mat, and a tripod and gauze over the Bunsen burner. Put a beaker of water on top of the tripod and heat the water until it is 35 °C (use a thermometer to measure the temperature). Try to keep the temperature of the water constant throughout the experiment.

You could use an electric water bath, instead of a Bunsen and a beaker of water, to control the temperature.

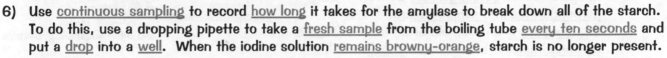

mixture sampled every 10 seconds

amylase, starch and buffer solution

dropping pipette

drop of iodine solution

spotting tile

3) Use a syringe to add 3 cm³ of amylase solution and 1 cm³ of a buffer solution with a pH of 5 to a boiling tube. Using test tube holders, put the boiling tube into the beaker of water and wait for five minutes.

4) Next, use a different syringe to add 3 cm³ of a starch solution to the boiling tube.

5) Immediately mix the contents of the boiling tube and start a stop clock.

6) Use continuous sampling to record how long it takes for the amylase to break down all of the starch. To do this, use a dropping pipette to take a fresh sample from the boiling tube every ten seconds and put a drop into a well. When the iodine solution remains browny-orange, starch is no longer present.

7) Repeat the whole experiment with buffer solutions of different pH values to see how pH affects the time taken for the starch to be broken down.

You could use a pH meter to accurately measure the pH of your solutions.

8) Remember to control any variables each time (e.g. concentration and volume of amylase solution) to make it a fair test.

Here's How to Calculate the Rate of Reaction

1) It's often useful to calculate the rate of reaction after an experiment. Rate is a measure of how much something changes over time.

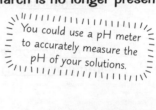

$$\text{Rate} = \frac{1000}{\text{time}}$$

2) For the experiment above, you can calculate the rate of reaction using this formula:

E.g.

> At pH 6, the time taken for amylase to break down all of the starch in a solution was 50 seconds. So the rate of the reaction = 1000 ÷ 50 = 20 s⁻¹

The units are in s⁻¹ since rate is given per unit time.

3) If an experiment measures how much something changes over time, you calculate the rate of reaction by dividing the amount that it has changed by the time taken.

EXAMPLE: The enzyme catalase catalyses the breakdown of hydrogen peroxide into water and oxygen. During an investigation into the activity of catalase, 24 cm³ of oxygen was released in 50 seconds (s). Calculate the rate of the reaction. Write your answer in cm³ s⁻¹.

Amount of product formed = change = 24 cm³

Rate of reaction = change ÷ time = 24 cm³ ÷ 50 s = 0.48 cm³ s⁻¹

If only enzymes could speed up revision...

You could easily adapt this experiment to investigate how factors other than pH affect the rate of amylase activity. For example, you could use a water bath set to different temperatures to investigate the effect of temperature.

Q1   An enzyme-controlled reaction was carried out at pH 4. After 60 seconds, 33 cm³ of product had been released. Calculate the rate of reaction in cm³ s⁻¹.   [1 mark]

Enzymes in Breakdown and Synthesis

Organisms can break big molecules down into smaller ones and build small molecules back up into bigger ones. It's pretty clever stuff, and all given a helping hand by our good friends, enzymes.

Enzymes Break Down Big Molecules

1) Proteins, lipids and some carbohydrates are big molecules.

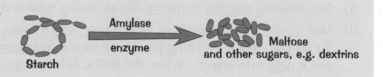
Lipids are fats and oils.

2) It's important that organisms are able to break them down into their smaller components so they can be used for growth and other life processes. For example:

- Many of the molecules in the food we eat are too big to pass through the walls of our digestive system, so digestive enzymes break them down into smaller, soluble molecules. These can pass easily through the walls of the digestive system, allowing them to be absorbed into the bloodstream. They can then pass into cells to be used by the body.

- Plants store energy in the form of starch (a carbohydrate). When plants need energy, enzymes break down the starch into smaller molecules (sugars). These can then be respired to transfer energy to be used by the cells (see p.92).

Different Types of Enzymes Break Down Carbohydrates, Proteins and Lipids

- Enzymes called carbohydrases convert carbohydrates into simple sugars. E.g. amylase is an example of a carbohydrase. It breaks down starch.

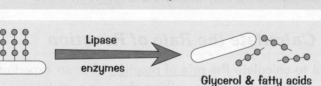
Starch — Amylase enzyme → Maltose and other sugars, e.g. dextrins

- Proteases convert proteins into amino acids.

Proteins — Protease enzymes → Amino acids

- Lipases convert lipids into glycerol and fatty acids.

Lipid — Lipase enzymes → Glycerol & fatty acids

When lipids are broken down, the fatty acids will lower the pH of the solution they are in.

Some Enzymes Join Molecules Together

Organisms need to be able to synthesise carbohydrates, proteins and lipids from their smaller components. Again, enzymes are used in this process.

- Carbohydrates can be synthesised by joining together simple sugars.

Glycogen synthase is an enzyme that joins together lots of chains of glucose molecules to make glycogen (a molecule used to store energy in animals).

- Proteins are made by joining amino acids together (see page 35). Enzymes catalyse the reactions needed to do this.

- Lots of enzymes are also involved in the synthesis of lipids from fatty acids and glycerol.

What do you call an acid that's eaten all the pies...

Make sure you know all the smaller components that make up the bigger carbohydrates, proteins and lipids and understand that enzymes play a role in both the breakdown and synthesis of the bigger molecules.

Q1   Name the molecules that result from the breakdown of: a) carbohydrates, b) proteins.   [2 marks]

Testing for Biological Molecules

Carbohydrates, lipids and proteins are all <u>biological molecules</u> (molecules found in living organisms). You need to know how you can <u>test for them</u> using different <u>chemicals</u>.

PRACTICAL

You Can Test for Sugars Using Benedict's Reagent

There are lots of different types of <u>sugar molecules</u>. Due to their <u>chemical properties</u>, many sugars (e.g. glucose) are called <u>reducing sugars</u>. You don't need to know exactly what reducing sugars are, but you do need to know how to <u>test</u> for them:

1) Add <u>Benedict's reagent</u> (which is <u>blue</u>) to a sample and <u>heat</u> it in a water bath that's set to <u>75 °C</u>. If the test's <u>positive</u> it will form a <u>coloured precipitate</u> (solid particles suspended in the solution).

2) The <u>higher</u> the <u>concentration</u> of reducing sugar, the <u>further</u> the colour change goes — you can use this to <u>compare</u> the amount of reducing sugar in different solutions.

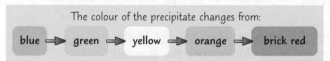

The colour of the precipitate changes from:

blue ⇒ green ⇒ yellow ⇒ orange ⇒ brick red

Starch is Tested for with Iodine

Just add <u>iodine solution</u> to the test sample.

1) If starch <u>is present</u>, the sample changes from <u>browny-orange</u> to a dark, <u>blue-black</u> colour.

2) If there's <u>no starch</u>, it stays browny-orange.

Iodine solution is iodine dissolved in potassium iodide solution.

Use the Emulsion Test for Lipids

An emulsion is when one liquid doesn't dissolve in another — it just forms little droplets.

To find out if there are any <u>lipids</u> in a sample:

1) <u>Shake</u> the test substance with <u>ethanol</u> for about a minute until it <u>dissolves</u>, then pour the solution into <u>water</u>.

2) If there <u>are</u> any <u>lipids present</u>, they will <u>precipitate</u> out of the liquid and show up as a <u>milky emulsion</u>.

3) The <u>more lipid</u> there is, the <u>more noticeable</u> the milky colour will be.

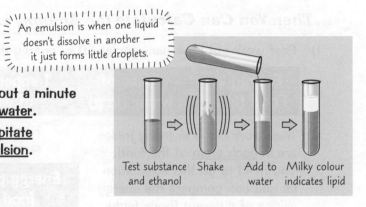

Test substance and ethanol Shake Add to water Milky colour indicates lipid

The Biuret Test is Used for Proteins

If you needed to find out if a substance contained <u>protein</u> you'd use the <u>biuret test</u>.

1) First, add a few drops of <u>potassium hydroxide</u> solution to make the solution <u>alkaline</u>.

2) Then add some <u>copper(II) sulfate</u> solution (which is <u>bright blue</u>).

- If there's <u>no protein</u>, the solution will stay <u>blue</u>.
- If protein <u>is present</u>, the solution will turn <u>purple</u>.

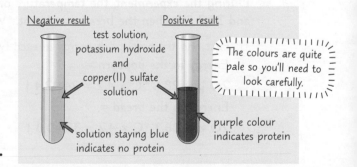

Negative result   Positive result

test solution, potassium hydroxide and copper(II) sulfate solution

The colours are quite pale so you'll need to look carefully.

solution staying blue indicates no protein

purple colour indicates protein

The Anger Test — annoy test subject. Red face = anger present...

OK, so this stuff isn't thrilling but learning it is better than being dissolved in a giant vat of vinegar. Yowch.

Q1   A solution that has been mixed with potassium hydroxide and copper(II) sulfate solution turns purple. What conclusion would you draw from this test?   [1 mark]

Energy in Food

I bet you've been told many a time not to play with your <u>food</u>. Well for this page I'm going to <u>encourage</u> you to do it, and play with <u>fire</u>, too. Actually it's a pretty <u>fun experiment</u>...

Food Can be Burnt to See How Much Energy it Contains

The posh name for this is <u>calorimetry</u>. You need to know how to do it with a <u>simple experiment</u>:

First You Need a Dry Food, Water and a Flame...

1) You need a <u>food</u> that'll <u>burn easily</u> — something that's dry, e.g. dried beans or pasta, will work best.

2) <u>Weigh</u> a small amount of the food and then <u>skewer</u> it on a <u>mounted needle</u>.

3) Next, add <u>a set volume</u> of water to a boiling tube (held with a clamp) — this will be used to <u>measure</u> the amount of <u>energy</u> that's transferred when the food is <u>burnt</u>.

4) Measure the <u>temperature</u> of the <u>water</u>, then <u>set fire</u> to the food using a <u>Bunsen burner flame</u>. Make sure the Bunsen isn't near the water or your results might be a bit wonky.

5) Immediately <u>hold</u> the burning food <u>under</u> the boiling tube until it <u>goes out</u>. Then <u>relight</u> the food and <u>hold</u> it under the tube — <u>keep doing this</u> until the food <u>won't</u> catch fire again.

6) The last thing to do is measure the <u>temperature</u> of the <u>water</u> again. Then you're ready for a bit of <u>maths</u>...

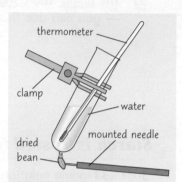

thermometer

clamp

water

dried bean

mounted needle

...Then You Can Calculate the Amount of Energy in the Food

1) First work out how many <u>joules</u> (J) of energy the food contains using this formula:

$$\text{Energy in Food (in J)} = \text{Mass of water (in g)} \times \text{Temperature change of water (in °C)} \times 4.2$$

1 cm³ of water is the same as 1 g of water.

Quite a bit of the energy in the food is transferred to the environment. You can minimise this by insulating the boiling tube, e.g. with foil.

2) Then work out how many joules are in <u>each gram</u> of the food. You need to do this calculation so you can <u>compare</u> the energy values of different foods <u>fairly</u>.

$$\text{Energy per gram of food (in J/g)} = \frac{\text{Energy in food (in J)}}{\text{Mass of food (in g)}}$$

> **EXAMPLE:**
> A student burned 0.2 g of popcorn and 0.5 g of bread separately under 20 cm³ of water. During the experiment, the temperature of the water increased by 28.6 °C when the popcorn was burnt and 38.7 °C when the bread was burnt. Which food has more energy per unit mass?
>
> 1) First find the amount of energy in each type of food:
> Energy in the popcorn =
> 20 g × 28.6 °C × 4.2 = 2402.4 J
> Energy in the bread =
> 20 g × 38.7 °C × 4.2 = 3250.8 J
>
> 2) Then convert this into joules per gram:
> Popcorn: 2402.4 ÷ 0.2
> = 12 012.0 J/g
> Bread: 3250.8 ÷ 0.5
> = 6501.6 J/g
>
> **Answer:** the popcorn has more energy per unit mass.

I think I accidentally measured the energy in my thumb...

Food scientists use fancy machines called calorimeters to measure the energy content of our food — they're insulated and sealed so produce much more accurate results than the experiment on this page. (But they're not as fun.)

Q1   A student performed a calorimetry experiment on a small piece of bread. Why is it important to record the increase in temperature as soon as possible after the bread is burnt in this experiment?   [1 mark]

Diffusion, Osmosis and Active Transport

Substances can move in and out of cells by <u>diffusion</u>, <u>osmosis</u> and <u>active transport</u>...

Diffusion — Don't be Put Off by the Fancy Word

1) <u>Diffusion</u> is simple. It's just the <u>gradual movement</u> of particles from places where there are <u>lots</u> of them to places where there are <u>fewer</u> of them. That's all it is — just the <u>natural tendency</u> for stuff to <u>spread out</u>. Here's the fancy <u>definition</u>:

> <u>DIFFUSION</u> is the <u>net (overall) movement</u> of <u>particles</u> from an area of <u>higher concentration</u> to an area of <u>lower concentration</u>.

If something moves from an area of higher concentration to an area of lower concentration it is said to have moved down a <u>concentration gradient</u>.

2) Diffusion happens in both <u>liquids</u> and <u>gases</u> — that's because the particles in these substances are free to <u>move about</u> randomly.

3) Only very <u>small</u> molecules can <u>diffuse</u> through <u>cell membranes</u> — things like <u>glucose</u>, <u>amino acids</u>, <u>water</u> and <u>oxygen</u>. <u>Big</u> molecules like <u>starch</u> and <u>proteins</u> can't fit through the membrane.

Osmosis is a Special Case of Diffusion, That's All

> <u>OSMOSIS</u> is the <u>net movement of water molecules</u> across a <u>partially permeable membrane</u> from a region of <u>higher water concentration</u> to a region of <u>lower water concentration</u>.

You could also describe osmosis as the net movement of water molecules across a partially permeable membrane from a region of <u>lower solute concentration</u> to a region of <u>higher solute concentration</u>.

1) A <u>partially permeable</u> membrane is just one with very small holes in it. So small, in fact, only tiny <u>molecules</u> (like water) can pass through them, and bigger molecules (e.g. <u>sucrose</u>) can't.

2) The water molecules actually pass <u>both ways</u> through the membrane during osmosis. This happens because water molecules <u>move about randomly</u> all the time.

3) But because there are <u>more</u> water molecules on one side than on the other, there's a steady <u>net flow</u> of water into the region with <u>fewer</u> water molecules, i.e. into the <u>more concentrated</u> solute solution.

4) This means the <u>solute</u> solution gets more <u>dilute</u>. The water acts like it's trying to "<u>even up</u>" the concentration either side of the membrane.

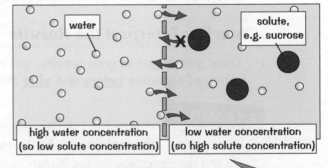

high water concentration (so low solute concentration) | low water concentration (so high solute concentration)

Net movement of water molecules

Active Transport Works Against a Concentration Gradient

> <u>ACTIVE TRANSPORT</u> is the <u>movement of particles</u> across a membrane against a concentration gradient (i.e. from an area of <u>lower</u> to an area of <u>higher concentration</u>) <u>using energy</u> transferred during respiration.

1) Active transport is a bit <u>different from diffusion</u> because particles are moved <u>up a concentration gradient</u> rather than down, and the process requires <u>energy</u> (unlike diffusion, which is a passive process).

2) Here's an example of active transport at work in the <u>digestive system</u>:

1) When there's a <u>higher concentration</u> of nutrients in the gut than in the blood, the nutrients <u>diffuse naturally</u> into the blood.

2) <u>BUT</u> — sometimes there's a <u>lower concentration</u> of nutrients in the gut than in the blood.

3) Active transport allows nutrients to be taken into the blood, despite the fact that the <u>concentration gradient</u> is the wrong way. This is essential to stop us starving.

Revision by diffusion — you wish...

Hopefully there'll have been a net movement of information from this page into your brain...

Q1   Give two differences between the processes of diffusion and active transport.   [2 marks]

PRACTICAL # Investigating Osmosis

For all you non-believers — here's an <u>experiment</u> you can do to see <u>osmosis in action</u>.

You Can Do an Experiment to Investigate Osmosis

This experiment involves putting <u>potato cylinders</u> into <u>different concentrations</u> of <u>sucrose solution</u> to see what effect different <u>water concentrations</u> have on them.

The higher the concentration of the sucrose solution, the lower the water concentration

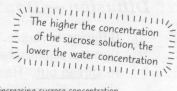

increasing sucrose concentration

0.0 M   0.2 M   0.4 M   0.6 M   0.8 M   1.0 M

First You Do the Experiment...

1) Prepare <u>sucrose solutions</u> of different concentrations ranging from <u>pure water</u> to a <u>very concentrated sucrose solution</u>.

2) Use a cork borer to cut a <u>potato</u> into the <u>same sized pieces</u> (The pieces need to be about <u>1 cm</u> in diameter and preferably from the <u>same potato</u>.)

'M' is a unit of concentration (you might also see it written as mol dm⁻³). The solution with a concentration of 0.0 M is pure water.

3) Divide the cylinders into <u>groups of three</u> and use a <u>mass balance</u> to measure the <u>mass</u> of each <u>group</u>.

4) Place <u>one group</u> in each solution.

5) <u>Leave</u> the cylinders in the solution for <u>at least 40 minutes</u> (making sure that they all get the <u>same amount</u> of time).

6) <u>Remove</u> the cylinders and <u>pat dry gently</u> with a paper towel. This removes <u>excess water</u> from the surface of the cylinders, so you get a more <u>accurate</u> measurement of their <u>final masses</u>.

7) <u>Weigh</u> each <u>group</u> again and record your results.

8) The <u>only</u> thing that you should <u>change</u> in this experiment is the <u>sucrose solution concentration</u>. Everything else (e.g. the volume of solution, the size of the potato cylinders, the type of potatoes used, the amount of drying, etc.) must be kept the <u>same</u> or your results <u>won't be valid</u>.

...Then You Interpret the Results

1) Once you've got all your results, you need to <u>calculate</u> the <u>percentage change in mass</u> for each group of cylinders <u>before</u> and <u>after</u> their time in the sucrose.

Calculating the percentage change allows you to compare the effect of sucrose concentration on cylinders that didn't have the same initial mass.

EXAMPLE:

A group of cylinders weighed 13.2 g at the start of the experiment. At the end they weighed 15.1 g. Calculate the percentage change in mass.

To find the <u>percentage change in mass</u>, use the following <u>formula</u>:

$$\text{percentage change} = \frac{\text{final mass} - \text{initial mass}}{\text{initial mass}} \times 100$$

$$\text{percentage change} = \frac{15.1 - 13.2}{13.2} \times 100 = 14.4\%$$

The positive result tells you the potato cylinders gained mass. If the answer was negative then the potato cylinders lost mass.

2) Then you can plot a <u>graph</u> and <u>analyse your results</u>:

At the points <u>above</u> <u>the x-axis</u>, the water concentration of the <u>sucrose solutions</u> is <u>higher</u> than in the <u>cylinders</u>. The cylinders <u>gain mass</u> as water is <u>drawn in</u> by osmosis.

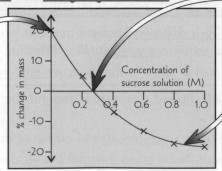

Concentration of sucrose solution (M)

Where there is <u>no change</u> in mass (where the curve <u>crosses the x-axis</u>) the fluid <u>inside</u> the cylinders and the <u>sucrose solution</u> are <u>isotonic</u> — they have the <u>same water concentration</u>.

At the points <u>below the x-axis</u>, the water concentration of the <u>sucrose solutions</u> is <u>lower</u> than in the <u>cylinders</u>. This causes the cylinders to <u>lose water</u> so their mass <u>decreases</u>.

So that's how they make skinny fries...

This experiment used sucrose as a solute, but you could do the experiment with different solutes (e.g. salt).

Q1   A group of potato cubes were placed in a sucrose solution and left for one hour. The cubes weighed 13.3 g at the start of the experiment and 11.4 g at the end. Calculate the percentage change in mass.   [2 marks]

Revision Questions for Topic 1

Make sure you learn all of Topic 1 good 'n' proper — many of the concepts will crop up again in other topics.

- Try these questions and <u>tick off each one</u> when you <u>get it right</u>.
- When you've done <u>all the questions</u> under a heading and are <u>completely happy</u>, tick it off.

Cells and Specialised Cells (p.12-13) ☑

1) What is the function of the cell membrane?
2) Give three structures found in plant cells but not in animal cells.
3) Name the subcellular structures in plant cells where photosynthesis takes place.
4) Name two structures that are found in both prokaryotic cells and eukaryotic cells.
5) What does the term 'haploid' mean?
6) Give three ways in which an egg cell is adapted to its function.
7) What are cilia?
8) What is the purpose of the ciliated epithelial cells that line the airways?

Microscopy (p.14-15) ☑

9) Give an advantage of electron microscopes over light microscopes.
10) Why is it necessary to use thin samples of tissue when viewing cells using a light microscope?
11) Write the equation you would use to find the size of a specimen using the magnification used and the size of the image seen through a microscope lens.
12) Describe how you would convert a measurement from mm to μm.
13) Which unit can be expressed in standard form as $\times 10^{-12}$ m?

Enzymes (p.16-18) ☑

14) What part of an enzyme makes it specific to a particular substrate?
15) Why can denatured enzymes no longer catalyse chemical reactions?
16) Explain how temperature affects enzyme activity.
17) Describe how you could investigate the effect of pH on the rate of amylase activity.
18) Which two molecules are produced when lipids are broken down?
19) Name a big molecule that's formed from simple sugars.

Testing for Biological Molecules and Energy in Food (p.19-20) ☑

20) Describe the colour change that occurs when Benedict's reagent is added to a substance containing reducing sugars.
21) What chemical reagent is used to test for the presence of starch?
22) How would you test for the presence of lipids in a sample?
23) Describe briefly how you could use calorimetry to measure the energy content of a peanut.

Diffusion, Osmosis and Active Transport (p.21-22) ☑

24) Define the following terms: a) diffusion,   b) osmosis,   c) active transport.
25) If a potato cylinder is placed in a solution with a very high sucrose concentration, what will happen to the mass of the potato cylinder over time? Explain why.

Mitosis

In order to survive and grow, our cells have got to be able to <u>divide</u>. And that means our DNA as well...

Chromosomes Contain Genetic Information

1) Most cells in your body have a <u>nucleus</u>. The nucleus contains your <u>genetic material</u> in the form of <u>chromosomes</u>. Chromosomes are <u>coiled up</u> lengths of <u>DNA molecules</u> (see p.34 for more on DNA).

2) <u>Body cells</u> normally have <u>two copies</u> of each <u>chromosome</u> — this makes them 'diploid' cells. One chromosome comes from the organism's '<u>mother</u>', and one comes from its '<u>father</u>'.

3) When a cell divides by <u>mitosis</u> (see below) it makes two cells <u>identical</u> to the original cell — the nucleus of each new cell contains the <u>same number of chromosomes</u> as the original cell.

The Cell Cycle Makes New Cells for Growth and Repair

1) <u>Body cells</u> in <u>multicellular</u> organisms <u>divide</u> to produce new cells during a process called the <u>cell cycle</u>. The stage of the cell cycle when the cell divides is called <u>mitosis</u>.

2) Multicellular organisms use <u>mitosis</u> to <u>grow</u> or to <u>replace cells</u> that have been <u>damaged</u>.

3) Some organisms use mitosis to <u>reproduce</u> — this is called <u>asexual reproduction</u>. E.g. strawberry plants form runners by mitosis, which become new plants.

4) You need to know about the main stages of the <u>cell cycle</u>:

Interphase

The
Cell
Cycle

Mitosis and
Cytokinesis

Interphase

In a cell that's not dividing, the DNA is all spread out in <u>long strings</u>. Before it divides, the cell has to <u>grow</u> and to <u>increase</u> the amount of <u>subcellular structures</u> such as <u>mitochondria</u> and <u>ribosomes</u>. It then <u>duplicates</u> its <u>DNA</u> — so there's one copy for each new cell. The DNA is copied and forms <u>X-shaped</u> chromosomes. Each 'arm' of the chromosome is an <u>exact duplicate</u> of the other.

The left arm has the same DNA as the right arm of the chromosome.

Mitosis and Cytokinesis

Once its contents and DNA have been copied, the cell is ready for <u>mitosis</u>. Mitosis is divided into <u>four stages</u>:

1) PROPHASE — The chromosomes <u>condense</u>, getting shorter and fatter. The <u>membrane</u> around the <u>nucleus breaks down</u> and the chromosomes <u>lie free</u> in the cytoplasm.

2) METAPHASE — The chromosomes <u>line up</u> at the centre of the cell.

3) ANAPHASE — <u>Cell fibres</u> pull the chromosomes apart. The <u>two arms</u> of each chromosome go to <u>opposite ends</u> of the cell.

4) TELOPHASE — Membranes form around each of the sets of chromosomes. These become the <u>nuclei</u> of the two new cells — the <u>nucleus</u> has <u>divided</u>.

Before telophase ends, the <u>cytoplasm</u> and <u>cell membrane</u> divide to form two separate cells — this process is called <u>cytokinesis</u>.

5) At the end of mitosis, the cell has produced <u>two new daughter cells</u>. Each daughter cell contains exactly the <u>same sets of chromosomes</u> in its nucleus as the other daughter cell — they're <u>genetically identical diploid cells</u>. They're also genetically identical to the <u>parent cell</u>.

6) You can <u>calculate</u> the <u>number of cells</u> there'll be after <u>multiple divisions</u> of a cell by mitosis. The formula you need is: <u>number of cells = 2^n</u>, where '<u>n</u>' is the <u>number of divisions</u> by mitosis.

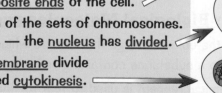

E.g. if you start with 1 cell, after <u>5</u> divisions of mitosis there'll be $\underline{2^5 = 2 \times 2 \times 2 \times 2 \times 2 = 32 \text{ cells}}$.

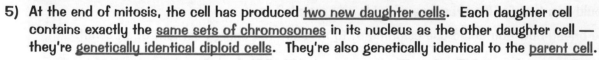

A cell's favourite computer game — divide and conquer...

Mitosis can seem tricky at first. But don't worry — just go through it slowly, one step at a time.

Q1   Describe what happens during the interphase stage of the cell cycle.   [2 marks]

Cell Division and Growth

Growth — it happens to us all. You need to know the <u>processes</u> involved in both <u>animal</u> and <u>plant</u> growth. Then, just for you, there's a beauty of a <u>graph</u> at the bottom of the page. Enjoy.

Growth Involves Cell Division, Differentiation and Elongation

1) <u>Growth</u> is an <u>increase</u> in <u>size</u> or <u>mass</u>. Plants and animals <u>grow</u> and <u>develop</u> due to these processes:

   - <u>CELL DIFFERENTIATION</u> — the process by which a cell <u>changes</u> to become <u>specialised</u> for its <u>job</u>. Having specialised cells allows multicellular organisms to work more <u>efficiently</u>.
   - <u>CELL DIVISION</u> — by <u>mitosis</u> (see previous page).

   Plants also grow by <u>CELL ELONGATION</u>. This is where a plant cell <u>expands</u>, making the cell <u>bigger</u> and so making the plant <u>grow</u>.

See page 13 for more on specialised cells.

2) <u>All growth</u> in <u>animals</u> happens by <u>cell division</u>. Animals tend to grow while they're <u>young</u>, and then they reach <u>full growth</u> and <u>stop</u> growing. So when you're young, cells divide at a <u>fast rate</u> but once you're an adult, most cell division is for <u>repair</u> — the cells divide to <u>replace</u> old or damaged cells. This also means, in most animals, <u>cell differentiation</u> is <u>lost</u> at an <u>early stage</u>.

3) In <u>plants</u>, growth in <u>height</u> is mainly due to cell <u>elongation</u> — cell <u>division</u> usually just happens in the <u>tips</u> of the <u>roots</u> and <u>shoots</u> (in areas called meristems — see next page). But <u>plants</u> often grow <u>continuously</u> — even really old trees will keep putting out <u>new branches</u>. So, plants continue to <u>differentiate</u> to <u>develop new parts</u>, e.g. leaves, roots.

Cancer is a Case of Uncontrolled Cell Division

1) The <u>rate</u> at which <u>cells divide</u> by <u>mitosis</u> is controlled by the chemical instructions (<u>genes</u>) in an organism's DNA.

2) If there's a <u>change</u> in one of the genes that controls cell division, the cell may start dividing <u>uncontrollably</u>.

3) This can result in a <u>mass of abnormal cells</u> called a <u>tumour</u>.

4) If the tumour <u>invades and destroys</u> surrounding tissue it is called <u>cancer</u>.

A random change in a gene is called a mutation — see page 35.

Percentile Charts are Used to Monitor Growth

1) <u>Growth charts</u> are used to assess a <u>child's growth</u> over time, so that an <u>overall pattern in development</u> can be seen and any <u>problems highlighted</u> (e.g. obesity, malnutrition, dwarfism).

2) For example, a baby's growth is regularly <u>monitored</u> after birth to make sure it's growing <u>normally</u>. Three measurements are taken — <u>length</u>, <u>mass</u> and <u>head circumference</u>.

3) These results are plotted on <u>growth charts</u>, like this one.

4) The chart shows a number of '<u>percentiles</u>'. E.g. the <u>50th percentile</u> shows the mass that <u>50%</u> of babies will have reached at a certain age.

5) Babies <u>vary</u> in size, but doctors are likely to investigate if a baby's size is above the <u>top</u> percentile line or below the <u>bottom</u> percentile line, their size increases or decreases by <u>two or more</u> percentile lines over time, or if there's an <u>inconsistent pattern</u> (e.g. a small baby with a very large head).

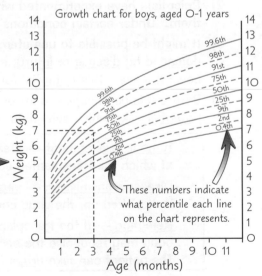

Growth chart for boys, aged 0-1 years

These numbers indicate what percentile each line on the chart represents.

E.g. a three-month-old who weighs 7 kg is just above 75th percentile — roughly 75% of three-month-olds are lighter and 25% are heavier.

I'm growing rather sick of this topic...

Growth is pretty important. Obviously. Without it, you wouldn't be able to reach anything on the top shelf.

Q1   a) Name a process that's used for growth in plants but not in animals.   [1 mark]
         b) Describe how a plant grows by the process you named in part a).   [1 mark]

Stem Cells

Your body is made up of all sorts of weird and wonderful cells. This page tells you where they all came from...

Stem Cells can Differentiate into Different Types of Cells

1) As you saw on the previous page, cells differentiate to become specialised cells.

2) Undifferentiated cells are called stem cells.

3) Depending on what instructions they're given, stem cells can divide by mitosis to become new cells, which then differentiate.

4) Stem cells are found in early human embryos. These embryonic stem cells have the potential to divide and produce any kind of cell at all. This makes sense — all the different types of cell found in a human have to come from those few cells in the early embryo.

5) This means stem cells are really important for the growth and development of organisms.

6) Adults also have stem cells, but they're only found in certain places, like bone marrow. These aren't as versatile as embryonic stem cells — they can't produce any cell type at all, only certain ones. In animals, adult stem cells are used to replace damaged cells, e.g. to make new skin or blood cells.

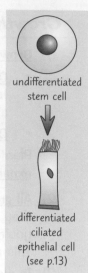

undifferentiated stem cell

differentiated ciliated epithelial cell (see p.13)

Meristems Contain Plant Stem Cells

1) In plants, the only cells that divide by mitosis are found in plant tissues called meristems.

2) Meristem tissue is found in the areas of a plant that are growing, e.g. the tips of the roots and shoots.

3) Meristems produce unspecialised cells that are able to divide and form any cell type in the plant — they act like embryonic stem cells. But unlike human stem cells, these cells can divide and differentiate to generate any type of cell for as long as the plant lives.

4) The unspecialised cells go on to form specialised tissues like xylem and phloem (see p.71).

A merry stem.

Stem Cells Can be Used in Medicine

1) Doctors already use adult stem cells to cure some diseases. E.g. sickle cell anaemia can sometimes be cured with a bone marrow transplant (containing adult stem cells which produce new blood cells).

2) Scientists have experimented with extracting stem cells from very early human embryos and growing them. Under certain conditions the stem cells can be stimulated to differentiate into specialised cells.

3) It might be possible to use stem cells to create specialised cells to replace those which have been damaged by disease or injury, e.g. new cardiac muscle cells could be transplanted into someone with heart disease. This potential for new cures is the reason for the huge scientific interest in stem cells.

4) Before this can happen, a lot of research needs to be done. There are many potential risks which scientists need to learn more about. For example:

- Tumour development — stem cells divide very quickly. If scientists are unable to control the rate at which the transplanted cells divide inside a patient, a tumour may develop (see previous page).

- Disease transmission — viruses live inside cells. If donor stem cells are infected with a virus and this isn't picked up, the virus could be passed on to the recipient and so make them sicker.

- Rejection — if the transplanted cells aren't grown using the patient's own stem cells, the patient's body may recognise the cells as foreign and trigger an immune response to try to get rid of them. The patient can take drugs to suppress this response, but this makes them susceptible to diseases.

5) Research using embryonic stem cells raises ethical issues. E.g. some people argue that human embryos shouldn't be used for experiments because each one is a potential human life. But others think that the aim of curing patients who are suffering should be more important than the potential life of the embryos.

Cheery cells, those merry-stems...

Turns out stem cells are pretty nifty. Now, let's see if you're specialised to answer this question...

Q1   If the tip is cut off a plant shoot, the tip can be used to grow a whole new plant. Explain why.   [3 marks]

The Brain and Spinal Cord

Scientists know a bit about the <u>brain</u> but <u>not as much</u> as they'd like. Read on — it's pretty amazing stuff.

The Brain and Spinal Cord make up the Central Nervous System (CNS)

1) The <u>spinal cord</u> is a long column of <u>neurones</u> (nerve cells) that run from the <u>base of the brain</u> down the <u>spine</u>. At several places down the cord, neurones <u>branch off</u> and <u>connect</u> with other parts of the body. The spinal cord <u>relays information</u> between the <u>brain</u> and the <u>rest of the body</u>.

2) The brain is made up of <u>billions</u> of <u>interconnected neurones</u>. Different brain <u>parts</u> have different <u>functions</u>:

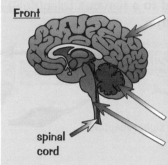

Front

<u>Cerebrum</u> — The <u>largest part</u> of the brain. It's divided into two halves called <u>cerebral hemispheres</u>. The <u>right</u> hemisphere controls <u>muscles</u> on the <u>left side</u> of the body and vice versa. Different parts of the cerebrum are responsible for different things, including <u>movement</u>, <u>intelligence</u>, <u>memory</u>, <u>language</u> and <u>vision</u>.

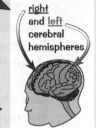

right and <u>left</u> cerebral hemispheres

<u>Cerebellum</u> — Responsible for <u>muscle coordination</u> and <u>balance</u>.

spinal cord

<u>Medulla oblongata</u> — Controls <u>unconscious</u> <u>activities</u> like <u>breathing</u> and your <u>heart rate</u>.

Scanners are used to Investigate Brain Function

To investigate the <u>function</u> of the brain you need to look <u>inside</u> it. Brain tissue can be accessed with <u>surgery</u> (by cutting the <u>skull open</u>), but it's pretty <u>risky</u>. The brain can be visualised <u>without surgery</u> using <u>scanners</u>.

CT SCANNING

1) A <u>CT scanner</u> uses <u>X-rays</u> to produce an <u>image</u> of the brain.

2) A CT scan shows the <u>main structures</u> in the brain, but it doesn't show the functions of them.

3) However, if a CT scan shows a <u>diseased</u> or <u>damaged</u> brain structure and the patient has <u>lost</u> some <u>function</u>, the function of that part of the brain can be <u>worked out</u>. For example, if an area of the brain is damaged and the patient <u>can't see</u>, then that area is involved in <u>vision</u>.

PET SCANNING

1) <u>PET scanners</u> are a bit <u>more fancy</u> than CT scanners. They use <u>radioactive chemicals</u> to show which parts of the brain are <u>active</u> when the person is inside the scanner.

2) PET scans are <u>very detailed</u> and can be used to investigate <u>both</u> the <u>structure</u> and the <u>function</u> of the brain in <u>real time</u>.

3) PET scans can show if areas in the brain are <u>unusually inactive or active</u>, so they are useful for <u>studying disorders</u> that change the <u>brain's activity</u>. E.g. in Alzheimer's disease, activity in certain areas of the brain is reduced — PET scans show this reduction when compared to a <u>normal brain</u>.

Treating Problems in the CNS Can be Tricky

There are many things that can <u>go wrong</u> with the <u>central nervous system (CNS)</u>, e.g. <u>injuries</u> to the <u>brain</u> or <u>spinal cord</u>, <u>tumours</u>, <u>diseases</u> (such as Alzheimer's and Parkinson's). These can be <u>difficult</u> to treat:

1) It's <u>hard to repair damage</u> to the nervous system — neurones in the CNS don't readily repair themselves and as of yet scientists <u>haven't</u> developed a way to <u>repair nervous tissue</u> in the <u>CNS</u>.

2) If a problem occurs in a part of the nervous system that's <u>not easy to access</u> it can be hard to treat, e.g. it's not possible to <u>surgically remove</u> tumours growing in certain parts of the brain.

3) Treatment for problems in the nervous system may lead to <u>permanent damage</u>. For example, a person who has injured their <u>spinal cord</u> may need <u>surgery</u> on their <u>spine</u> near to the injury. There is a risk that the spinal cord could be <u>damaged further</u> during the operation, leading to permanent damage.

Brain surgeons must talk quietly — they handle nervous tissue...

As technology improves, scientists are learning more and more about what goes on up there in your skull.

Q1   Give one function of: a) the medulla oblongata, b) the cerebellum.   [2 marks]

The Nervous System

The <u>nervous system</u> is what lets you <u>react</u> to what goes on around you, so you'd find life tough without it.

The CNS Coordinates a Response

1) The nervous system is made up of <u>neurones</u> (nerve cells) which go to <u>all parts</u> of the body.

2) The body has lots of sensory <u>receptors</u> — groups of <u>cells</u> that can detect a <u>change in your environment</u> (a <u>stimulus</u>). Different receptors detect different stimuli. For example, receptors in your <u>eyes</u> detect <u>light</u>, while receptors in your <u>skin</u> detect <u>touch</u> (pressure) and <u>temperature change</u>.

3) When a <u>stimulus</u> is detected by <u>receptors</u>, the information is <u>converted</u> to a <u>nervous (electrical) impulse</u> and sent along <u>sensory neurones</u> to the <u>CNS</u> (the brain and spinal cord).

4) The CNS <u>coordinates</u> the response (in other words, it <u>decides what to do</u> about the stimulus and tells something to do it). Impulses travel through the CNS along <u>relay neurones</u>.

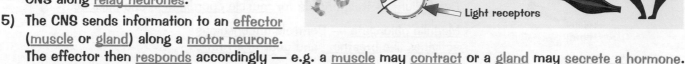

5) The CNS sends information to an <u>effector</u> (<u>muscle</u> or <u>gland</u>) along a <u>motor neurone</u>. The effector then <u>responds</u> accordingly — e.g. a <u>muscle</u> may <u>contract</u> or a <u>gland</u> may <u>secrete a hormone</u>.

6) The <u>time</u> it takes you to <u>respond</u> to a stimulus is called your <u>reaction time</u>.

Neurones Transmit Information Rapidly as Electrical Impulses

1) All neurones have a <u>cell body</u> with a <u>nucleus</u> (plus cytoplasm and other subcellular structures).

2) The cell body has <u>extensions</u> that <u>connect to other neurones</u> — <u>dendrites</u> and <u>dendrons</u> carry nerve impulses <u>towards</u> the cell body, and <u>axons</u> carry nerve impulses <u>away</u> from the cell body.

3) Some axons are surrounded by a <u>myelin sheath</u>. This acts as an <u>electrical insulator</u>, <u>speeding up</u> the electrical impulse.

4) Neurones can be very <u>long</u>, which also <u>speeds up</u> the impulse (<u>connecting</u> with <u>another neurone</u> slows the impulse down, so one long neurone is much <u>quicker</u> than lots of short ones joined together).

5) You need to know the <u>structure</u> and <u>function</u> of <u>sensory</u>, <u>motor</u> and <u>relay</u> neurones.

SENSORY NEURONE
- One <u>long dendron</u> carries nerve impulses from <u>receptor cells</u> to the <u>cell body</u>, which is located in the <u>middle</u> of the neurone.
- One <u>short axon</u> carries nerve impulses from the <u>cell body</u> to the <u>CNS</u>.

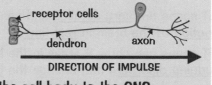

MOTOR NEURONE
- Many <u>short dendrites</u> carry nerve impulses from the <u>CNS</u> to the <u>cell body</u>.
- One <u>long axon</u> carries nerve impulses from the <u>cell body</u> to <u>effector cells</u>.

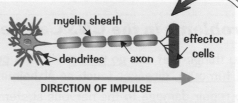

The diagram shows a <u>myelinated</u> motor neurone but you can get unmyelinated ones too. <u>Sensory</u> and <u>relay neurones</u> can also be myelinated.

RELAY NEURONE
- Many <u>short dendrites</u> carry nerve impulses from <u>sensory neurones</u> to the <u>cell body</u>.
- An <u>axon</u> carries nerve impulses from the <u>cell body</u> to <u>motor neurones</u>.

Don't let the thought of exams play on your nerves...

Make sure you understand how the different parts of the nervous system work together to coordinate a response.

Q1   Describe the structure and function of a sensory neurone.   [3 marks]

Synapses and Reflexes

Information is passed between neurones <u>really quickly</u>, especially when there's a <u>reflex</u> involved...

Synapses Connect Neurones

1) The <u>connection</u> between <u>two neurones</u> is called a <u>synapse</u>.

2) The nerve signal is transferred by chemicals called <u>neurotransmitters</u>, which <u>diffuse</u> (move) across the gap.

3) The neurotransmitters then set off a <u>new electrical signal</u> in the <u>next</u> neurone.

4) The <u>transmission</u> of a nervous <u>impulse</u> is <u>very fast</u>, but it is <u>slowed down</u> a bit at the synapse because the <u>diffusion</u> of neurotransmitters across the gap takes <u>time</u>.

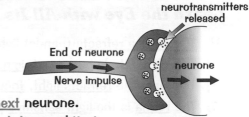

Reflexes Help Prevent Injury

1) <u>Reflexes</u> are <u>automatic</u>, <u>rapid</u> responses to stimuli — they can reduce the chances of being injured.

2) The passage of information in a reflex (from receptor to effector) is called a <u>reflex arc</u>.

3) The neurones in reflex arcs go through the <u>spinal cord</u> or through an <u>unconscious part of the brain</u>.

4) When a <u>stimulus</u> (e.g. a bee sting) is detected by receptors, <u>impulses</u> are sent along a <u>sensory neurone</u> to a <u>relay neurone</u> in the CNS.

5) When the impulses reach a <u>synapse</u> between the sensory neurone and the relay neurone, they trigger <u>neurotransmitters</u> to be released (see above). These cause impulses to be sent along the <u>relay neurone</u>.

6) When the impulses reach a <u>synapse</u> between the relay neurone and a motor neurone, the same thing happens. Neurotransmitters are released and cause impulses to be sent along the <u>motor neurone</u>.

7) The impulses then travel along the motor neurone to the <u>effector</u> (in this example it's a muscle, but it could be a gland).

8) The <u>muscle</u> then <u>contracts</u> and moves your hand away from the bee.

9) Because you don't have to spend time thinking about the response, it's <u>quicker</u> than normal responses.

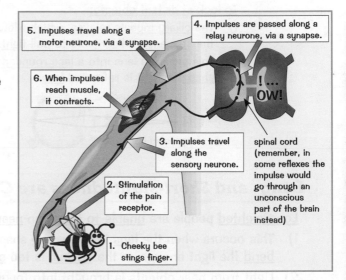

A Reflex Helps to Protect the Eye

1) <u>Very bright light</u> can <u>damage</u> the eye — so you have a reflex to protect it.

2) <u>Light receptors</u> in the eye detect very bright light and send a message along a <u>sensory neurone</u> to the brain.

3) The message then travels along a <u>relay neurone</u> to a <u>motor neurone</u>, which tells <u>circular muscles</u> in the <u>iris</u> (the coloured part of the eye) to <u>contract</u>, making the pupil smaller.

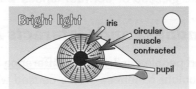

There's more about the structure of the eye on the next page.

Don't get all twitchy — just learn it...

Reflexes bypass conscious parts of your brain completely when a super quick response is essential — your body just gets on with things. If you had to stop and think first, you'd end up a lot more sore (or worse).

Q1   A chef touches a hot tray. A reflex reaction causes him to immediately move his hand away. Describe the pathway of the reflex arc from receptors to effector.   [5 marks]

The Eye

The <u>eye</u> is <u>sensitive to light</u> and responsible for <u>sight</u>. Eye problems are certainly not uncommon though...

Learn the Eye with All Its Labels:

1) The <u>cornea refracts</u> (bends) light into the eye.

2) The <u>iris</u> controls <u>how much light</u> enters the <u>pupil</u> (the <u>hole</u> in the <u>middle</u>).

3) The <u>lens</u> also <u>refracts light</u>, <u>focusing</u> it onto the <u>retina</u>.

4) The <u>retina</u> is the <u>light sensitive</u> part and it's covered in receptor cells called <u>rods</u> and <u>cones</u>, which detect light.

5) <u>Rods</u> are more sensitive in <u>dim light</u> but <u>can't</u> sense colour.

6) <u>Cones</u> are sensitive to different <u>colours</u> but are not so good in dim light.

7) The <u>information</u> from light is <u>converted</u> into <u>electrical impulses</u>. The <u>optic nerve</u> carries these impulses from the receptors to the <u>brain</u>.

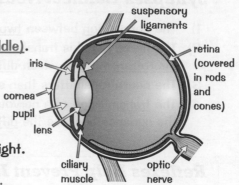

Focusing on Near and Distant Objects

The lens is <u>elastic</u>, so the eye can focus light onto the retina by <u>changing</u> the <u>shape</u> of the <u>lens</u>.

To look at distant objects:

1) The <u>ciliary muscle relaxes</u>, which allows the <u>suspensory ligaments</u> to <u>pull tight</u>.

2) This pulls the lens into a <u>less rounded shape</u> so light is refracted <u>less</u>.

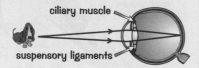

To look at close objects:

1) The <u>ciliary muscle contracts</u>, which slackens the <u>suspensory ligaments</u>.

2) The lens becomes a <u>more rounded shape</u>, so light is refracted <u>more</u>.

Long- and Short-sightedness are Caused by Structural Abnormalities

<u>Long-sighted</u> people are <u>unable to focus</u> on <u>near</u> objects:

1) This occurs when the <u>lens</u> is the wrong shape and doesn't <u>bend</u> the light enough or the <u>eyeball</u> is too <u>short</u>.

2) Light from near objects is brought into focus <u>behind</u> the <u>retina</u>.

3) You can use glasses or contact lenses with a <u>convex lens</u> to correct it.

<u>Short-sighted</u> people are <u>unable to focus</u> on <u>distant</u> objects:

1) This occurs when the <u>lens</u> is the wrong shape and bends the light <u>too much</u> or the <u>eyeball</u> is too <u>long</u>.

2) Light from distant objects is brought into focus <u>in front</u> of the <u>retina</u>.

3) You can use glasses or contact lenses with a <u>concave lens</u> to correct it.

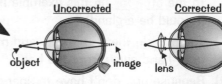

Colour Blindness and Cataracts Also Cause Vision Problems

1) Colour blind people <u>can't tell the difference</u> between <u>certain colours</u>. The most common form of the disorder is <u>red-green</u> colour blindness — it's caused when red or green <u>cones</u> in the <u>retina</u> are <u>not working properly</u>. There's <u>no cure</u> for colour blindness at the moment because the cone cells <u>can't</u> be <u>replaced</u>.

2) A <u>cataract</u> is a <u>cloudy patch</u> on the <u>lens</u>, which stops light from being able to <u>enter the eye</u> normally. People with cataracts are likely to have <u>blurred vision</u>. They may also experience colours looking <u>less vivid</u> and have difficulty seeing in <u>bright light</u>. A cataract can be <u>treated</u> by replacing the faulty lens with an <u>artificial one</u>.

I think I'm a little long-sighted...

If you can read this you've got better eyesight than me!

When light isn't focused on the retina, the brain can't interpret the image properly, so it appears blurry.

Q1   Explain how a structural problem with the eye may cause a person to be long-sighted.   [2 marks]

Revision Questions for Topic 2

Well, that sure was a brain-tingling, nerve-jangling, eye-popping topic. Thank goodness you're at the end.

• Try these questions and <u>tick off each one</u> when you <u>get it right</u>.

• When you've done <u>all the questions</u> under a heading and are <u>completely happy</u>, tick it off.

Mitosis and Growth (p.24-25) ☑

1) What is the cell cycle?

2) Give three uses of mitosis in organisms.

3) Name the four stages of mitosis. Describe what happens in each one.

4) Is the following statement true or false?
"The cells produced at the end of mitosis are identical to each other and the parent cell."

5) Describe how animals grow.

6) What major illness can result from uncontrolled cell division?

7) Describe how a percentile chart is used to monitor growth.

Stem Cells (p.26) ☑

8) What is a stem cell?

9) How are embryonic stem cells different to adult stem cells?

10) What are meristems? Where are they found?

11) What are the potential benefits of stem cells being used in medicine?

12) Give three potential risks associated with using stem cells in medicine.

The Brain and The Nervous System (p.27-29) ☑

13) Produce a sketch of the brain and label the cerebrum, cerebellum and medulla oblongata.

14) Give four things that the cerebrum is responsible for.

15) Describe what a PET scan shows.

16) Give three reasons why it may be tricky to treat problems with the brain and spinal cord.

17) What effect does a myelin sheath have on the speed of an electrical impulse?

18) Draw and label a motor neurone.

19) What is a synapse?

20) Describe the role of neurotransmitters in the transmission of nervous impulses.

21) What is a reflex arc?

22) Why are reflexes faster than normal nervous responses?

The Eye (p.30) ☑

23) Describe the function of these structures in the eye: a) cornea,   b) lens.

24) Which part of the eye controls the amount of light entering the pupil?

25) How are the functions of rods and cones different?

26) Describe how short-sightedness can be treated.

27) Why is there currently no cure for colour blindness?

28) What is a cataract?

Sexual Reproduction and Meiosis

Ever wondered why you look <u>like</u> your <u>family members</u>, but <u>not exactly the same</u>? Well today's your lucky day.

Sexual Reproduction Produces Genetically Different Cells

1) <u>Sexual reproduction</u> is where genetic information from <u>two</u> organisms (a <u>father</u> and a <u>mother</u>) is combined to produce offspring which are <u>genetically different</u> to either parent.

2) In <u>sexual reproduction</u>, the father and mother produce <u>gametes</u> (reproductive cells). In animals these are <u>sperm</u> and <u>egg cells</u>.

3) Gametes only contain <u>half the number</u> of <u>chromosomes</u> of normal cells — they are <u>haploid</u>. <u>Normal cells</u> (with the full number of chromosomes) are <u>diploid</u> (see p.24).

4) At <u>fertilisation</u>, a male gamete <u>fuses</u> with a female gamete to produce a <u>fertilised egg</u>, also known as a <u>zygote</u>. The zygote ends up with the <u>full set</u> of chromosomes (so it is diploid).

5) The zygote then undergoes <u>cell division</u> (by mitosis — see p.24) and develops into an <u>embryo</u>.

6) The embryo <u>inherits characteristics</u> from <u>both parents</u>, as it has received a <u>mixture of chromosomes</u> (and therefore <u>genes</u>) from its mum and its dad.

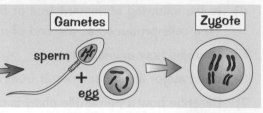

A human cell nucleus contains 46 chromosomes — so the diploid number for a human is 46 and the haploid number is 23.

Gametes	Zygote
sperm + egg	

In flowering plants, the male gametes are found in the pollen and the female gametes are found in the ovaries at the bottom of the stigma.

Gametes are Produced by Meiosis

Meiosis is a type of <u>cell division</u>. It's different to mitosis because it <u>doesn't produce identical cells</u>. In humans, meiosis <u>only</u> happens in the <u>reproductive organs</u> (ovaries and testes).

Division 1

1) Before the cell starts to divide, it <u>duplicates</u> its <u>DNA</u> (so there's enough for each new cell). One arm of each X-shaped chromosome is an <u>exact copy</u> of the other arm.

2) In the <u>first division</u> in meiosis (there are two divisions) the chromosomes <u>line up</u> in pairs in the centre of the cell. One chromosome in each pair came from the organism's mother and one came from its father.

3) The <u>pairs</u> are then <u>pulled apart</u>, so each new cell only has one copy of each chromosome. <u>Some</u> of the father's chromosomes and <u>some</u> of the mother's chromosomes go into each new cell.

4) Each new cell will have a <u>mixture</u> of the mother's and father's chromosomes. Mixing up the genes like this is <u>really important</u> — it creates <u>genetic variation</u> in the offspring.

Division 2

5) In the <u>second division</u> the chromosomes <u>line up</u> again in the centre of the cell. It's a lot like mitosis. The <u>arms</u> of the chromosomes are <u>pulled apart</u>.

6) You get <u>four haploid daughter cells</u> — these are the <u>gametes</u>. Each <u>gamete</u> only has a <u>single set</u> of chromosomes. The gametes are all <u>genetically different</u>.

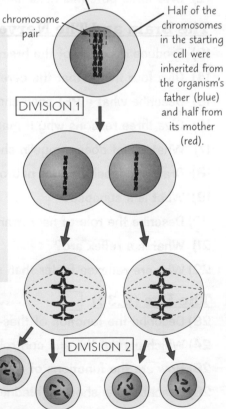

This cell has duplicated each chromosome — each arm of the X-shape is identical.

chromosome pair

Half of the chromosomes in the starting cell were inherited from the organism's father (blue) and half from its mother (red).

DIVISION 1

DIVISION 2

Now that I have your undivided attention...

Remember — in humans, meiosis only occurs in the reproductive organs.

Q1   The haploid gamete of a plant species has 12 chromosomes. Two of these gametes fuse to make a zygote. How many chromosomes will there be in the zygote?   [1 mark]

Q2   How does meiosis introduce genetic variation?   [2 marks]

Asexual and Sexual Reproduction

Humans can only reproduce <u>sexually</u>, but some organisms can reproduce by either <u>sexual</u> or <u>asexual</u> reproduction, e.g. some species of plant. Here's a handy page <u>comparing</u> both.

Asexual and Sexual Reproduction Have Advantages and Disadvantages

1) Reproducing is <u>very important</u> to all organisms — it's how they <u>pass on</u> their <u>genes</u>.

2) Some organisms reproduce <u>sexually</u>, some reproduce <u>asexually</u>, and some can do <u>both</u>.

3) When cells reproduce <u>asexually</u>, they divide by <u>mitosis</u> — this results in <u>two diploid daughter cells</u>, which are genetically <u>identical</u> to each other and to the parent cell (see page 24).

4) <u>Sexual reproduction</u> involves <u>meiosis</u> and the production of <u>genetically different</u> haploid gametes, which fuse to form a diploid cell at <u>fertilisation</u> (see previous page).

5) You need to be able to describe some of the <u>advantages</u> and <u>disadvantages</u> of asexual and sexual reproduction. For example:

	ASEXUAL REPRODUCTION	SEXUAL REPRODUCTION
ADVANTAGES	• Asexual reproduction can produce <u>lots</u> of offspring <u>very quickly</u> because the <u>reproductive cycle</u> (the time it takes to produce independent offspring) is so <u>fast</u>. • For example, bacteria, such as *E. coli*, can divide <u>every half an hour</u>. • This can allow organisms to <u>colonise a new area</u> very <u>rapidly</u>. • Only <u>one parent</u> is needed — this means organisms can reproduce whenever conditions are <u>favourable</u>, <u>without</u> having to wait for a <u>mate</u>. • For example, aphids reproduce asexually during <u>summer</u> when there is <u>plenty of food</u>.	• Sexual reproduction creates <u>genetic variation</u> within the population, which means different individuals have <u>different characteristics</u>. • This means that if the environmental conditions <u>change</u>, it's <u>more likely</u> that at least <u>some individuals</u> in the population will have the characteristics to <u>survive</u> the change. • Over time, this can lead to <u>natural selection</u> and <u>evolution</u> (see p.45) as species become <u>better adapted</u> to their new environment.
DISADVANTAGES	• There's <u>no genetic variation</u> between offspring in the population. • So, if the <u>environment changes</u> and conditions become <u>unfavourable</u>, the <u>whole population</u> may be affected. • For example, Black Sigatoka is a disease that affects <u>banana</u> plants, which reproduce <u>asexually</u>. So, if there's an outbreak of the <u>disease</u>, it's likely that <u>all</u> banana plants in the population will be <u>affected</u> as there are <u>none</u> that are <u>resistant</u> to it.	• Sexual reproduction takes more <u>time</u> and <u>energy</u> than asexual reproduction, so organisms produce <u>fewer offspring</u> in their lifetime. • For example, organisms need to <u>find</u> and <u>attract</u> mates, which takes time and energy. E.g. male bowerbirds <u>build</u> structures out of twigs and then <u>dance</u> to impress females. • <u>Two parents</u> are needed for sexual reproduction. This can be a problem if individuals are <u>isolated</u>. • For example, polar bears often live <u>alone</u>, so male polar bears may have to walk up to <u>100 miles</u> to find a mate.

Asexual reproduction — an aphid's answer to life in the fast lane...

So, both sexual and asexual reproduction have their pros and cons — which is why some organisms can do both.

Q1 Strawberry plants can reproduce asexually.
Discuss the advantages and disadvantages of this form of reproduction. [4 marks]

DNA

Reproduction is all about <u>passing on your DNA</u> to the next generation. This molecule carries all the <u>instructions</u> for your characteristics — so it's a big part of what makes you <u>you</u>.

DNA is Made Up of Nucleotides

1) DNA strands are <u>polymers</u> made up of lots of repeating units called <u>nucleotides</u>.

2) Each nucleotide consists of <u>one sugar molecule</u>, <u>one phosphate molecule</u> and <u>one 'base'</u>.

3) The <u>sugar</u> and <u>phosphate</u> molecules in the nucleotides form a <u>'backbone'</u> to the DNA strands. The sugar and phosphate molecules <u>alternate</u>.

4) One of <u>four</u> different <u>bases</u> joins to each <u>sugar</u>. The bases are: <u>A</u> (adenine), <u>T</u> (thymine), <u>C</u> (cytosine) and <u>G</u> (guanine).

5) A DNA molecule has <u>two strands coiled together</u> in the shape of a <u>double helix</u> (a double stranded spiral).

6) Each base <u>links</u> to a base on the opposite strand in the helix.

7) A <u>always pairs up</u> with T, and C <u>always pairs up</u> with G. This is called <u>complementary base pairing</u>.

8) The complementary base pairs are joined together by <u>weak hydrogen bonds</u>.

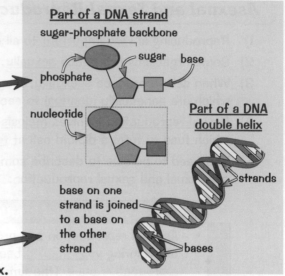

Part of a DNA strand

sugar-phosphate backbone

phosphate • sugar • base • nucleotide

Part of a DNA double helix

base on one strand is joined to a base on the other strand • strands • bases

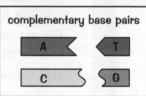

complementary base pairs

A — T

C — G

DNA is Stored as Chromosomes and Contains Genes

1) <u>Chromosomes</u> are <u>long</u>, <u>coiled up</u> molecules of <u>DNA</u>. They're found in the <u>nucleus</u> of <u>eukaryotic cells</u>.

2) A <u>gene</u> is a <u>section</u> of DNA on a chromosome that codes for a <u>particular protein</u>.

3) <u>All</u> of an organism's DNA makes up its <u>genome</u>.

You Need to Know How to Extract DNA From Fruit Cells

Don't believe that cells contain DNA? Well here's a practical you can do to get it out...

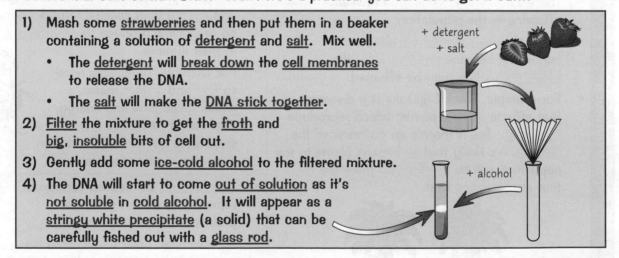

1) Mash some <u>strawberries</u> and then put them in a beaker containing a solution of <u>detergent</u> and <u>salt</u>. Mix well.

- The <u>detergent</u> will <u>break down</u> the <u>cell membranes</u> to release the DNA.
- The <u>salt</u> will make the <u>DNA stick together</u>.

2) <u>Filter</u> the mixture to get the <u>froth</u> and <u>big</u>, <u>insoluble</u> bits of cell out.

3) Gently add some <u>ice-cold alcohol</u> to the filtered mixture.

4) The DNA will start to come <u>out of solution</u> as it's <u>not soluble</u> in <u>cold alcohol</u>. It will appear as a <u>stringy white precipitate</u> (a solid) that can be carefully fished out with a <u>glass rod</u>.

+ detergent + salt

+ alcohol

My band has a great rhythm section — it has paired basses...

Hope you enjoyed extracting all that DNA and learning about its structure. Sadly, though, you won't be getting a Nobel Prize for your efforts — you're too late. Crick, Watson and Wilkins were awarded the Nobel Prize for their work in determining the structure of DNA in 1962. Typical. I'm always late for everything...

Q1 Which DNA bases pair up according to complementary base pairing? [2 marks]

Q2 Why is it useful to use salt when extracting DNA from fruit cells? [1 mark]

Protein Synthesis

So here's how life works — DNA molecules contain a genetic code that determines which proteins are built. The proteins determine how all the cells in the body function. Simple, eh.

Proteins are Made by Reading the Code in DNA

1) DNA controls the production of proteins (protein synthesis) in a cell.
2) Proteins are made up of chains of molecules called amino acids. Each different protein has its own particular number and order of amino acids.
3) The amino acid chains fold up to give each protein a different, specific shape — which means each protein can have a different function. This is why enzymes have active sites with a specific shape, and so only catalyse a specific reaction (see page 16).
4) Remember, a section of DNA that codes for a particular protein is called a gene (see previous page). It's the order of the bases in a gene that decides the order of amino acids in a protein.
5) Each amino acid is coded for by a sequence of three bases in the gene — this is called a base triplet.
6) The amino acids are joined together to make proteins, following the order of the bases in the gene.

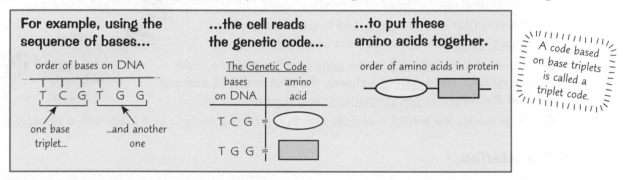

For example, using the sequence of bases... the cell reads the genetic code... to put these amino acids together.

A code based on base triplets is called a triplet code.

7) Each gene contains a different sequence of bases — which is what allows it to code for a particular protein.

DNA Also Contains Non-Coding Regions

1) Many regions of DNA are non-coding — that means that they don't code for any amino acids.
2) Despite this, some of these regions are still involved in protein synthesis (see next page).
3) All of an organism's DNA (including the non-coding regions) makes up the organism's genome.

Genetic Variants Can Arise By Mutations

1) A mutation is a rare, random change to an organism's DNA base sequence that can be inherited.
2) If a mutation happens in a gene, it produces a genetic variant — a different version of the gene.
3) The genetic variant may code for a different sequence of amino acids, which may change the shape of the final protein and so its activity.

Genetic variants are also called alleles — see p.38.

4) For example, the activity of an enzyme might increase, decrease or stop altogether.
5) This could end up changing the characteristics (phenotype, see p.38) of an organism. E.g. XDH is an enzyme. Fruit flies with normal XDH activity have red eyes. Fruit flies with no XDH activity have brown eyes because they can't produce the red eye pigment.
6) Mutations can also happen in non-coding regions of DNA. There's more on the influence of variants in non-coding DNA on the next page.

A triplet of bases — three-tiered cheesecake anyone...

Definitely been watching too much Bake Off. Now, make sure you can do these questions before you move on.

Q1   Explain how a gene can code for a particular protein.   [2 marks]
Q2   Explain how a genetic variant can result in a protein with a very low level of activity.   [2 marks]

More on Protein Synthesis

This page is all about how you actually <u>use</u> the DNA code to <u>make</u> the proteins that you need.

Proteins are Made in Two Stages

1) Transcription

1) Proteins are made in the <u>cell cytoplasm</u> by subcellular structures called <u>ribosomes</u> (see p.12). DNA is found in the cell <u>nucleus</u> and can't move out of it because it's <u>really big</u>. The cell needs to get the information from the DNA to the ribosome in the cytoplasm.

2) This is done using a molecule called <u>messenger RNA</u> (<u>mRNA</u>). Like DNA, mRNA is a <u>polymer</u> of <u>nucleotides</u>, but it's <u>shorter</u> and only a <u>single strand</u>. It also uses <u>uracil</u> (U) instead of <u>thymine</u> (T) as a <u>base</u>.

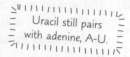
Uracil still pairs with adenine, A-U.

3) <u>RNA polymerase</u> is the <u>enzyme</u> involved in <u>joining together</u> RNA nucleotides to make mRNA. This stage of protein synthesis is called <u>transcription</u>. Here's how it works:

1) <u>RNA polymerase</u> binds to a region of <u>non-coding DNA</u> in front of a gene.

2) The two DNA strands <u>unzip</u> and the RNA polymerase <u>moves along</u> one of the strands of the DNA.

3) It uses the <u>coding DNA</u> in the <u>gene</u> as a <u>template</u> to make the <u>mRNA</u>. <u>Base pairing</u> between the DNA and RNA ensures that the mRNA is <u>complementary</u> to the gene.

4) Once made, the mRNA molecule moves <u>out</u> of the nucleus and joins with a <u>ribosome</u>.

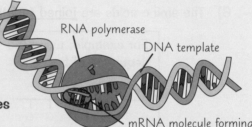
RNA polymerase
DNA template
mRNA molecule forming

2) Translation

Once the <u>mRNA</u> is bound to a ribosome, the <u>protein</u> can be assembled. This stage is called <u>translation</u>.

1) <u>Amino acids</u> are brought to the <u>ribosome</u> by another RNA molecule called <u>transfer RNA</u> (<u>tRNA</u>).

2) The <u>order</u> in which the amino acids are brought to the ribosome <u>matches</u> the order of the <u>base triplets</u> in mRNA. Base triplets in mRNA are also known as <u>codons</u>.

3) Part of the tRNA's structure is called an <u>anticodon</u> — it is <u>complementary</u> to the <u>codon</u> for the amino acid. The pairing of the codon and anticodon makes sure that the amino acids are brought to the ribosome in the <u>correct order</u>.

4) The amino acids are <u>joined together</u> by the ribosome. This makes a <u>polypeptide</u> (protein).

amino acids
tRNA
protein
anticodon
mRNA
ribosome

Non-Coding DNA Affects the Binding of RNA Polymerase

1) Before any transcription can happen, <u>RNA polymerase</u> has to bind to a region of non-coding DNA <u>in front</u> of a gene. If a <u>mutation</u> happens in this region of DNA, then it could affect the <u>ability</u> of RNA polymerase to bind to it. It might make it <u>easier</u> to bind to, or <u>more difficult</u>.

2) How well RNA polymerase can bind to this region of DNA will affect <u>how much</u> mRNA is <u>transcribed</u> and therefore how much of the <u>protein</u> is <u>produced</u>. And, depending on the <u>function</u> of the protein, the <u>phenotype</u> of the organism may be affected by <u>how much</u> of it is made.

3) So genetic variants in <u>non-coding regions</u> can still affect the <u>phenotype</u> of an organism, even if they don't <u>code</u> for proteins <u>themselves</u>.

Alors, j'adore l'ADN, et les protéines sont aussi bien...

Get it? You have to <u>translate</u> it... Never mind. Remember — the non-coding DNA is in on the action here too.

Q1   Describe how a gene is transcribed to form mRNA.   [3 marks]

The Work of Mendel

Some people forget about Mendel but I reckon he's the <u>Granddaddy of Genetics</u>. Here's a whole page on him.

Mendel Did Genetic Experiments with Pea Plants

1) <u>Gregor Mendel</u> was an Austrian monk who trained in <u>mathematics</u> and <u>natural history</u>. On his garden plot at the monastery in the <u>mid 19th century</u>, Mendel noted how <u>characteristics</u> in <u>plants</u> were <u>passed on</u> from one generation to the next.

2) The results of his research were published in <u>1866</u> and eventually became the <u>foundation</u> of modern <u>genetics</u>. Here's an example of one of his experiments:

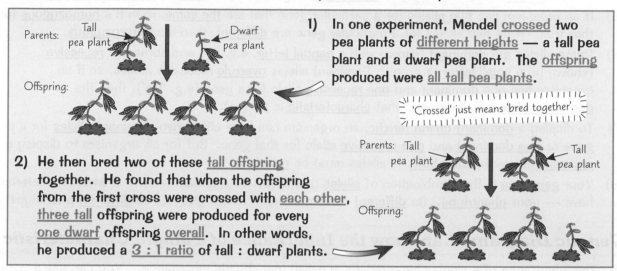

1) In one experiment, Mendel <u>crossed</u> two pea plants of <u>different heights</u> — a tall pea plant and a dwarf pea plant. The <u>offspring</u> produced were <u>all tall pea plants</u>.

'Crossed' just means 'bred together'.

2) He then bred two of these <u>tall offspring</u> together. He found that when the offspring from the first cross were crossed with <u>each other</u>, <u>three tall</u> offspring were produced for every <u>one dwarf</u> offspring <u>overall</u>. In other words, he produced a <u>3 : 1 ratio</u> of tall : dwarf plants.

> Mendel had shown that the height characteristic in pea plants was determined by separately inherited "<u>hereditary units</u>" passed on from each parent. The ratios of tall and dwarf plants in the offspring showed that the unit for tall plants, <u>T</u>, was <u>dominant</u> over the unit for dwarf plants, <u>t</u>.

We now know that the pea plants in the first cross were each <u>homozygous</u> for their trait and that their tall offspring were <u>heterozygous</u> for their trait — these terms are explained on the next page.

3) As well as height, Mendel also showed that <u>other characteristics</u> of pea plants were inherited in the <u>same way</u>, e.g. he found that a purple flower colour was <u>dominant</u> over a white colour.

Mendel Reached Three Important Conclusions

Mendel reached these three important conclusions about <u>heredity in plants</u>:

1) Characteristics in plants are determined by "<u>hereditary units</u>".

2) Hereditary units are passed on to offspring <u>unchanged</u> from both parents, <u>one unit</u> from <u>each parent</u>.

3) Hereditary units can be <u>dominant</u> or <u>recessive</u> — if an individual has <u>both</u> the dominant and the recessive unit for a characteristic, the <u>dominant</u> characteristic will be expressed.

Although Mendel didn't perform experiments on animals, similar experiments have since shown that heredity in animals works the same way.

It Took a While For People to Understand His Work

1) Mendel's work was <u>cutting edge</u> and <u>new</u> to the scientists of the day.

2) We now know that his "hereditary units" are of course <u>genes</u>. But at the time, scientists didn't have the background knowledge to <u>properly understand</u> Mendel's findings — they had <u>no idea</u> about <u>genes</u>, <u>DNA</u> and <u>chromosomes</u>.

3) It wasn't until <u>after his death</u> that people realised how <u>significant</u> his work was and that the <u>mechanism</u> of <u>inheritance</u> could be fully explained.

peas out

Clearly, being a monk in the 1800s was a right laugh...

There was no TV in those days, you see, so Mendel filled his time by growing lots and lots of pea plants.

Q1 Suggest why the importance of Mendel's work wasn't realised straight away. [1 mark]

Genetic Diagrams

You can use genetic diagrams to <u>predict</u> how different <u>characteristics</u> will be <u>inherited</u>.

Alleles Are Different Versions of the Same Gene

1) What <u>genes</u> you <u>inherit</u> control what <u>characteristics</u> you <u>develop</u>.

2) <u>Different</u> genes control <u>different</u> characteristics. <u>Some</u> characteristics are controlled by a <u>single</u> gene. However most characteristics are controlled by <u>several genes interacting</u>.

3) All genes exist in different <u>versions</u> called <u>alleles</u> (which are represented by <u>letters</u> in genetic diagrams).

4) You have <u>two</u> versions (alleles) of <u>every gene</u> in your body — <u>one</u> on <u>each chromosome</u> in a pair.

5) If an organism has <u>two alleles</u> for a particular gene that are <u>the same</u>, then it's <u>homozygous</u> for that trait. If its two alleles for a particular gene are <u>different</u>, then it's <u>heterozygous</u>.

6) Some alleles are <u>dominant</u> (shown with a <u>capital letter</u>, e.g. '<u>C</u>') and some are <u>recessive</u> (shown by a <u>small letter</u>, e.g. '<u>c</u>'). Dominant alleles <u>overrule</u> recessive alleles, so if an organism has <u>one dominant</u> and <u>one recessive</u> allele for a gene (e.g. '<u>Cc</u>'), then the <u>dominant allele</u> will determine what <u>characteristic</u> is present.

7) To display a <u>dominant characteristic</u>, an organism can have either <u>two dominant alleles</u> for a particular gene or <u>one dominant</u> and <u>one recessive</u> allele for that gene. But for an organism to display a <u>recessive</u> characteristic, <u>both</u> its alleles must be <u>recessive</u>.

8) Your <u>genotype</u> is the combination of <u>alleles</u> you have. Your alleles determine what characteristics you have — your <u>phenotype</u>. So <u>different</u> combinations of alleles give rise to <u>different</u> phenotypes.

Genetic Diagrams Can Show the Inheritance of a Single Characteristic

1) The inheritance of a <u>single</u> characteristic is called <u>monohybrid inheritance</u>. You can use a <u>monohybrid cross</u> to show how <u>recessive</u> and <u>dominant</u> traits for a <u>single characteristic</u> are inherited.

2) For example, let's say an allele that causes hamsters to have superpowers is <u>recessive</u> ("b"), and that <u>normal</u> (boring) hamsters don't have superpowers due to a <u>dominant</u> allele ("B"). Here's how you could use a monohybrid cross to show the <u>probability</u> of either the <u>dominant</u> or <u>recessive</u> trait being <u>inherited</u>:

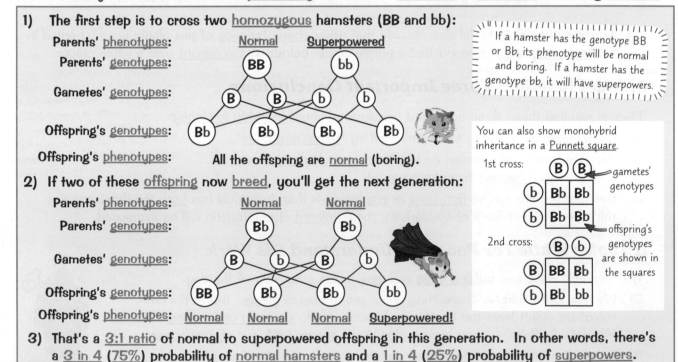

1) The first step is to cross two <u>homozygous</u> hamsters (BB and bb):

Parents' <u>phenotypes</u>:   Normal   Superpowered

Parents' <u>genotypes</u>:   (BB)   (bb)

Gametes' <u>genotypes</u>:   (B) (B)   (b) (b)

Offspring's <u>genotypes</u>: (Bb) (Bb) (Bb) (Bb)

Offspring's <u>phenotypes</u>:   All the offspring are <u>normal</u> (boring).

If a hamster has the genotype BB or Bb, its phenotype will be normal and boring. If a hamster has the genotype bb, it will have superpowers.

2) If two of these <u>offspring</u> now <u>breed</u>, you'll get the next generation:

Parents' <u>phenotypes</u>:   Normal   Normal

Parents' <u>genotypes</u>:   (Bb)   (Bb)

Gametes' <u>genotypes</u>:   (B) (b)   (B) (b)

Offspring's <u>genotypes</u>: (BB) (Bb) (Bb) (bb)

Offspring's <u>phenotypes</u>: Normal   Normal   Normal   Superpowered!

You can also show monohybrid inheritance in a <u>Punnett square</u>.

1st cross: (B) (B) ← gametes' genotypes
(b) Bb Bb
(b) Bb Bb

2nd cross: (B) (b)
(B) BB Bb
(b) Bb bb

← offspring's genotypes are shown in the squares

3) That's a <u>3:1 ratio</u> of normal to superpowered offspring in this generation. In other words, there's a <u>3 in 4</u> (<u>75%</u>) probability of <u>normal hamsters</u> and a <u>1 in 4</u> (<u>25%</u>) probability of <u>superpowers</u>.

Your meanotype determines how nice you are to your sibling...

Remember, genetic diagrams only tell you probabilities. They don't say what will definitely happen.

Q1   Define genotype and phenotype.   [2 marks]

More Genetic Diagrams

Here's <u>another</u> page of funny diagrams with squares, circles and lines going everywhere. And it's not the last...

A Genetic Diagram Can Show How Sex is Determined in Humans

1) There are <u>23 matched pairs</u> of chromosomes in every human body cell. The <u>23rd pair</u> is labelled <u>XX</u> or <u>XY</u>. They're the two chromosomes that decide whether you turn out <u>male</u> or <u>female</u>.

2) Males have an <u>X</u> and a <u>Y</u> chromosome (XY). The <u>Y</u> chromosome causes <u>male</u> characteristics.

3) Females have <u>two X chromosomes</u> (XX). The <u>XX combination</u> allows <u>female characteristics</u> to develop.

4) Because of this, there's an <u>equal chance</u> of having either a <u>boy</u> or a <u>girl</u>. Here's a <u>genetic diagram</u> to prove it:

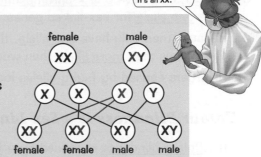

1) Even though we're talking about inheriting <u>chromosomes</u> here and not <u>single genes</u>, the <u>genetic diagram</u> still works the same way.

2) When you plug all the letters into the diagram, it shows that there are <u>two XX</u> results and <u>two XY</u> results, so there's the <u>same probability</u> of getting a boy or a girl.

3) Don't forget that this <u>50 : 50 ratio</u> is <u>only a probability</u>. If you had four kids they could all be boys.

5) All <u>eggs</u> have one <u>X chromosome</u>, but a <u>sperm</u> can have either an <u>X chromosome</u> or a <u>Y chromosome</u>. So <u>sex determination</u> in humans depends on whether the <u>sperm</u> that <u>fertilises</u> an egg carries an <u>X</u> or a <u>Y</u>.

Family Pedigrees Can Also Show Monohybrid Inheritance

Knowing how inheritance works helps you to interpret a <u>family pedigree</u> (a family tree of genetic disorders). Here's a worked example using <u>cystic fibrosis</u> — a genetic disorder of the cell membranes.

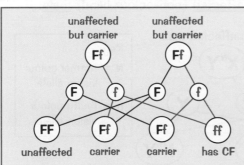

1) The allele which causes cystic fibrosis (CF) is a <u>recessive allele</u>, 'f', carried by about <u>1 person in 30</u>.

2) Because it's recessive, people with only <u>one copy</u> of the allele <u>won't</u> have the disorder — they're known as <u>carriers</u>.

3) For a child to have a chance of inheriting the disorder, <u>both parents</u> must either have the disorder themselves or be <u>carriers</u>.

4) As the diagram shows, there's a <u>1 in 4 chance</u> of a child having the disorder if <u>both</u> parents are <u>carriers</u>.

Below is a <u>family pedigree</u> for a family that includes <u>carriers</u> of <u>cystic fibrosis</u>. The lines on the pedigree link the parents to each other (horizontal) and to their children (vertical).

1) You can see from the pedigree that the <u>allele</u> for cystic fibrosis <u>isn't</u> dominant because plenty of the family <u>carry</u> the allele but don't have the disorder.

2) There is a 1 in 4 (<u>25%</u>) chance that the new baby will have <u>cystic fibrosis</u> and a 1 in 2 (<u>50%</u>) chance that it will be a <u>carrier</u> because <u>both</u> of its parents are carriers but don't have the disorder.

3) The case of the new baby is just the same as in the genetic diagram above — so the baby could be <u>unaffected</u> (FF), a <u>carrier</u> (Ff) or have the <u>disorder</u> (ff).

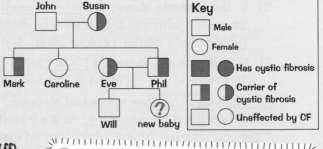

The probability of each outcome can also be expressed as a ratio — 1 : 2 : 1 for unaffected : carrier : disorder.

Have you got the Y-factor...

I bet you're sick of genetic diagrams by now. Still, that family pedigree makes a nice change. Umm... sort of.

Q1 Use the family pedigree above for the following question. Mark and his wife (who is not shown in the diagram) have a baby with cystic fibrosis. What are the possible genotypes of Mark's wife? [1 mark]

Sex-Linked Genetic Disorders

There are some genetic disorders that you're more likely to end up with if you're male — and it's all thanks to your X and Y chromosomes. Who'd have thought the little blighters could cause so much trouble...

Some Genetic Characteristics Are Sex-Linked

1) A characteristic is sex-linked if the allele that codes for it is located on a sex chromosome (X or Y).

2) The Y chromosome is smaller than the X chromosome and carries fewer genes. So most genes on the sex chromosomes are only carried on the X chromosome.

3) As men only have one X chromosome they often only have one allele for sex-linked genes.

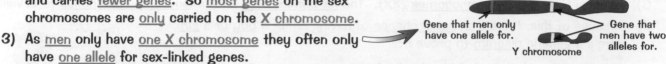

4) Because men only have one allele, the characteristic of this allele is shown even if it is recessive. This makes men more likely than women to show recessive characteristics for genes that are sex-linked.

5) Disorders caused by faulty alleles located on sex chromosomes are called sex-linked genetic disorders.

Colour Blindness is a Sex-Linked Disorder

1) Colour blindness is caused by a faulty allele carried on the X chromosome.

2) As it's sex-linked, both the chromosome and the allele are written in the genetic diagram, e.g. X^n, where X represents the X chromosome and n the faulty allele for colour vision. The Y chromosome doesn't have an allele for colour vision so is just represented by Y.

3) Women need two copies of the recessive allele to be colour blind, while men only need one copy. This means colour blindness is much rarer in women than men.

4) A woman with only one copy of the recessive allele is a carrier of colour blindness. This means that she isn't colour blind herself, but she can pass the allele on to her offspring.

5) Here's a genetic cross between a carrier female and an unaffected (non-colour blind) male:

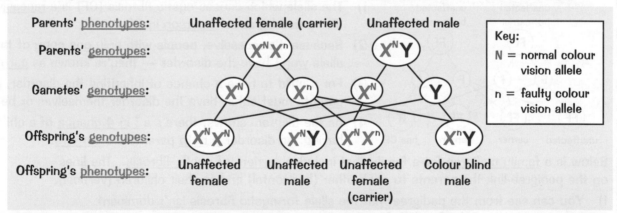

6) In the example above, the ratio of unaffected : colour blind offspring is 3 : 1. Be careful with this one, it may be disguised as a 2 : 1 : 1 ratio (unaffected : carrier : colour blind), but it means the same thing.

7) In other words, there's a 1 in 4 (25%) chance of a child being colour blind. This rises to 1 in 2 (50%) if you know that the child will be a boy.

Haemophilia is another sex-linked disorder. It's also caused by a faulty allele carried on the X chromosome, so it's inherited in the same way as colour blindness. A genetic diagram for the inheritance of haemophilia will look the same as the one above.

Haemophilia is a disease where the blood doesn't clot properly.

I keep tripping up — I've got a socks-linked disorder...

This diagram is nothing new — just remember that you're dealing with the inheritance of whole chromosomes.

Q1   Haemophilia is caused by a recessive allele located on the X chromosome. A couple are having a baby. The mother is a carrier of haemophilia. The father does not have the disorder. What is the probability that the couple will have: a) a son with haemophilia?   b) a daughter with haemophilia?   [2 marks]

Inheritance of Blood Groups

This is a bit more <u>complicated</u> than the examples on previous pages, but don't worry, you'll be fine. I'm here...

There Are Multiple Alleles That Determine Blood Group

1) So far you've probably only come across cases where there are <u>two possible alleles</u> for a gene — one that's <u>recessive</u> and one that's <u>dominant</u>.

2) Well, sometimes you'll get <u>more than two</u> (multiple) <u>alleles</u> for a <u>single gene</u>. This makes studying the inheritance of characteristics controlled by these genes a little more <u>complicated</u>.

3) For example, humans have <u>four</u> potential <u>blood types</u> — <u>O</u>, <u>A</u>, <u>B</u> and <u>AB</u>. The <u>gene</u> for blood type in humans has <u>three different alleles</u> — I^O, I^A and I^B.

4) I^A and I^B are <u>codominant</u> with each other. That means that when an individual has <u>both</u> of these alleles (genotype I^AI^B), then they'll have the blood type <u>AB</u> — one allele <u>isn't</u> dominant over the other one.

5) However, I^O is <u>recessive</u>. So when you get I^O with, say, I^A (genotype I^AI^O) then you <u>only</u> see the effect of I^A — giving blood type <u>A</u>.

6) You only get <u>blood type O</u> when you have <u>two of the recessive alleles</u> (I^OI^O).

> Recessive blood groups are normally really rare, but it just so happens that loads of people in Britain are descended from people who were $I^O I^O$, so O's really common.

You Can Predict Blood Groups Using Genetic Diagrams

1) You can draw <u>genetic diagrams</u> for <u>codominant</u> alleles in the same way that you would for alleles that are <u>recessive</u> and <u>dominant</u>.

2) The tricky bit is predicting the potential <u>phenotypes</u> in the offspring once you've worked out what the potential <u>genotypes</u> are. You need to remember how the different alleles <u>interact with each other</u> to produce a phenotype.

3) Here's an example showing how you can use <u>genetic diagrams</u> to predict the <u>blood type</u> inherited by the offspring:

1) A man is <u>blood group A</u>. His genotype is I^AI^O. A woman is <u>blood group B</u>. Her genotype is I^BI^O. The diagram shows the <u>alleles</u> that they can produce.

Parents' phenotypes — Heterozygous Blood group A — Heterozygous Blood group B

Parents' genotypes — I^AI^O — I^BI^O

Gametes' alleles — I^A I^O — I^B I^O

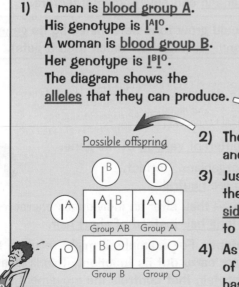

Possible offspring

	I^B	I^O
I^A	I^AI^B Group AB	I^AI^O Group A
I^O	I^BI^O Group B	I^OI^O Group O

2) The man and the woman have a child. The possible <u>genotypes</u> and <u>phenotypes</u> are shown in the Punnett square on the left.

3) Just like in the Punnett square you saw on page 38, the parents' <u>gametes</u> are written along the <u>top</u> and the <u>sides</u> of the square. They're <u>combined</u> in the middle to show the <u>possible genotypes</u> of the <u>offspring</u>.

4) As you can see from the diagram, the child could have any one of <u>four</u> different blood groups (<u>AB</u>, <u>A</u>, <u>B</u> or <u>O</u>). The child also has an <u>equal chance</u> (1 in 4 or 25%) of having each blood group.

What did the two recessive alleles say to the writer...

...sorry about the Type-O. Phew. That's the last of those diagrams, thank goodness. You might find this page a bit confusing — just remember, there can be multiple possible alleles for a gene, but an individual will only ever have two because they get one from each parent. Now before you have a well-earned rest, have a go at this question.

Q1 Explain how a mother with blood group A and a father with blood group B can have a child with blood group O.

[3 marks]

Variation

There's been a lot of talk about <u>genes</u> in this here uhh... genetics... section — but when it comes to <u>variation</u> in organisms, the <u>environment</u> is also really <u>important</u>. So make sure you don't forget about it.

Organisms of the Same Species Have Differences

1) Different species look... well... different — my dog definitely doesn't look like a daisy.

2) But even organisms of the <u>same species</u> will usually look at least slightly <u>different</u> — e.g. all dogs are the <u>same species</u>, but a <u>Dalmatian</u> looks quite different to a <u>Pug</u>.

3) These differences are called the <u>variation</u> within a species. It can be <u>genetic</u> or <u>environmental</u>.

4) <u>Genetic variation</u> within a species is caused by organisms having <u>different alleles</u> (versions of genes) which can lead to differences in <u>phenotype</u> (the <u>characteristics</u> an organism displays).

5) Genetic variation can be caused by <u>new alleles</u> arising through <u>mutations</u> (see below). <u>Sexual reproduction</u> also causes genetic variation since it results in alleles being <u>combined</u> in lots of <u>different ways</u> in offspring.

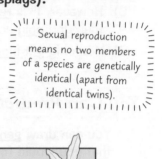

Sexual reproduction means no two members of a species are genetically identical (apart from identical twins).

6) There tends to be <u>a lot</u> of genetic variation <u>within a population</u> of a species. This is mostly due to <u>neutral mutations</u> (see below).

7) <u>Variation</u> within a species can also be caused by the <u>environment</u> (the conditions in which organisms live). For example:

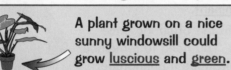

A plant grown on a nice sunny windowsill could grow <u>luscious</u> and <u>green</u>.

The same plant grown in darkness would grow <u>tall</u> and <u>spindly</u> and its leaves would turn <u>yellow</u>.

These <u>environmental variations</u> in phenotype are also known as <u>acquired characteristics</u>. They're characteristics that organisms acquire (get) during their lifetimes.

8) Most variation in phenotype is determined by a <u>mixture</u> of <u>genetic</u> and <u>environmental</u> factors.

For example, the <u>maximum height</u> that an animal or plant could grow to is determined by its <u>genes</u>. But whether it actually grows that tall depends on its <u>environment</u> (e.g. how much food it gets).

Alleles Arise Due to Genetic Mutations

There's more about the structure of DNA and mutations on pages 34 and 35.

1) <u>Mutations</u> are changes to the <u>base sequence</u> of DNA.

2) When they occur within a <u>gene</u> they result in an <u>allele</u>, or a <u>different version</u> of the gene.

3) They don't always have a <u>big</u> effect on the <u>phenotype</u> of an organism. In fact, <u>most</u> mutations don't have <u>any effect</u> — in other words they are <u>neutral</u>.

4) But <u>some</u> mutations do have a <u>small effect</u> on the phenotype — they alter an individual's characteristics, but only very slightly. E.g. a mutation might give a hamster <u>long hair</u> instead of <u>short hair</u>.

5) Very <u>rarely</u>, a single mutation will have a <u>big effect</u> on phenotype. For example, it might result in the production of a protein that is <u>so different</u> that it can <u>no longer</u> carry out its function. This is what happens in <u>cystic fibrosis</u> (see p.39). A mutation causes a <u>protein</u> that controls the <u>movement</u> of salt and water into and out of cells to <u>stop working</u> properly. This leads to the production of <u>thick, sticky</u> <u>mucus</u> in the lungs and digestive system, which can make it <u>difficult</u> to <u>breathe</u> and <u>digest food</u>.

6) New <u>combinations</u> of alleles may also <u>interact</u> with each other to produce <u>new phenotypes</u>.

Environmental variation — pretty much sums up British weather...

So, all the variation that you see around you is a complicated mixture of environmental and genetic influences. In fact, it's often really tricky to decide which factor is more influential, your genes or the environment.

Q1   Why does sexual reproduction result in genetic variation in a population?   [1 mark]

The Human Genome Project

The Human Genome Project is one of the most exciting things to have happened in science in recent years. Some people even called it "more exciting than the first moon landing"...

Researchers Managed to Map Over 20 000 Human Genes

1) Thousands of scientists from all over the world collaborated (worked together) on the Human Genome Project. The big idea was to find every single human gene.

2) The project officially started in 1990 and a complete map of the human genome, including the locations of around 20 500 genes, was completed in 2003.

3) Now that the genes have all been found, scientists are trying to figure out what they all do.

4) So far, the project has helped to identify about 1800 genes related to disease, which has huge potential benefits for medicine (see below).

There are Lots of Medical Applications for the Project's Research

Prediction and prevention of diseases

Many common diseases like cancers and heart disease are caused by the interaction of different genes, as well as lifestyle factors. If doctors knew what genes predisposed people to what diseases, we could all get individually tailored advice on the best diet and lifestyle to avoid our likely problems. Doctors could also check us regularly to ensure early treatment if we do develop the diseases we're susceptible to.

Testing and treatment for inherited disorders

1) Inherited disorders (e.g. cystic fibrosis) are caused by the presence of one or more faulty alleles in a person's genome.

2) Thanks to the Human Genome Project, scientists are now able to identify the genes and alleles that are suspected of causing an inherited disorder much more quickly than they could do in the past.

3) Once an allele that causes an inherited disorder has been identified, people can be tested for it and it may be possible to develop better treatments or even (eventually) a cure for the disease.

New and better medicines

1) Genome research has highlighted some common genetic variations between people. Some variations affect how our individual bodies will react to certain diseases and to the possible treatments for them.

2) Scientists can use this knowledge to design new drugs that are specifically tailored to people with a particular genetic variation. They can also determine how well an existing drug will work for an individual. Tests can already identify whether or not someone with breast cancer will respond to a particular drug, and what dosage is most appropriate for certain drugs in different patients.

3) More generally, knowing how a disease affects us on a molecular level should make it possible to design more effective treatments with fewer side-effects.

But There Could Also be Drawbacks

1) Increased stress — if someone knew from an early age that they're susceptible to a nasty brain disease, they could panic every time they get a headache (even if they never get the disease).

2) Gene-ism — people with genetic problems could come under pressure not to have children.

3) Discrimination by employers and insurers — life insurance could become impossible to get (or blummin' expensive at least) if you have any genetic likelihood of serious disease. And employers may discriminate against people who are genetically likely to get a disease.

DNA lipstick is part of my genetic make-up...

The Human Genome Project has resulted in some pretty useful discoveries, but there's still loads of work to do.

Q1   How could information from the Human Genome Project be used
      to help prevent individuals from developing certain diseases?   [2 marks]

Revision Questions for Topic 3

The next section's got more geneticsy bits — so make sure you can answer all these questions before going on.

- Try these questions and <u>tick off each one</u> when you <u>get it right</u>.
- When you've done <u>all the questions</u> under a heading and are <u>completely happy</u>, tick it off.

Reproduction and Meiosis (p.32-33) ☑

1) Name the gametes in humans. ☑
2) What happens to the DNA in a cell before the first division in meiosis? ☑
3) What is the advantage of having genetic variation in a population? ☑
4) Give a reason why sexual reproduction can take more time than asexual reproduction. ☑

DNA and Protein Synthesis (p.34-36) ☑

5) Draw a single nucleotide. ☑
6) What is meant by the term 'double helix'? ☑
7) When extracting DNA from a fruit, what is the purpose of mixing the fruit with detergent? ☑
8) What effect does ice-cold alcohol have on a solution containing free DNA molecules? ☑
9) Fill in the blank: Proteins are made up of _____ joined together in a chain. ☑
10) How do DNA bases code for specific amino acids? ☑
11) Name the enzyme that joins together RNA nucleotides to make mRNA. ☑
12) How can a mutation in non-coding DNA affect the phenotype of an organism? ☑

The Work of Mendel and Genetic Diagrams (p.37-39) ☑

13) Describe the experiment that Mendel used to study the inheritance of height in pea plants. ☑
14) Give three conclusions that Mendel reached by performing his experiments. ☑
15) What does it mean if an organism is
    a) homozygous for a gene?
    b) heterozygous for a gene? ☑
16) What is monohybrid inheritance? ☑
17) A couple have a child.
    What's the probability that the child will have the **XX** combination of sex chromosomes? ☑
18) How are carriers shown on a family pedigree? ☑

Sex-Linked Genetic Disorders and Inheritance of Blood Groups (p.40-41) ☑

19) Why are there more genes on the X chromosome than the Y chromosome? ☑
20) Why are men more likely to show recessive characteristics that are sex-linked? ☑
21) What is the name given to a person with only one copy of a recessive allele for a genetic disorder? ☑
22) What is meant by the term 'codominance'? ☑
23) What blood group does an individual have if they have the genotype $I^A I^O$? ☑

Variation and The Human Genome Project (p.42-43) ☑

24) What causes genetic variation in a species? ☑
25) What is an acquired characteristic? ☑
26) Write down three applications of the knowledge gained from the Human Genome Project. ☑
27) Describe three potential drawbacks of being able to read a person's genome. ☑

Natural Selection and Evidence for Evolution

Evolution is the <u>slow and continuous change</u> of organisms from one generation to the next.
<u>Charles Darwin</u> came up with the theory of <u>natural selection</u> to explain how <u>evolution</u> occurs.

Natural Selection Means "Survival of the Fittest"

1) Individuals in a population show <u>genetic variation</u> because of differences in their <u>alleles</u> (see page 42). New alleles arise through <u>mutations</u>.

Alleles are versions of genes — see page 38.

2) Things like <u>predation</u>, <u>competition</u> for resources (e.g. food, water, mates, etc.) and <u>disease</u> act as <u>selection pressures</u>. This means they affect an organism's chance of <u>surviving</u> and <u>reproducing</u>.

3) Those individuals with <u>characteristics</u> that make them <u>better adapted</u> to the selection pressures in their environment have a <u>better chance of survival</u> and so are more likely to <u>breed</u> successfully.

4) This means the <u>alleles</u> that are responsible for the useful characteristics are more likely to be <u>passed on</u> to the <u>next generation</u>.

5) However, some individuals will be <u>less well adapted</u> to the selection pressures in their environment and may be less able to <u>compete</u>. These individuals are <u>less likely</u> to survive and reproduce.

6) The <u>beneficial characteristics</u> become more <u>common</u> in the population over time.

A species that can't compete is likely to go extinct.

Bacteria Provide Evidence for Evolution

1) Like all organisms, bacteria sometimes develop <u>random mutations</u> in their DNA. These can create <u>new alleles</u>, which can <u>change</u> the bacteria's <u>characteristics</u> — e.g. a bacterium could become <u>less affected</u> by a particular <u>antibiotic</u> (a drug designed to kill bacteria or prevent them from reproducing).

2) For the bacterium, the ability to <u>resist</u> this antibiotic is a big <u>advantage</u>. In a host who's being treated to get rid of the infection, a resistant bacterium is <u>better able to survive</u> than a non-resistant bacterium — and so it lives for longer and <u>reproduces</u> many more times.

It's easy to see evolution happening in bacteria because they reproduce so rapidly.

3) This leads to the allele for antibiotic resistance being <u>passed on</u> to lots of offspring — it's just <u>natural selection</u>. This is how it spreads and becomes <u>more common</u> in a population of bacteria over time.

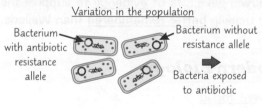
Variation in the population

Bacterium with antibiotic resistance allele — Bacterium without resistance allele — Bacteria exposed to antibiotic

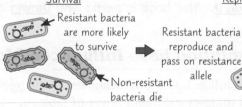
Survival

Resistant bacteria are more likely to survive — Non-resistant bacteria die

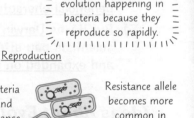
Reproduction

Resistant bacteria reproduce and pass on resistance allele — Resistance allele becomes more common in the population

4) Antibiotic resistance provides <u>evidence</u> for evolution because it makes the bacteria <u>better adapted</u> to an <u>environment</u> in which <u>antibiotics</u> (a <u>selection pressure</u>) are <u>present</u>. And as a result, antibiotic resistance becomes <u>more common</u> in the population over time. The emergence of <u>other</u> resistant organisms (e.g. <u>rats</u> resistant to the poison <u>warfarin</u>) <u>also</u> provides evidence for evolution.

Fossils Provide More Evidence for Evolution

1) A fossil is <u>any trace</u> of an animal or plant that lived <u>a long time ago</u> (e.g. over a thousand years). They are most commonly found in <u>rocks</u>. Generally, the <u>deeper</u> the rock, the <u>older</u> the fossil.

2) By arranging fossils in <u>chronological</u> (date) order, <u>gradual changes</u> in organisms can be observed. This provides <u>evidence</u> for evolution, because it shows how species have <u>changed</u> and <u>developed</u> over billions of years. Fossils that provide evidence for <u>human evolution</u> are covered on page 47.

Natural Selection — sounds like vegan chocolates...

So the evidence for evolution is right under our feet. Literally... But you've got to know what you're looking for.

Q1   How do fossils provide evidence that organisms evolved from simpler life forms?   [1 mark]

Darwin and Wallace

It was two clever chaps — <u>Darwin</u> and <u>Wallace</u> — who first developed the <u>theory of evolution by</u> <u>natural selection</u>. Little did they know we'd still be harping on about them <u>150 years later</u>...

Darwin Came up With The Theory of Evolution by Natural Selection...

Charles Darwin

1) <u>Charles Darwin</u> was the guy that came up with the <u>theory of evolution</u> <u>by natural selection</u>.

2) He spent 5 years on a <u>voyage</u> around the world <u>studying</u> <u>plants</u> and <u>animals</u> on a ship called <u>HMS Beagle</u>.

3) He noticed that there was <u>variation</u> in members of the <u>same species</u> and that those with characteristics <u>most suited</u> to the <u>environment</u> were more likely to <u>survive</u>.

4) He also noticed that characteristics could be <u>passed on</u> to offspring.

5) He wrote his <u>theory of evolution by natural selection</u> to explain his observations.

DNA and genes hadn't been discovered when Darwin was doing his work, so he didn't know exactly how characteristics were passed on — these details were added to the theory much later on.

...and Wallace Contributed Too

1) <u>Alfred Russel Wallace</u> was a scientist working at the <u>same time</u> as Darwin.

2) He also came up with the idea of natural selection, <u>independently</u> of Darwin.

3) He and Darwin <u>published</u> their papers on evolution <u>together</u> and <u>acknowledged</u> each other's work — although they didn't always <u>agree</u> on the <u>mechanisms</u> involved in <u>natural selection</u>.

4) Wallace's <u>observations</u> provided lots of <u>evidence</u> to help support the theory of evolution by natural selection. E.g. he realised that <u>warning colours</u> are used by some species (e.g. butterflies) to <u>deter predators</u> from eating them — an example of a <u>beneficial characteristic</u> that had <u>evolved</u> by natural selection.

5) But it was <u>Darwin's famous book</u> 'On the Origin of Species' (published in 1859) that made other scientists pay attention to the theory. In this book Darwin gave lots of <u>evidence</u> to support the theory and <u>expanded on it</u>. This book is partly why <u>Darwin</u> is usually <u>better remembered</u> than Wallace.

Ideas About Evolution have Influenced Modern Biology

1) The theory of evolution by natural selection is still <u>relevant today</u> — it helps us to <u>understand</u> many areas of <u>biology</u>.

2) We now understand that all life <u>changes</u> through the process of evolution, and that the evidence suggests we have <u>all descended</u> from a <u>common ancestor</u>.

3) This has affected lots of <u>different areas</u> of biology, including:

- <u>classification</u> — if all living organisms have descended from a common ancestor, then we're all <u>related</u> in some way. We now <u>classify</u> organisms (arrange them into groups) based on how <u>closely related</u> they are (see page 49).

- <u>antibiotic resistance</u> (see previous page) — we now understand the importance of <u>finishing</u> the course of drugs to <u>prevent</u> resistant bacteria <u>spreading</u> and we know we need to <u>constantly</u> develop <u>new antibiotics</u> to fight <u>newly evolved</u> resistant bacteria.

- <u>conservation</u> — we now understand the importance of <u>genetic diversity</u> and how it helps populations <u>adapt to changing environments</u>. This has led to <u>conservation projects</u> to protect species.

Darwin was a darlin', and Wallace was well ace...

Biology wouldn't be what it is today without Darwin and Wallace, but at the time their ideas were revolutionary.

Q1   Describe Wallace's role in developing the theory of evolution by natural selection.   [2 marks]

Fossil Evidence for Human Evolution

There's a lot of fossil evidence that suggests that humans evolved from a common ancestor with other apes.

Fossils Give Us Clues About What Human Ancestors Were Like...

1) Evidence from fossils suggests that humans and chimpanzees evolved from a common ancestor that existed around 6 million years ago.

2) Human beings and their ancestors are known as hominids. Fossils of several different hominid species have been found.

3) These fossils have characteristics that are between apes and humans — by looking at hominid fossils you can see how humans have evolved over time.

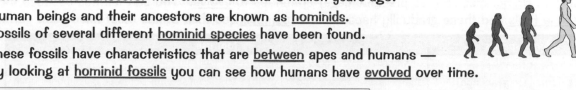

'Ardi' is a Fossil Hominid 4.4 Million Years Old

Ardi is a fossil of the species *Ardipithecus ramidus*. She was found in Ethiopia and is 4.4 million years old. Ardi's features are a mixture of those found in humans and in apes:

1) The structure of her feet suggests she climbed trees — she had an ape-like big toe to grasp branches.

2) She also had long arms and short legs (more like an ape than a human).

3) Her brain size was about the same as a chimpanzee's.

4) But the structure of her legs suggests that she walked upright. Her hand bone structure also suggests she didn't use her hands to help her walk (like apes do).

> Brain size is found by working out 'cranial capacity' — the space taken up by the brain in the skull.

'Lucy' is a Fossil Hominid 3.2 Million Years Old

Lucy is a fossil of the species *Australopithecus afarensis*. She was found in Ethiopia and is 3.2 million years old. Lucy also has a mixture of human and ape features, but she is more human-like than Ardi.

1) Lucy had arched feet, more adapted to walking than climbing, and no ape-like big toe.

2) The size of her arms and legs was between what you would expect to find in apes and humans.

3) Her brain was slightly larger than Ardi's but still similar in size to a chimp's brain.

4) The structure of Lucy's leg bones and feet suggest she walked upright, but more efficiently than Ardi.

Leakey and His Team Found Fossil Hominids 1.6 Million Years Old

In 1984 scientist Richard Leakey organised an expedition to Kenya to look for hominid fossils. He and his team discovered many important fossils of different *Australopithecus* and *Homo* species.

1) One of their finds was Turkana Boy — a 1.6 million year old fossil skeleton of the species *Homo erectus*. He has a mixture of human and ape-like features, but is more human-like than Lucy.

2) His short arms and long legs are much more like a human than an ape, and his brain size was much larger than Lucy's — similar to human brain size.

3) The structure of his legs and feet suggest he was even better adapted to walking upright than Lucy.

...and Can be Put on a Timeline to Show Human Evolution

So you know that the *Ardipithecus* and *Australopithecus* species were more ape-like, compared to the *Homo* species, which are human-like. They can all be put on a time line, showing how humans have evolved:

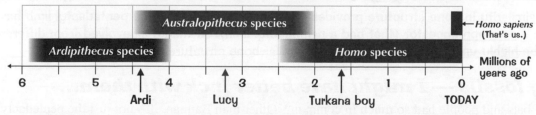

Hang on a minute — how do they know her name was Lucy?

You should know how these fossils provide evidence for human evolution. Typical. Bet Lucy never had to revise...

Q1   Outline the major changes observed between the fossils of 'Ardi' and 'Lucy' in the fossil record of hominids.

[3 marks]

More Evidence for Evolution

It's not just fossils — you can find evidence for human evolution from the <u>tools</u> they used too. What's more, the structures in <u>living organisms</u> also provide evidence for evolution. Fun stuff...

Development of Stone Tools Provides Evidence For Human Evolution

The different <u>Homo</u> species (see previous page) continued to <u>evolve</u>. You can tell this because they started using <u>stone tools</u> and these gradually became more <u>complex</u> (so their brains must have been getting <u>larger</u>):

Homo species	Tool use
Homo habilis (2.5-1.5 million years ago)	Made simple stone tools called pebble tools by hitting rocks together to make sharp flakes. These could be used to scrape meat from bones or crack bones open.
Homo erectus (2-0.3 million years ago)	Sculpted rocks into shapes to produce more complex tools like simple hand-axes. These could be used to hunt, dig, chop and scrape meat from bones.
Homo neanderthalis (300 000-25 000 years ago)	More complex tools. Evidence of flint tools, pointed tools and wooden spears.
Homo sapiens (200 000 years ago-present)	Flint tools widely used. Pointed tools including arrowheads, fish hooks, buttons and needles appeared around 50 000 years ago.

When an ancient stone tool or hominid fossil (see previous page) is found, there are several <u>different ways</u> scientists can work out <u>how old it is</u>. These include:

Dating tools and fossils isn't always very accurate, e.g. rock layers can move over time.

1)   Looking at the <u>structural features</u> of the tool or fossil.
     For example, <u>simpler tools</u> are likely to be <u>older</u> than more complex tools.

2)   Using <u>stratigraphy</u> — the study of <u>rock layers</u>. <u>Older</u> rock layers are normally found <u>below</u> younger layers, so tools or fossils in <u>deeper</u> layers are usually <u>older</u>.

3)   Stone tools are often found with <u>carbon-containing material</u>, e.g. a wooden handle. <u>Carbon-14 dating</u> can be used to date this material.

The Pentadactyl Limb Also Provides Evidence for Evolution

1)   A <u>pentadactyl limb</u> is a limb with <u>five digits</u>.

2)   You can see the pentadactyl limb in <u>many species</u>, e.g. mammals, reptiles, amphibians.

3)   In each of these species the pentadactyl limb has a <u>similar bone structure</u>, but usually a <u>different function</u>. For example, a <u>human's hand</u> and a <u>bat's wing</u> are both pentadactyl limbs — and they look pretty alike...

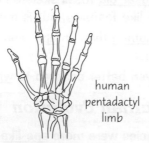

human pentadactyl limb

bat pentadactyl limb

© X-Ray of Pteropus also known as Flying Fox or Fruit Bat / Nick Veasey / Getty Images

...but we can't use ours to <u>fly</u>. D'oh.

4)   The <u>similarity</u> in bone structure provides <u>evidence</u> that species with a pentadactyl limb have all <u>evolved</u> from a <u>common ancestor</u> (that had a pentadactyl limb). If they'd all evolved from different ancestors, it'd be <u>highly unlikely</u> that they'd share a similar bone structure.

Dating fossils — I might have better luck with them...

Who knew bats and people had so much in common? Other than Batman. It's not just the pentadactyl limb either, we share loads of similar features with other mammals — ears, eyes, noses... The list is endless really.

Q1   An archaeologist discovered a fossil-rich site for hominid skeletons.
      She discovered what appeared to be pieces of pointed stone tools among the bones.
      a)   What does the shape of the stone tools suggest about the fossils present at the site?   [1 mark]
      b)   State one method that the scientist could use to find the age of the stone tools.   [1 mark]

Classification

It seems to be a basic human urge to want to <u>classify</u> things — that's the case in biology anyway...

Classification is Organising Living Organisms into Groups

1) Traditionally, organisms were <u>classified</u> according to similarities and differences in their <u>observable characteristics</u>, i.e. things you can see (like how many legs something has). As <u>technology improved</u>, this included things you can see with a <u>microscope</u>, e.g. <u>cell structure</u>.

2) These characteristics were used to classify organisms in the <u>five kingdom classification system</u>. In this system, living things are first divided into <u>five groups</u> called <u>kingdoms</u>. These are:

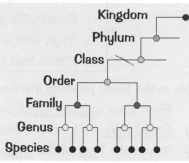

- <u>Animals</u> — fish, mammals, reptiles, etc.
- <u>Plants</u> — grasses, trees, etc.
- <u>Fungi</u> — mushrooms and toadstools, yeasts, all that mouldy stuff on your loaf of bread (yuck).
- <u>Prokaryotes</u> — all <u>single-celled</u> organisms <u>without</u> a nucleus.
- <u>Protists</u> — <u>eukaryotic single-celled</u> organisms, e.g. algae.

3) The <u>kingdoms</u> are then subdivided into smaller and smaller groups that have common features — <u>phylum</u>, <u>class</u>, <u>order</u>, <u>family</u>, <u>genus</u>, <u>species</u>.

There's more on prokaryotes and eukaryotes on p.12.

Classification Systems Change Over Time

1) The <u>five kingdom</u> classification system is still used, but it's now a bit <u>out of date</u>.

2) Over time, <u>technology</u> has developed further and our understanding of things like <u>biochemical processes</u> and <u>genetics</u> has increased. For example, we are now able to determine the <u>sequence of DNA bases</u> in different organisms' <u>genes</u> and <u>compare them</u> — the more <u>similar</u> the sequence of a gene, the more <u>closely related</u> the organisms. Scientists are also able to compare <u>RNA sequences</u> in a similar way.

3) This led to a bit of a rethink about the way organisms are <u>classified</u> and to the proposal of the <u>three domain system</u> of classification by a scientist called Carl Woese.

There's more on DNA and RNA on pages 34-36.

4) Using <u>RNA sequencing</u>, Woese found that some members of the <u>Prokaryote kingdom</u> were not as closely related as first thought. He proposed that this kingdom should be split into two groups called <u>Archaea</u> and <u>Bacteria</u>.

5) In fact, Woese suggested that all organisms should first be divided into <u>three large groups</u> called <u>domains</u>. Archaea and Bacteria are <u>two</u> of these domains. The third domain is <u>Eukarya</u>.

1) ARCHAEA — Organisms in this domain <u>look similar</u> to <u>bacteria</u> but are actually quite <u>different</u> — as differences in their <u>DNA and RNA sequences</u> show. They were first found in <u>extreme places</u> such as hot springs and salt lakes.

2) BACTERIA — This domain contains <u>true bacteria</u> like *E. coli* and *Staphylococcus*.

3) EUKARYA — This domain includes a <u>broad range</u> of organisms including <u>fungi</u>, <u>plants</u>, <u>animals</u> and <u>protists</u>.

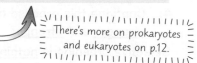

6) The three domains are then <u>subdivided</u> into <u>smaller groups</u> used in the <u>five kingdom system</u> (beginning with kingdom and finishing with species).

Why did the Bacterium break up with the Archaean?

...they didn't have much in common. Biologists have the best jokes. It's strange to think that Archaea and Bacteria, which look really similar, are actually more different than we are to a mushroom.

Q1   Give one example of how advances in technology allowed
       scientists to distinguish between Archaea and Bacteria.   [1 mark]

Selective Breeding

'Selective breeding' sounds like it has the potential to be a tricky topic, but it's actually dead simple. You take the best plants or animals and breed them together to get the best possible offspring. That's it.

Selective Breeding is Very Simple

Selective breeding is when humans artificially select the plants or animals that are going to breed so that the genes for particular characteristics remain in the population. Organisms are selectively bred to develop features that are useful or attractive, for example:

- Animals that produce more meat or milk.
- Crops with disease resistance.
- Dogs with a good, gentle temperament.
- Plants that produce bigger fruit.

This is the basic process involved in selective breeding:

1) From your existing stock select the ones which have the characteristics you're after.
2) Breed them with each other.
3) Select the best of the offspring, and breed them together.
4) Continue this process over several generations, and the desirable trait gets stronger and stronger. Eventually, all the offspring will have the characteristic.

Selective breeding is also known as 'artificial selection'.

Selective breeding is nothing new — people have been doing it for thousands of years. It's how we ended up with edible crops from wild plants and how we got domesticated animals like cows and dogs.

Selective Breeding is Useful...

Selective breeding is important in agriculture. For example:

Genetic variation means some cattle will have better characteristics for producing meat than others (e.g. a larger size). To improve meat yields, a farmer could select cows and bulls with these characteristics and breed them together. After doing this, and selecting the best of the offspring for several generations, the farmer would get cows with a very high meat yield.

It's also used in medical research. For example:

In several studies investigating the reasons behind alcoholism, rats have been bred with either a strong preference for alcohol or a weak preference for alcohol. This has allowed researchers to compare the differences between the two different types of rats, including differences in their behaviour and in the way that their brains work.

...but Also Has Disadvantages

1) The main problem with selective breeding is that it reduces the gene pool — the number of different alleles (forms of a gene) in a population. This is because the "best" animals or plants are always used for breeding — and they are all closely related. This is known as inbreeding.

2) Inbreeding can cause health problems because there's more chance of the organisms inheriting harmful genetic defects when the gene pool is limited. Some dog breeds are susceptible to certain defects because of inbreeding, e.g. pugs often have breathing problems. This leads to ethical considerations — particularly if animals are deliberately bred to have negative characteristics for medical research.

3) There can also be serious problems if a new disease appears. There's not much variation in the population, so there's less chance of resistance alleles being present. All the stock are closely related to each other, so if one is going to be killed by a new disease, the others are also likely to succumb to it.

I use the same genes all the time too — they flatter my hips...

Different breeds of dog came from selective breeding. For example, somebody thought 'I really like this small, yappy wolf — I'll breed it with this other one'. After thousands of generations, we got poodles.

Q1 Give three potential problems selective breeding can cause.   [3 marks]

Tissue Culture

By taking little bits of tissues and <u>growing them</u>, scientists are able to reproduce tissue from a <u>single individual</u> — so they don't have to go through the lengthy process of selective breeding.

Plants Can be Grown Using Tissue Culture

1) Tissue culture involves growing cells on an <u>artificial growth medium</u>.

2) <u>Whole plants</u> can be grown via tissue culture — it's really <u>easy</u> and really <u>useful</u> too.
   Plants grown this way can be made very <u>quickly</u>, in <u>very little space</u> and can be grown <u>all year</u>.

3) The plants produced via tissue culture are also <u>clones</u> — <u>genetically identical</u> organisms.
   This means you can use tissue culture to create <u>lines</u> of clones all with the <u>same beneficial</u>
   <u>features</u>, e.g. <u>pesticide resistance</u>, <u>tasty fruit</u>, etc. Here's how it works:

1) First you choose the plant you want to clone based on its <u>characteristics</u> —
   e.g. a beautiful flower, a good fruit crop.

2) You <u>remove</u> several <u>small pieces</u> of <u>tissue</u> from the <u>parent plant</u>. You get the best results if you
   take tissue from <u>fast-growing root or shoot tips</u>.

3) You grow the tissue in a <u>growth medium</u> containing <u>nutrients</u> and <u>growth hormones</u>. This is done
   under <u>aseptic</u> (sterile) conditions to prevent growth of <u>microbes</u> that could harm the plants.

4) As the tissues produce shoots and roots they can be moved to <u>potting compost</u> to carry on growing.

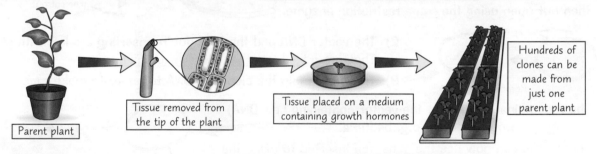

Parent plant

Tissue removed from
the tip of the plant

Tissue placed on a medium
containing growth hormones

Hundreds of
clones can be
made from
just one
parent plant

Animal Tissue Culture is Useful for Medical Research

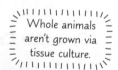

Whole animals
aren't grown via
tissue culture.

1) <u>Animal</u> tissue culture is often used in <u>medical research</u> because it means that you can
   carry out all kinds of <u>experiments</u> on tissues in <u>isolation</u>. E.g. you can investigate the
   effect of <u>glucose</u> on cells in the <u>pancreas</u> by growing pancreatic cells in culture.

2) It means that you can look at the effects of a <u>particular substance</u> or <u>environmental change</u> on
   the cells of a <u>single tissue</u>, without <u>complications</u> from other processes in the <u>whole</u> organism.

3) Tissue culture of <u>animal cells</u> is carried out as follows:

1) First, a <u>sample</u> of the <u>tissue</u> you want to study, e.g. tissue
   from the pancreas, is <u>extracted from</u> the animal.

2) The cells in the sample are <u>separated</u> from each
   other using <u>enzymes</u>.

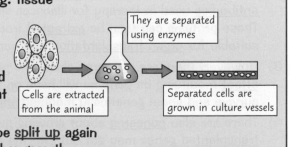

They are separated
using enzymes

Cells are extracted
from the animal

Separated cells are
grown in culture vessels

3) Then they are placed in a <u>culture vessel</u> and bathed
   in a <u>growth medium</u> containing all the <u>nutrients</u> that
   they need. This allows them to <u>grow</u> and <u>multiply</u>.

4) After several rounds of <u>cell division</u>, the cells can be <u>split up</u> again
   and placed into <u>separate vessels</u> to encourage <u>further growth</u>.

5) Once the tissue culture has been grown, it can be <u>stored</u> for future use.

How do you culture a tissue? Take it to the theatre, dahling...

So there you have it, being able to make clones of a tissue or an organism is really useful.

Q1 A farmer discovers an apple tree in his orchard that produces a new kind of pink apple.
    Describe the method of tissue culture he could use to make clones of this tree. [4 marks]

Genetic Engineering

Genetic engineering involves modifying an organism's genome (its DNA) to introduce desirable characteristics. This involves the use of enzymes and vectors (carriers).

Enzymes Can Be Used To Cut Up DNA or Join DNA Pieces Together

1) Restriction enzymes recognise specific sequences of DNA and cut the DNA at these points — the pieces of DNA are left with sticky ends where they have been cut.

2) Ligase enzymes are used to join two pieces of DNA together at their sticky ends.

3) Two different bits of DNA stuck together are known as recombinant DNA.

Vectors Can Be Used To Insert DNA Into Other Organisms

A vector is something that's used to transfer DNA into a cell. There are two sorts — plasmids and viruses:

- Plasmids are small, circular molecules of DNA that can be transferred between bacteria.

- Viruses insert DNA into the organisms they infect.

Here's how genetic engineering works:

1) The DNA you want to insert (e.g. the gene for human insulin) is cut out with a restriction enzyme. The vector DNA is then cut open using the same restriction enzyme.

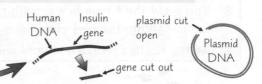

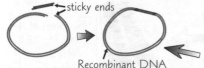

2) The vector DNA and the DNA you're inserting are left with sticky ends. They are mixed together with ligase enzymes.

3) The ligases join the pieces of DNA together to make recombinant DNA.

4) The recombinant DNA (i.e. the vector containing new DNA) is inserted into other cells, e.g. bacteria.

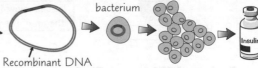

5) These cells can now use the gene you inserted to make the protein you want. E.g. bacteria containing the gene for human insulin can be grown in huge numbers in a fermenter to produce insulin for people with diabetes.

Genetic Engineering is Useful in Agriculture and Medicine

1) For example, in agriculture, crops can be genetically modified to be resistant to herbicides (chemicals that kill plants). Making crops herbicide-resistant means farmers can spray their crops to kill weeds, without affecting the crop itself. This can also increase crop yield.

2) In medicine, as well as genetically engineering bacteria to produce human insulin, researchers have managed to transfer human genes that produce useful proteins into sheep and cows. E.g. human antibodies used in therapy for illnesses like arthritis, some types of cancer and multiple sclerosis. These proteins can then be extracted from the animal, e.g. from their milk. Animals that have organs suitable for organ transplantation into humans might also be produced in the future.

3) However, there are concerns about the genetic engineering of animals. It can be hard to predict what effect modifying its genome will have on the organism — many genetically modified embryos don't survive and some genetically modified animals suffer from health problems later in life.

4) There are also concerns about growing genetically modified crops. One is that transplanted genes may get out into the environment. E.g. a herbicide resistance gene may be picked up by weeds, creating a new 'superweed' variety. Another concern is that genetically modified crops could adversely affect food chains — or even human health.

If only there was a gene to make revision easier...

Genetically modified organisms have a lot of potential to be very useful. But we don't yet know what all the consequences of using them might be — so it's good to be familiar with the arguments for and against them.

Q1   Explain one benefit of being able to genetically engineer herbicide-resistant crops.   [2 marks]

Topic 4 — Natural Selection and Genetic Modification

GMOs and Human Population Growth

Genetically modified organisms are also known as GM organisms or GMOs.
GMOs are being used to help provide food for many people in the world that suffer from hunger.

Crops can be Genetically Modified to be Resistant to Insects

1) One reason why people might want to genetically engineer crops is to make them resistant to insect pests. This can improve crop yields and reduce the need for chemical pesticides.

2) There's a bacterium called *Bacillus thuringiensis* (Bt) which produces a toxin (poison) that kills many of the insect larvae that are harmful to crops.

3) The gene for the Bt toxin is inserted into crops, such as corn and cotton, which then produce the toxin in their stems and leaves — making them resistant to the insect pests.

4) The toxin is specific to insect pests — it's harmless to humans, animals and other insects. However, the long-term effects of exposure to Bt crops aren't yet known.

5) The insects that feed on the crops are constantly exposed to the toxin, so there's a danger they'll develop resistance and no longer be killed by it. Farmers try to avoid this happening by using other insecticides too.

GMOs Can Be Used to Provide More Food for People

1) The world's population is rising very quickly — and it's not slowing down.

2) This means that global food production must increase too so that we all have access to enough food that is safe for us to eat and has the right balance of nutrition — this is known as 'food security'.

3) GM crops can be used to help increase food production — e.g. crops that are genetically engineered to be resistant to pests or to grow better in drought conditions can help to improve crop yields.

4) Some crops can be engineered to combat certain deficiency diseases, e.g. Golden Rice™ has been genetically engineered to produce a chemical that's converted in the body to vitamin A.

5) Unfortunately, not everyone thinks this is a good idea:

   1) Many people argue that people go hungry because they can't afford to buy food, not because there isn't any food about. So they argue that you need to tackle poverty first.

   2) There are fears that countries may become dependent on companies who sell GM seeds.

   3) Sometimes poor soil is the main reason why crops fail, and even GM crops won't survive.

Other Techniques Can Also be Used to Increase Food Production

1) Using GMOs is a relatively new way of improving crop yields — and it might not always be helpful.

2) For example, if soils are poor, applying fertilisers is likely to be the best way to increase yields. Fertilisers contain minerals that are essential for plant growth, e.g. nitrates and phosphates. They replace the nutrients that have been lost from the soils to previous crops. However, excess fertilisers can cause problems in rivers and lakes through the process of eutrophication — see p.99.

3) Pests can also be controlled without the use of GM crops or chemical pesticides. Biological control methods use other organisms (including predators and parasites) to reduce pest numbers. For example, cane toads were introduced into Australia to eat beetles that were damaging crops.

4) Biological control can have longer-lasting effects than chemical pesticides and be less harmful to wildlife, but introducing new organisms can cause problems, e.g. cane toads are now a pest themselves in Australia because they poison the native species that eat them.

Cabbage that tastes like chocolate — there's a GMO I'll support...

There probably isn't one solution to providing enough food for everyone — each method of improving crop yields has its advantages and disadvantages, so you should learn what they all are.

Q1   Suggest three methods that could be used to help provide food for a growing human population. [3 marks]

Revision Questions for Topic 4

A lot of names to remember for this one — it's like some kind of fancy "meet and greet" with fossils...

* Try these questions and <u>tick off each one</u> when you <u>get it right</u>.
* When you've done <u>all the questions</u> under a heading and are <u>completely happy</u>, tick it off.

<u>Natural Selection and Evolution (p.45-48)</u> ☑

1) Describe how organisms evolve by the process of natural selection. ☑
2) How do antibiotic-resistant bacteria provide evidence for evolution? ☑
3) Name three important areas of modern biology that have been influenced by
   Darwin and Wallace's theory of evolution by natural selection. ☑
4) What are hominids? ☑
5) Which fossil is older — "Ardi" or "Lucy"? ☑
6) Who was Richard Leakey? What important discoveries did he make in relation to human evolution? ☑
7) What is stratigraphy? How might it be used to date stone tools? ☑
8) How do pentadactyl limbs provide evidence for evolution? ☑

<u>Classification (p.49)</u> ☑

9) Describe how organisms were classified using the five kingdom classification system. ☑
10) What classification system was proposed by Carl Woese and what led him to propose it? ☑

<u>Selective Breeding (p.50)</u> ☑

11) What is artificial selection? ☑
12) How can selective breeding be used to improve yields in the meat industry? ☑
13) Describe one way in which selective breeding can be useful outside of agriculture. ☑
14) What is a gene pool? ☑
15) Why does selective breeding reduce gene pools? ☑

<u>Tissue Culture (p.51)</u> ☑

16) What is a clone? ☑
17) Why is it useful to be able to make many clones of a single plant? ☑
18) What are the benefits of using animal tissue culture for medical research? ☑

<u>Genetic Engineering and Human Population Growth (p.52-53)</u> ☑

19) What are restriction enzymes used for in genetic engineering? ☑
20) What is a vector? ☑
21) What are the concerns over creating genetically modified organisms? ☑
22) Complete the sentence:
    A gene from *Bacillus thuringiensis* is used to make crops more resistant to _____. ☑
23) How can poor soils be improved to increase crop yields? ☑
24) Give an example of a biological pest control method. ☑

Health and Disease

If you're hoping I'll ease you gently into this new topic... no such luck. Straight on to the <u>baddies</u> of biology.

You Need to Know How 'Health' is Defined

1) It might surprise you to know that <u>being healthy</u> is about <u>more</u> than just <u>not being sick</u>.

2) The <u>World Health Organisation</u> (the <u>WHO</u>) defines health as "a state of <u>complete physical</u>, <u>mental</u> and <u>social well-being</u>, and not merely the absence of disease or infirmity".

3) This means that even if someone is very <u>physically fit</u>, they still might be <u>unhealthy</u> if, e.g. they have <u>mental health</u> issues or are <u>socially isolated</u>.

Infirmity means weakness or frailness, commonly due to old age.

Diseases Can be Communicable or Non-Communicable

1) A disease is a <u>condition</u> where <u>part</u> of an organism <u>doesn't function</u> properly. There are <u>two sorts</u> of disease — <u>communicable</u> and <u>non-communicable</u>.

2) <u>Communicable diseases</u> are diseases that can be spread <u>between</u> individuals. See the table below.

3) <u>Non-communicable diseases</u> can't be transmitted between individuals. They include things like <u>cancer</u> and <u>heart disease</u>. There's more on these on page 65.

4) If you are affected by <u>one</u> disease, it could make you <u>more susceptible</u> to others — your body may become <u>weakened</u> by the disease, so it's less able to fight off others.

Being susceptible to a disease, means that you have an increased chance of getting it.

Communicable Diseases are Caused by Pathogens

<u>Pathogens</u> are <u>organisms</u> such as <u>viruses</u>, <u>bacteria</u>, <u>fungi</u> and <u>protists</u> (see p.49) that cause <u>communicable</u> <u>diseases</u>. Here are some examples of <u>communicable diseases</u> that you need to know about for your exam:

Disease	Pathogen	Symptoms/ Effects	How it spreads	How to reduce/prevent transmission
Cholera	A <u>bacterium</u> called *Vibrio cholerae*.	Diarrhoea.	Via contaminated <u>water</u> sources.	Making sure that people have access to <u>clean water supplies</u>.
Tuberculosis	A <u>bacterium</u> called *Mycobacterium tuberculosis*.	Coughing and <u>lung damage</u>.	Through the <u>air</u> when infected individuals cough.	Infected people should <u>avoid crowded public spaces</u>, <u>practise good hygiene</u> and <u>sleep alone</u>. Their homes should also be <u>well-ventilated</u>.
Malaria	A <u>protist</u>.	Damage to <u>red blood cells</u> and, in severe cases, to the <u>liver</u>.	<u>Mosquitoes</u> act as animal <u>vectors</u> (carriers) — they pass on the <u>protist</u> to humans but don't get the disease <u>themselves</u>.	Use of <u>mosquito nets</u> and <u>insect repellent</u> to prevent mosquitoes carrying the pathogen from <u>biting</u> people.
Stomach ulcers	A <u>bacterium</u> called *Helicobacter pylori*.	<u>Stomach pain</u>, <u>nausea</u> and <u>vomiting</u>.	<u>Oral transmission</u>, e.g. swallowing contaminated water or food.	Having <u>clean water</u> supplies and <u>hygienic</u> living conditions.
Ebola	Ebola <u>virus</u>.	<u>Haemorrhagic fever</u> (a fever with <u>bleeding</u>).	Via <u>bodily fluids</u>.	By <u>isolating infected individuals</u> and <u>sterilising</u> any areas where the virus may be present.
Chalara ash dieback	A <u>fungus</u> that infects ash trees.	<u>Leaf loss</u> and <u>bark lesions</u> (wounds).	Carried through the <u>air</u> by the <u>wind</u>. (It also spreads when <u>diseased ash trees</u> are <u>moved</u> between areas.)	<u>Removing young, infected ash trees</u> and <u>replanting</u> with different species. <u>Restricting</u> the <u>import</u> or <u>movement</u> of ash trees.

Coughs and sneezes spread diseases...

Yuck, lots of nasties out there that can cause disease. Plants need to be worried too, as you can see.

Q1   Describe how the Ebola virus is spread and what can be done to prevent its spread.   [3 marks]

Viruses and STIs

Viruses such as <u>HIV</u> and some <u>bacteria</u>, like *Chlamydia*, take advantage of our cells in some nasty ways...

Viruses Can Only Reproduce Inside Living Cells

1) Viruses <u>aren't cells</u>. They're usually no more than a <u>protein coat</u> around a strand of <u>genetic material</u>.

2) They have to <u>infect living cells</u> (called host cells) in order to <u>reproduce</u>. <u>Specific</u> types of viruses will only infect <u>specific cells</u>.

3) The <u>life cycle</u> of a virus starts with when it infects a <u>new host cell</u>. Many will then reproduce by the <u>lytic pathway</u>, but some can enter the <u>lysogenic</u> pathway <u>first</u>:

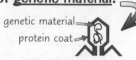

genetic material
protein coat
A typical virus

The lytic pathway

1) The virus attaches itself to a <u>specific host cell</u> and <u>injects</u> its <u>genetic material</u> into the cell.

2) The virus uses <u>proteins</u> and <u>enzymes</u> in the host cell to <u>replicate</u> its <u>genetic material</u> and produce the <u>components</u> of new viruses.

3) The viral components <u>assemble</u>.

4) The host cell <u>splits open</u>, releasing the new viruses, which infect <u>more cells</u>.

The lysogenic pathway

1) The injected <u>genetic material</u> is <u>incorporated</u> into the <u>genome</u> (DNA) of the host cell.

2) The viral <u>genetic material</u> gets <u>replicated</u> along with the <u>host DNA</u> every time the host cell <u>divides</u> — but the virus is <u>dormant</u> (inactive) and <u>no new viruses</u> are made.

3) Eventually a <u>trigger</u> (e.g. the presence of a <u>chemical</u>) causes the viral genetic material to <u>leave</u> the genome and enter the <u>lytic pathway</u>.

virus
host cell
eek!
Lytic Pathway
viral DNA
host cell DNA
new viruses
viral DNA within host cell genome
Lysogenic Pathway
dividing host cell

STIs are Sexually Transmitted Infections

<u>STIs</u> are infections that are spread through <u>sexual contact</u>, including <u>sexual intercourse</u>. Here are <u>two</u> STIs that you need to know about:

Some STIs, including Chlamydia, are spread by genital contact, not just sexual intercourse.

1) *Chlamydia* is a kind of <u>bacterium</u>, but it behaves in a similar way to a <u>virus</u> because it can only reproduce <u>inside host cells</u>.

2) Although it doesn't always cause <u>symptoms</u>, it can result in <u>infertility</u> in men and women.

3) The <u>spread</u> of *Chlamydia* can be <u>reduced</u> by wearing a <u>condom</u> when having sex, <u>screening</u> individuals so they can be <u>treated</u> for the infection or <u>avoiding sexual contact</u>.

1) HIV is the <u>Human Immunodeficiency Virus</u> — it kills <u>white blood cells</u>, which are really important in the <u>immune response</u>.

2) HIV infection eventually leads to <u>AIDS</u> (Acquired Immune Deficiency Syndrome).

3) This is when the infected person's immune system <u>deteriorates</u> and eventually <u>fails</u> — because of this, the person becomes very <u>vulnerable</u> to opportunistic infections by <u>other pathogens</u>.

4) HIV is spread via infected <u>bodily fluids</u> (e.g. blood, semen, vaginal fluids). One of the main ways to prevent its spread is to use a <u>condom</u> when having sex. <u>Drug users</u> should also avoid <u>sharing needles</u>. Medication can <u>reduce the risk</u> of an infected individual passing the virus on to others during sex (or of a mother passing the virus to her baby during pregnancy) so <u>screening</u> and <u>proper treatment</u> are also important.

Typical. Can't do anything by themselves, so they pick on us...

You'll be pleased to hear the next page is about plant diseases, not human ones. Learn this lot, then you can move on.

Q1 Describe the lytic pathway in the life cycle of a virus. [4 marks]

Plant Diseases

Plants have some pretty nifty ways of <u>defending</u> themselves against <u>disease</u> — in fact we use many of their <u>chemical defences</u> to make our <u>medicines</u>. Hurrah for plants, helping to <u>fight</u> against those pesky <u>pathogens</u>.

Plants Have Physical Defences Against Pathogens and Pests...

1) Most plant <u>leaves</u> and <u>stems</u> have a <u>waxy cuticle</u>, which provides a <u>barrier</u> to stop pathogens <u>entering</u> them or pests from <u>damaging</u> them. It may also stop <u>water collecting</u> on the leaf, which could reduce the risk of infection by pathogens that are <u>transferred</u> between plants <u>in water</u>.

2) Plant cells themselves are surrounded by <u>cell walls</u> made from <u>cellulose</u>. These form a <u>physical barrier</u> against pathogens that make it past the waxy cuticle.

...as Well as Chemical Ones

1) Plants don't just rely on <u>physical defences</u>. They also produce <u>chemicals</u> that help prevent <u>damage</u> to the plant. For example, they produce chemicals called <u>antiseptics</u>, which <u>kill</u> bacterial and fungal <u>pathogens</u>. They also produce <u>chemicals</u> to <u>deter pests</u> (e.g. insects) from <u>feeding</u> on their leaves.

2) Some of these chemicals can be used as <u>drugs</u> to <u>treat human diseases</u> or <u>relieve symptoms</u>. E.g.

> • <u>Quinine</u> comes from the <u>bark</u> of the cinchona tree. For years it was the main <u>treatment</u> for <u>malaria</u>.
> • <u>Aspirin</u> is used to relieve <u>pain</u> and <u>fever</u>. It was developed from a chemical found in the <u>bark</u> and <u>leaves</u> of <u>willow trees</u>.

Plant Diseases Can be Detected in the Field and in the Lab

1) In the <u>field</u>, plant diseases are usually detected by <u>observations</u>. Plant <u>pathologists</u> (experts in plant disease) recognise the <u>symptoms</u>. E.g. <u>galls</u> (abnormal growths) might indicate <u>crown gall disease</u> in many different types of plant, including <u>apple</u> and other <u>fruit trees</u>.

2) Sometimes plants may show <u>symptoms</u> of a <u>disease</u> (e.g. yellow leaves) which are actually due to <u>environmental causes</u>, such as a <u>nutrient deficiency</u>. By changing the <u>environmental conditions</u> (e.g. adding nutrients to the soil) and observing any <u>change</u> in the plant's symptoms, it can be possible to determine whether a plant is <u>diseased</u> or if the symptoms were due to something else.

3) Different pathogens are spread in <u>different ways</u> — so plant pathologists can analyse the <u>distribution</u> of <u>diseased plants</u> to identify the kind of pathogen involved. E.g. <u>patches</u> of diseased plants may suggest that the disease is spread through the <u>soil</u> and a <u>random distribution</u> may suggest an airborne pathogen.

4) Laboratory-based <u>diagnostic testing</u> allows accurate <u>identification</u> of specific pathogens. It might involve:

Detecting Antigens	• <u>Pathogens</u> have unique <u>molecules</u> on their surface called <u>antigens</u> (see next page). • Antigens from a particular <u>pathogen</u> will be <u>present</u> in a plant <u>infected</u> with that pathogen and can be <u>detected</u> in a sample of plant tissue (using <u>monoclonal antibodies</u>, see p.60). • The detection of an <u>antigen</u> unique to a particular pathogen allows that <u>pathogen</u> to be <u>identified</u> and the <u>disease diagnosed</u>.

Detecting DNA	• If a plant is <u>infected</u> with a pathogen, the pathogen's DNA will be present in the plant's <u>tissues</u>. • Scientists have techniques that allow them to detect even <u>small amounts</u> of <u>pathogen DNA</u> in a sample of plant tissue, allowing them to <u>identify</u> the particular pathogen that is present.

My garden looks really poorly — it's got terrible treesles...

Admit it — plants are cleverer than you thought. Hold on to that whilst you drill this page into your brain.

Q1   Give two physical methods that plants use to defend themselves against pathogens.   [2 marks]

Fighting Disease

The human body has some pretty neat features when it comes to <u>fighting disease</u>.

Physical and Chemical Barriers Stop Pathogens Entering the Body

Like plants (see previous page) the <u>human body</u> has <u>physical</u> and <u>chemical</u> defences against pathogen entry.

Physical barriers

1) The skin acts as a <u>barrier</u> to pathogens, and, if it gets <u>damaged</u>, <u>blood clots</u> quickly <u>seal cuts</u> and keep microorganisms <u>out</u>.

2) <u>Hairs</u> and <u>mucus</u> in your nose <u>trap</u> particles that could contain <u>pathogens</u>.

3) <u>Cells</u> in your <u>trachea</u> and <u>bronchi</u> (airways in the lungs) also produce <u>mucus</u>, which traps pathogens. <u>Other cells</u> that line the trachea and bronchi have <u>cilia</u>. These are <u>hair-like structures</u> which waft the mucus up to the <u>back of the throat</u> where it can be <u>swallowed</u>.

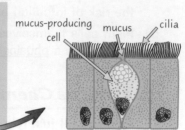

Chemical barriers

1) The <u>stomach</u> produces <u>hydrochloric acid</u>. This <u>kills</u> most pathogens that are swallowed.

2) The <u>eyes</u> produce a chemical called <u>lysozyme</u> (in tears) which <u>kills bacteria</u> on the <u>surface</u> of the eye.

These physical and chemical barriers are non-specific — they work against many different types of pathogens.

Your Immune System Can Attack Pathogens

1) If pathogens do make it into your body, your <u>immune system</u> kicks in to <u>destroy</u> them.

2) The most important part of your immune system is the <u>white blood cells</u>. They travel around in your <u>blood</u> and crawl into every part of you, patrolling for <u>pathogens</u>.

3) <u>B-lymphocytes</u> are a type of white blood cell that are involved in the <u>specific immune response</u> — this is the immune response to a <u>specific pathogen</u>. Here's how it works:

1) Every pathogen has <u>unique molecules</u> (e.g. proteins) on its surface called <u>antigens</u>.

2) When your B-lymphocytes come across an antigen on a <u>pathogen</u>, they start to produce <u>proteins</u> called <u>antibodies</u>. Antibodies <u>bind</u> (lock on) to the new invading <u>pathogen</u>, so it can be <u>found</u> and <u>destroyed</u> by other white blood cells. The antibodies produced are <u>specific</u> to that pathogen — they won't lock on to any <u>other</u> pathogens.

3) The <u>antibodies</u> are then produced <u>rapidly</u> and flow all round the body to find all similar <u>pathogens</u>.

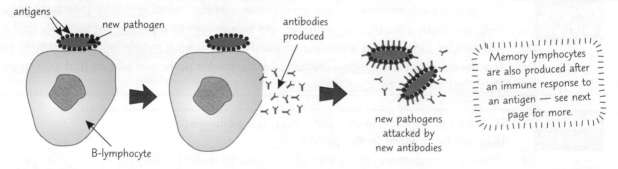

Memory lymphocytes are also produced after an immune response to an antigen — see next page for more.

Fight disease — blow your nose with boxing gloves...

If you have a low level of white blood cells, you'll be more susceptible to infections. HIV attacks white blood cells and weakens the immune system, making it easier for other pathogens to invade.

Q1   Describe how the trachea and bronchi are adapted to defend against the entry of pathogens.   [3 marks]

Q2   What are B-lymphocytes?   [1 mark]

Memory Lymphocytes and Immunisation

Forgive and forget, they always say. Fortunately for us, though, our immune system tends to hold grudges...

Memory Lymphocytes Give Immunity To Later Infection

1) When a pathogen enters the body for the first time the response is slow because there aren't many B-lymphocytes that can make the antibody needed to lock on to the antigen.

2) Eventually the body will produce enough of the right antibody to overcome the infection. Meanwhile the infected person will show symptoms of the disease.

3) As well as antibodies, memory lymphocytes are also produced in response to a foreign antigen. Memory lymphocytes remain in the body for a long time, and 'remember' a specific antigen.

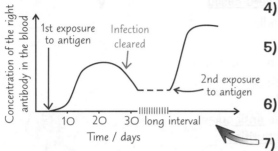

4) The person is now immune — their immune system has the ability to respond quickly to a second infection.

5) If the same pathogen enters the body again, there are more cells that will recognise it and produce antibodies against it. This secondary immune response is faster and stronger.

6) The secondary response often gets rid of the pathogen before you begin to show any symptoms.

7) This can all be shown in a lovely graph like the one here.

Immunisation Stops You Getting Infections

1) To avoid getting ill, you can be immunised against some diseases, e.g. measles.

2) Immunisation usually involves injecting dead or inactive pathogens into the body. These are antigenic (they carry antigens), so even though they're harmless your body makes antibodies to help destroy them.

3) The antigens also trigger memory lymphocytes to be made.

4) So, if live pathogens of the same type get into the body, there will already be memory lymphocytes that can cause a fast secondary immune response. This means that you're less likely to get the disease. Cool.

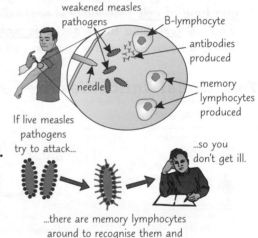

There are Pros and Cons of Immunisation

Pros:

1) Big outbreaks of diseases, called epidemics, can be prevented if a large percentage of the population are immunised. Even the people who aren't immunised are unlikely to catch the disease because there are fewer people able to pass it on — this is known as 'herd immunity'. But if a significant number of people aren't immunised, the disease can spread quickly through them and lots of people will be ill at the same time.

2) Some diseases, e.g. smallpox, have been virtually wiped out by immunisation programmes.

Cons:

1) Immunisation doesn't always work — sometimes it doesn't give you immunity.

2) You can sometimes have a bad reaction to a vaccine (e.g. swelling, or maybe something more serious like a fever or seizures). But bad reactions are very rare.

Take that, you evil antigen...

Immunisation's great. It's helped to save millions of lives all around the world — and all because of those nifty antibodies and memory cells. You need to know how immunisation works and how it can create 'herd immunity'.

Q1 Why is the secondary immune response to a pathogen much faster than the first response? [2 marks]

Monoclonal Antibodies

Antibodies aren't only used by the immune system — scientists have engineered them for lots of new uses.

Monoclonal Antibodies are Identical Antibodies

1) Antibodies are produced by B-lymphocytes — a type of white blood cell (see page 58).

2) Monoclonal antibodies are produced from lots of clones of a single B-lymphocyte. This means all the antibodies are identical and will only target one specific protein antigen.

3) However, you can't just grab the lymphocyte that made the antibody and grow more — lymphocytes don't divide very easily.

4) Tumour cells, on the other hand, don't produce antibodies but divide lots — so they can be grown really easily.

5) It's possible to fuse a mouse B-lymphocyte with a type of tumour cell called a myeloma cell, to create a cell called a hybridoma.

6) Hybridomas can be cloned to get lots of identical cells. These can all divide really quickly to produce the same antibodies (monoclonal antibodies). These can be collected and purified.

7) You can make monoclonal antibodies that bind to anything you want, e.g. an antigen that's only found on the surface of one type of cell. Monoclonal antibodies are really useful because they will only bind to (target) this molecule — this means you can use them to target a specific cell or chemical in the body.

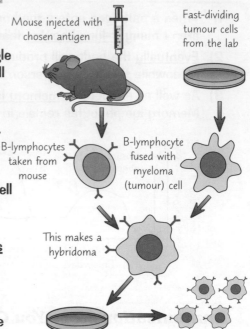

Mouse injected with chosen antigen

Fast-dividing tumour cells from the lab

B-lymphocytes taken from mouse

B-lymphocyte fused with myeloma (tumour) cell

This makes a hybridoma

It divides quickly to produce lots of clones that produce monoclonal antibodies

Monoclonal Antibodies Are Used In Pregnancy Tests

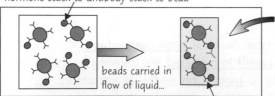

bit where you wee

antibody stuck to blue bead

test strip

antibody stuck down

If you're pregnant:

hormone stuck to antibody stuck to bead

beads carried in flow of liquid...

...and stick to strip

If you're not pregnant:

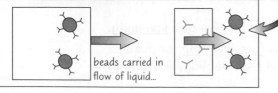

beads carried in flow of liquid...

...but don't stick

A hormone (HCG) is found in the urine of women only when they are pregnant. Pregnancy testing sticks detect this hormone. Here's how they work:

1) The bit of the stick you wee on has some antibodies to the hormone, with blue beads attached.

2) The test strip (the bit of the stick that turns blue if you're pregnant) has some more antibodies to the hormone stuck onto it (so that they can't move).

3) If you're pregnant and you wee on the stick:
   • The hormone binds to the antibodies on the blue beads.
   • The urine moves up the stick, carrying the hormone and the beads.
   • The beads and hormone bind to the antibodies on the strip.
   • So the blue beads get stuck on the strip, turning it blue.

4) If you're not pregnant and you wee on the stick, the urine still moves up the stick, carrying the blue beads. But there's nothing to stick the blue beads onto the test strip, so it doesn't go blue.

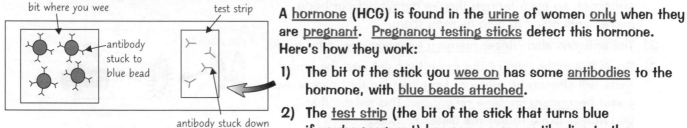

By using different antibodies, you can use this test to find other substances in a sample of urine, e.g. antigens on pathogens.

The one time when you can write "wee on a stick" in an exam...

There's more on monoclonal antibodies coming next, but don't move on until you understand this page.

Q1   What is a hybridoma cell made from?   [2 marks]

More on Monoclonal Antibodies

Because monoclonal antibodies can be produced to <u>target</u> a <u>specific</u> chemical or cell, they have loads of uses.

You Can Make Monoclonal Antibodies That Target Cancer Cells

1) <u>Cancer cells</u> have <u>proteins</u> on their cell membranes that <u>aren't</u> found on <u>normal</u> body cells. They're called <u>tumour markers</u>.

2) In the <u>lab</u>, you can make monoclonal antibodies that will <u>bind</u> to these tumour markers. They can be used to help <u>diagnose</u> and <u>treat cancer</u>.

Monoclonal Antibodies Can Be Used To Diagnose Cancer...

1) First, the antibodies are labelled with a <u>radioactive element</u>.

2) Then, the <u>labelled antibodies</u> are given to a patient through a <u>drip</u>. They go into the <u>blood</u> and are <u>carried around</u> the body.

3) When the antibodies come into <u>contact</u> with the cancer cells they <u>bind</u> to the <u>tumour markers</u>.

4) A <u>picture</u> of the patient's body is taken using a special camera that detects <u>radioactivity</u>. Anywhere there are <u>cancer cells</u> will show up as a <u>bright spot</u>.

5) Doctors can see <u>exactly</u> where the cancer is, what <u>size</u> it is, and find out if it is <u>spreading</u>.

...and to Target Drugs to Cancer Cells

1) An <u>anti-cancer drug</u> is attached to <u>monoclonal antibodies</u>.

2) The antibodies are given to the patient through a <u>drip</u>.

3) The antibodies <u>target specific cells</u> (the cancer cells) because they <u>only bind</u> to the tumour markers.

4) The drug <u>kills</u> the cancer cells but <u>doesn't kill</u> any <u>normal body cells</u> near the tumour.

5) Other cancer treatments (like other <u>drugs</u> and <u>radiotherapy</u>) can affect <u>normal</u> body cells <u>as well as</u> killing cancer cells.

6) So the <u>side effects</u> of an <u>antibody-based</u> drug are <u>lower</u> than for other drugs or radiotherapy.

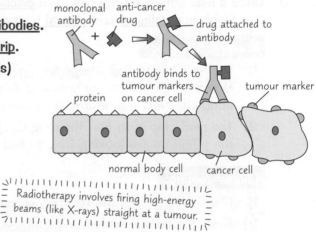

Radiotherapy involves firing high-energy beams (like X-rays) straight at a tumour.

Monoclonal Antibodies Can Also Be Used To Find Blood Clots

1) When blood <u>clots</u>, <u>proteins</u> in the blood <u>join together</u> to form a <u>solid mesh</u>.

2) <u>Monoclonal antibodies</u> have been developed that <u>bind</u> to these proteins.

3) You can attach a <u>radioactive element</u> to these antibodies.

4) Then, if you <u>inject</u> them into the body and <u>take a picture</u> using a camera that picks up the <u>radiation</u>, that picture will have a really bright spot where there is a blood clot.

5) This is useful because you can easily find a <u>potentially harmful</u> blood clot (and <u>get rid of it</u> before it harms the patient).

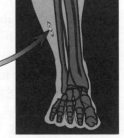

Bonoclonal antibodies — used to detect Irish rock stars...

As you've just found out, monoclonal antibodies are really useful for finding stuff. Imagine having a horde of trained fireflies to search for your lost keys or phone. Instead of you having to search under everything, you just release the fireflies and wait for them to cluster around your lost stuff, in a big obvious glowing mass. Genius.

Q1 Explain how monoclonal antibodies are used in treating cancer. [4 marks]

Antibiotics and Other Medicines

New medicines are constantly being <u>developed</u>. This nifty little page tells you all about how that happens.

Antibiotics Are Used to Treat Bacterial Infections

1) Antibiotics work by <u>inhibiting processes</u> in <u>bacterial cells</u>, but <u>not</u> in the <u>host organism</u>. For example, some antibiotics inhibit the <u>building</u> of bacterial <u>cell walls</u> — this <u>prevents</u> the bacteria from <u>dividing</u>, and eventually <u>kills them</u>, but has <u>no effect</u> on cells in the <u>human host</u> (which <u>don't</u> have cell walls).

2) <u>Different antibiotics</u> kill <u>different types</u> of bacteria, so it's important to be treated with the <u>right one</u>.

3) But antibiotics <u>don't destroy viruses</u> (e.g. <u>flu</u> or <u>cold</u> viruses). Viruses reproduce <u>using your body cells</u>, which makes it <u>very difficult</u> to develop drugs that destroy just the virus <u>without</u> killing the body's cells.

There Are Several Stages in the Development of New Drugs

1) First a drug has to be <u>discovered</u>. This can happen in lots of different ways — for example:

> <u>Penicillin</u> is an <u>antibiotic</u>. It was discovered by Alexander Fleming when he was clearing out Petri dishes containing <u>bacteria</u>. He noticed that one of the dishes had <u>mould</u> on it and that the area around the mould was <u>free</u> of bacteria. The mould was producing <u>penicillin</u>, which was <u>killing</u> the bacteria.

2) Nowadays, most scientists use their knowledge of how a disease <u>works</u> to try and identify <u>molecules</u> that could be used as drugs to <u>fight</u> the disease.

3) Once a new potential drug has been <u>discovered</u>, it needs to be <u>developed</u>. This involves <u>preclinical</u> and <u>clinical testing</u>.

Preclinical testing:

1) In preclinical testing, drugs are <u>first</u> tested on <u>human cells and tissues</u> in the lab. However, you can't use human cells and tissues to test drugs that affect whole or multiple body systems, e.g. a drug for blood pressure must be tested on a whole animal.

2) The next step is to test the drug on <u>live animals</u>. This is to <u>test</u> that the drug <u>works</u> (produces the <u>effect</u> you're looking for), to find out how <u>toxic</u> (<u>harmful</u>) it is and to find the best <u>dosage</u>.

Clinical testing:

1) If the drug <u>passes</u> the tests on animals then it's tested on <u>human volunteers</u> in a <u>clinical trial</u>.

2) First, the drug is tested on <u>healthy volunteers</u> to make sure that it doesn't have any <u>harmful side effects</u> when the body is working <u>normally</u>.

3) If the results of the tests on healthy volunteers are good, the drugs can be tested on people suffering from the <u>illness</u>. The <u>optimum dose</u> is found — this is the dose of drug that is the <u>most effective</u> and has the <u>fewest side effects</u>.

4) Patients are <u>randomly</u> put into <u>two groups</u>. One is given the <u>new drug</u>, the other is given a <u>placebo</u> (a substance that <u>looks like</u> the drug being tested but <u>doesn't do anything</u>, e.g. a sugar pill). This is to allow for the <u>placebo effect</u> (when the patient expects the treatment to work and so <u>feels better</u>, even though the treatment isn't doing anything).

5) Clinical trials are <u>blind</u> — the patient in the study <u>doesn't know</u> whether they're getting the <u>drug</u> or the <u>placebo</u>. In fact, they're often <u>double-blind</u> — neither the <u>patient</u> nor the <u>doctor</u> knows until all the <u>results</u> have been gathered. This is so the doctors <u>monitoring</u> the patients and <u>analysing</u> the results aren't <u>subconsciously influenced</u> by their knowledge.

4) When a drug has finally passed all of these tests, it still needs to be <u>approved</u> by a <u>medical agency</u> before it can be used to <u>treat</u> patients. All of this means that drugs are as <u>effective</u> and <u>safe</u> as possible.

The placebo effect doesn't work with revision...

Testing, retesting and then...yep, more testing. You'd know all about that anyway, it's just like being in school...

Q1   Explain how a double-blind trial would be carried out.   [2 marks]

Topic 5 — Health, Disease and the Development of Medicines

Investigating Antibiotics and Antiseptics

And now for some hands-on stuff. Time to grow your own microorganisms...

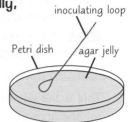

PRACTICAL

You Can Grow Bacteria in the Lab

1) Bacteria (and some other microorganisms) are cultured (grown) in a growth medium, which contains the carbohydrates, minerals, proteins and vitamins they need to grow.

2) The growth medium used can be a nutrient broth solution or solid agar jelly.

3) Bacteria grown on agar 'plates' will form visible colonies on the surface of the jelly, or will spread out to give an even covering.

> To make an agar plate, hot agar jelly is poured into shallow round plastic dishes called Petri dishes. When the jelly's cooled and set, inoculating loops (wire loops) can be used to transfer microorganisms to the agar jelly. Alternatively, a sterile dropping pipette and spreader can be used to get an even covering of bacteria. The microorganisms then multiply.

4) In the lab at school, cultures of microorganisms are kept at about 25 °C because harmful pathogens are less likely to grow at this temperature. Outside of schools, scientists may culture microorganisms at higher temperatures to provide optimum conditions for growth.

You Can Investigate the Effect of Substances on Bacterial Growth

Antibiotics kill bacteria inside the body. Antiseptics kill bacteria outside the body (e.g. on the skin). You can investigate the effect of antibiotics and antiseptics on cultures of bacteria. Since many plants produce antiseptics in self-defence (see p.57) you can also test the effects of different plant extracts in a similar way. Here's how it can be done, using antibiotics as an example:

1) Place paper discs soaked in different types of antibiotics on an agar plate that has an even covering of bacteria. Leave some space between the discs.

2) The antibiotic should diffuse (soak) into the agar jelly. Antibiotic-resistant bacteria (i.e. bacteria that aren't affected by the antibiotic — see p.45) will continue to grow on the agar around the paper discs, but non-resistant strains will die. A clear area will be left where the bacteria have died — this is called an inhibition zone.

3) Make sure you use a control. This is a paper disc that has not been soaked in an antibiotic. You can then be sure that any difference between the growth of the bacteria around the control disc and around one of the antibiotic discs is due to the effect of the antibiotic alone (and not something weird in the paper, for example).

4) Leave the plate for 48 hours at 25 °C.

5) The more effective the antibiotic is against the bacteria, the larger the inhibition zone will be (see p.64).

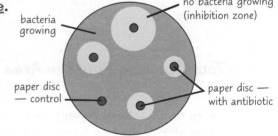

You Need to Use Aseptic Techniques

Contamination by unwanted microorganisms will affect your results and can potentially result in the growth of pathogens. To avoid this, the following aseptic techniques should be used:

1) The Petri dishes and growth medium must be sterilised before use. This can be done by placing them in a machine called an autoclave, which uses steam at a high pressure and temperature to kill any microorganisms present.

2) Before being used to transfer bacteria, an inoculating loop should be sterilised by passing it through a hot flame, so that any unwanted microorganisms are killed.

3) Liquid bacterial cultures should be kept in a culture vial with a lid. The lid should only be removed briefly when transferring the bacteria, to prevent other microbes getting in.

4) After transferring bacteria to it, a Petri dish should be covered with a lid, which should be lightly taped on. This is to stop microorganisms from the air getting in.

5) The Petri dish should be stored upside down to stop drops of condensation falling onto the agar.

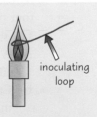
inoculating loop

storing a Petri dish

Topic 5 — Health, Disease and the Development of Medicines

Investigating Antibiotics and Antiseptics

Calculate the Sizes of the Inhibition Zones to Compare Results

You can <u>compare</u> the <u>effectiveness</u> of different <u>antibiotics</u> (or <u>antiseptics</u> or <u>plant extracts</u>) on bacteria by looking at the <u>relative sizes</u> of the <u>inhibition zones</u>. The <u>larger</u> the inhibition zone around a disc, the <u>more bacteria killed</u> and so the <u>more effective</u> the antibiotic is against the bacteria.

You can do this <u>by eye</u> if there are large differences in size. But to get more accurate results it's a good idea to calculate the <u>areas</u> of the inhibition zones using their <u>diameter</u> (the distance <u>across</u>).

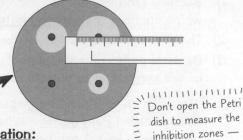

Don't open the Petri dish to measure the inhibition zones — they should be visible through the bottom of the dish.

To calculate the area of an inhibition zone, you need to use <u>this equation</u>:

This is the equation for the area of a circle. You're likely to use the units cm² or mm².

$$\text{Area} = \pi r^2$$

r is the radius of the inhibition zone — it's equal to half the diameter.

π is just a number. You should have a button for it on your calculator. If not, just use the value 3.14.

EXAMPLE:

The diagram below shows the inhibition zones produced by antibiotics A and B. Use the areas of the inhibition zones to compare the effectiveness of the antibiotics.

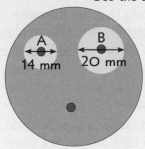

A 14 mm B 20 mm

1) Divide the diameter of zone A by <u>two</u> to find the <u>radius</u>.

Radius of A $= 14 \div 2 = 7$ mm

2) Stick the radius value into the <u>equation</u> area = πr^2.

Area of A $= \pi \times 7^2 = 154$ mm²

3) <u>Repeat</u> steps 1 and 2 for zone B.

Radius of B $= 20 \div 2 = 10$ mm

4) <u>Compare</u> the <u>sizes</u> of the <u>areas</u>. 314 mm² is just over twice 154 mm², so you could say that:

Area of B $= \pi \times 10^2 = 314$ mm²

The inhibition zone of antibiotic B is roughly twice the size of the inhibition zone of antibiotic A.

You Can Also Find the Area of a Colony

The equation above can also be used to calculate the <u>area</u> of a bacterial <u>colony</u>. You just need to measure the <u>diameter</u> of the colony you are interested in first.

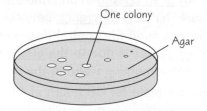

One colony

Agar

Imagine the hilarity when my Dad's sister married Mr Biotic...

Microorganisms might be the perfect pets. You don't have to walk them, they won't get lonely and they hardly cost anything to feed. But whatever you do, do not feed them after midnight.

Q1 A researcher was investigating the effect of different antiseptics on the growth of bacteria. She placed four paper discs, each soaked in a different antiseptic, on an agar plate with an even covering of bacteria. The diagram shows the results.

a) Which antiseptic was most effective against the bacteria? [1 mark]

b) Calculate the size of the inhibition zone for Antiseptic C. Give your answer in mm². [2 marks]

c) Describe a control that could have been used for this investigation. [1 mark]

d) Explain why a control should be used. [1 mark]

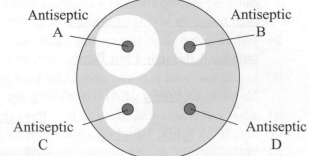

Antiseptic A

Antiseptic B

Antiseptic C

Antiseptic D

Non-Communicable Diseases

Non-communicable diseases <u>aren't caused by pathogens</u>. Instead, there are <u>risk factors</u> associated with them.

Lifestyle Factors May Increase the Risk of a Non-Communicable Disease

1) <u>Risk factors</u> are things that are linked to an <u>increase</u> in the <u>likelihood</u> that a person will develop a certain disease during their lifetime. They <u>don't guarantee</u> that someone <u>will</u> get the disease.

2) Risk factors can be <u>unavoidable</u>, e.g. a person's <u>age</u> or <u>gender</u> may make them <u>more likely</u> to get a disease. But some are <u>lifestyle factors</u> that people <u>can change</u>. For example:

> Smoking is a <u>major risk factor</u> associated with <u>cardiovascular disease</u> — any disease associated with the heart or blood vessels, e.g. a <u>heart attack</u> or <u>stroke</u> (see p.67). This is because:
> - <u>Nicotine</u> in cigarette smoke <u>increases heart rate</u>, which <u>increases blood pressure</u>.
> - High blood pressure <u>damages artery walls</u>, which contributes to the build up of <u>fatty deposits</u> in the arteries. These deposits restrict blood flow and increase the risk of a <u>heart attack</u> or <u>stroke</u>.
> - Smoking increases the risk of <u>blood clots</u> forming in arteries, which can <u>restrict</u> or <u>block</u> blood flow, leading to a <u>heart attack</u> or <u>stroke</u>.

3) Other lifestyle factors are associated with different <u>diseases</u>. E.g.
   - a diet with <u>too many</u> or <u>too few nutrients</u> can lead to <u>malnutrition</u> (and diseases associated with <u>malnutrition</u>, e.g. <u>scurvy</u> — a <u>vitamin C deficiency</u> disease.)

   Malnutrition doesn't just mean not getting enough nutrients. Getting too many nutrients is also a form of malnutrition, and it can lead to obesity.

   - not getting enough <u>exercise</u> and having a diet <u>high</u> in <u>fat</u> and <u>sugar</u> are risk factors for <u>obesity</u>.
   - drinking too much <u>alcohol</u> is a major risk factor for the development of <u>liver disease</u>, e.g. <u>cirrhosis</u> (scarring of the liver). This is because alcohol is <u>broken down</u> by enzymes in the liver and some of the <u>products</u> are <u>toxic</u>. Drinking too much over a long period of time can cause <u>permanent liver damage</u>.

Non-Communicable Diseases Have Many Risk Factors

1) As well as <u>smoking</u>, there are lots of other risk factors associated with <u>cardiovascular disease</u>, including: drinking too much <u>alcohol</u>, <u>lack of exercise</u>, and a diet <u>high</u> in saturated <u>fat</u>.

2) In fact, many <u>non-communicable</u> diseases are caused by <u>several different</u> risk factors <u>interacting</u> with each other, rather than <u>one factor alone</u>, including <u>cancer</u>, <u>liver</u> and <u>lung diseases</u> and <u>obesity</u>. Obesity is also a risk factor for <u>other</u> non-communicable diseases, e.g. <u>type 2 diabetes</u> (see p.82) and <u>cardiovascular disease</u>.

Non-Communicable Diseases Can Have Wide-Ranging Effects

1) Non-communicable diseases can have <u>knock-on effects</u> for local areas. For example, in areas where there are <u>high levels</u> of <u>obesity</u>, <u>smoking</u> or <u>excess alcohol consumption</u>, there's likely to be a <u>high occurrence</u> of certain <u>non-communicable diseases</u>, e.g. cardiovascular or liver disease. This can put <u>pressure</u> on the <u>resources</u> (money, beds, staff, etc.) of <u>local hospitals</u>.

2) Non-communicable diseases are also costly at a <u>national level</u> because the <u>National Health Service</u> provides the <u>resources</u> for the treatment of patients all over the UK. And sometimes, people <u>suffering</u> from a non-communicable disease may not be able to <u>work</u>. A <u>reduction</u> in the number of people able to work can affect a country's <u>economy</u>.

3) As well as being costly, non-communicable diseases are <u>very common</u>, e.g. <u>cardiovascular disease</u> is the <u>number one</u> cause of death <u>worldwide</u>. In <u>developing countries</u>, <u>malnutrition</u> is also a big problem because people are not able to access <u>enough food</u>. The high cost and occurrence of these diseases can hold back the <u>development</u> of a <u>country</u> — so they have an effect at a <u>global</u> level.

Best put down that cake and go for a run...

You may be given data about risk factors in the exam — see p.10 for how you can draw conclusions using data.

Q1 Give one example of a lifestyle factor that increases the risk of cardiovascular disease. [1 mark]

Measures of Obesity

People come in all sorts of <u>shapes</u> and <u>sizes</u>, so you can't just say that anyone <u>over a particular weight</u> is <u>obese</u>. You have to use <u>indices</u> and <u>ratios</u> to figure this out instead — which is what this page is all about.

A Body Mass Index Indicates If You're Under- or Overweight

1) The <u>Body Mass Index</u> (<u>BMI</u>) is used as a guide to help decide whether someone is <u>underweight</u>, <u>normal</u>, <u>overweight</u> or <u>obese</u>. It's calculated from their <u>height</u> and <u>weight</u>:

$$BMI = \frac{weight\ (kg)}{(height\ (m))^2}$$

Body Mass Index	Weight Description
below 18.5	underweight
18.5 - 24.9	normal
25 - 29.9	overweight
30 - 40	moderately obese
above 40	severely obese

2) Once you have a <u>value</u> for a person's BMI, you can refer to a <u>table</u> that shows how the different values are <u>classified</u>.

EXAMPLE: Calculate the BMI of a person who weighs 63.0 kg and is 1.70 m tall. Is this person overweight?

$$BMI = \frac{weight\ (kg)}{(height\ (m))^2} \quad = 63.0\ kg \div 1.70\ m^2$$
$$= 21.8\ kg\ m^{-2}$$

This person is not overweight — their BMI lies between 18.5 and 24.9 (the normal weight range).

3) If you eat a <u>high fat</u>, <u>high sugar diet</u> and you <u>don't do</u> enough <u>exercise</u>, you're likely to <u>take in</u> more energy than you <u>use</u>. The <u>excess</u> energy is <u>stored</u> as <u>fat</u>, so you're more likely to have a <u>high BMI</u> and be obese.

4) BMI <u>isn't</u> always a <u>reliable</u> measure of obesity. For example, athletes have lots of <u>muscle</u>, which <u>weighs more</u> than fat, so they can come out with a <u>high BMI</u> even though they're <u>not overweight</u>.

Martin prefers to use a "Body Splash Index".

A Waist-to-Hip Ratio Can Also Be Used

1) By measuring the <u>circumference</u> of a person's <u>waist</u> and <u>hips</u>, you can use the following formula to figure out their <u>waist-to-hip ratio</u>.

$$waist\text{-}to\text{-}hip\ ratio = \frac{waist\ circumference}{hip\ circumference}$$

(e.g. in cm)
(e.g. in cm)

The <u>circumference</u> of a person's waist or hips is the distance the whole way around their body at that point.

2) The <u>higher</u> your waist-to-hip ratio, the <u>more weight</u> you're likely to be carrying around your middle.

3) A ratio <u>above 1.0</u> for <u>males</u> and <u>above 0.85</u> for <u>females</u> indicates you're carrying <u>too much weight</u> around your middle — this is known as <u>abdominal obesity</u>. It puts you at a <u>greater risk</u> of developing obesity-related <u>health problems</u>, such as type 2 diabetes (see p.82).

EXAMPLE: A woman has a waist measurement of 29 cm and a hip measurement of 36 cm. Find her waist-to-hip ratio.

$$waist\text{-}to\text{-}hip\ ratio = \frac{waist\ circumference\ (cm)}{hip\ circumference\ (cm)} \quad \begin{aligned}&= 29 \div 36 \\ &= 0.81\end{aligned}$$

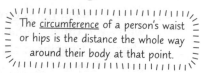

Shakira was really onto something then...

...it's true. Hips don't lie. Seriously though, obesity is a major health issue. BMI and waist-to-hip ratios might not be perfect but they do provide a good guide for helping people know when it's time to lose weight.

Q1   Before beginning a new diet and exercise routine, a person weighs 76.0 kg and has a height of 1.58 m. Three weeks later their weight has dropped to 73.0 kg.

a) Calculate the person's BMI at the beginning and the end of the three week period.   [2 marks]

b) Use the table at the top of the page to determine the weight description of the person before and after the three week period.   [2 marks]

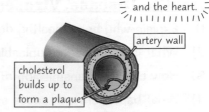

Treatments for Cardiovascular Disease

Cardiovascular disease is a big, big problem in the UK. The good news is there are lots of ways to treat it.

Cardiovascular Disease Affects Your Heart and Blood Vessels

See p.90-91 for more on blood vessels and the heart.

Cardiovascular disease (CVD) is any disease associated with your heart and blood vessels.

1) Arteries are blood vessels that carry blood away from the heart.

2) Cholesterol is a fatty substance that the body needs to make things like cell membranes. But too much cholesterol in the blood can cause fatty deposits to build up in arteries, restricting blood flow.

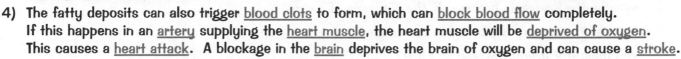

artery wall

cholesterol builds up to form a plaque

3) Deposits occur in areas where the artery wall has been damaged, e.g. by high blood pressure.

4) The fatty deposits can also trigger blood clots to form, which can block blood flow completely. If this happens in an artery supplying the heart muscle, the heart muscle will be deprived of oxygen. This causes a heart attack. A blockage in the brain deprives the brain of oxygen and can cause a stroke.

Lifestyle Changes Can be Used to Treat CVD

1) Making changes to your lifestyle can reduce your risk of developing CVD. If you already have CVD, these changes can form part of the treatment, helping to reduce the risk of a further heart attack or stroke.

2) People with (or at risk of) CVD may be encouraged to eat a healthy, balanced diet, which is low in saturated fat (as saturated fat can increase blood cholesterol level). They may also be encouraged to exercise regularly, lose weight if necessary and stop smoking.

3) Lifestyle changes are often recommended first because they don't really have any downsides.

Some Drugs Can Reduce the Risk of a Heart Attack or Stroke

Lifestyle changes aren't always enough to treat CVD. Sometimes medicines are needed too. Some people may need to take these medicines for the rest of their lives.

1) Statins reduce the amount of cholesterol in the bloodstream. This slows down the rate at which fatty deposits form — reducing the risk of heart attacks and strokes. However, they can sometimes cause negative side effects, e.g. aching muscles. Some of these side effects can be serious, e.g. liver damage.

2) Anticoagulants (e.g. Warfarin™) are drugs which make blood clots less likely to form. However, this can cause excessive bleeding if the person is hurt in an accident.

3) Antihypertensives reduce blood pressure. This helps to prevent damage to blood vessels and so reduces the risk of fatty deposits forming. However, they can cause side effects, e.g. headaches and fainting.

Surgical Procedures are Sometimes Necessary to Repair Damage

1) Stents are tubes that are inserted inside arteries. They keep them open, making sure blood can pass through to the heart muscles, lowering the risk of a heart attack. But over time, the artery can narrow again as stents can irritate the artery and make scar tissue grow. The patient also has to take drugs to stop blood clotting on the stent.

2) If part of a blood vessel is blocked, a piece of healthy vessel taken from elsewhere can be used to bypass the blocked section. This is known as coronary bypass surgery.

3) The whole heart can be replaced with a donor heart. However, the new heart does not always start pumping properly and drugs have to be taken to stop the body rejecting it. These drugs can have side effects, e.g. making you more vulnerable to infections.

Any heart surgery is a major procedure and there is risk of bleeding, clots and infection.

Look after yerselves me hearties...

Make sure you're aware of the drawbacks of each treatment for cardiovascular disease, as well as the advantages.

Q1   Why might surgery be considered to be a last resort when treating cardiovascular disease?   [2 marks]

Topic 5 — Health, Disease and the Development of Medicines

Revision Questions for Topic 5

Well, now that you've been warned about all these nasty diseases, make sure you learn all of the material.

- Try these questions and tick off each one when you get it right.
- When you've done all the questions under a heading and are completely happy, tick it off.

Health, Disease, Viruses and STIs (p.55-56) ☐

1) Explain why being healthy doesn't just mean not being sick. ☑
2) What is a 'non-communicable' disease? ☑
3) How can the transmission of malaria be prevented? ☑
4) What bacterium can cause stomach ulcers? ☑
5) Describe the lysogenic pathway in the life cycle of a virus. ☑
6) How can the spread of *Chlamydia* be reduced? ☑
7) Why does HIV eventually lead to AIDS? ☑

Plant Diseases (p.57) ☑

8) Why do plants produce antiseptic chemicals? ☑
9) Give an example of a drug used in medicine which is extracted from plants. ☑
10) Give four ways in which a plant disease can be identified. ☑

Fighting Disease, Immunisation and Monoclonal Antibodies (p.58-61) ☐

11) Give two types of chemical defence that prevent pathogens from infecting humans. ☑
12) What is an antigen? ☑
13) What does a B-lymphocyte do when it recognises a pathogen? ☑
14) How do vaccines prepare the immune system against infection by a particular pathogen? ☑
15) What is 'herd immunity'? ☑
16) What are monoclonal antibodies? ☑
17) Why are tumour cells used to make hybridoma cells in the production of monoclonal antibodies? ☑
18) Explain how a positive result in a pregnancy test is detected using antibodies. ☑
19) How can you use monoclonal antibodies to identify cancer cells? ☑
20) You can use monoclonal antibodies to identify blood clots.
    Why does the antibody need to be attached to a radioactive element? ☑

Antibiotics and Other Medicines (p.62-64) ☐

21) Which type of pathogen can antibiotics be used to kill? ☑
22) What is the placebo effect? ☑
23) Describe how you could test the effect of an antibiotic on a particular strain of bacteria. ☑
24) What is the purpose of using aseptic techniques when studying
    the effect of substances on the growth of microorganisms? ☑
25) How would you calculate the size of an inhibition zone around an antibiotic in a culture of bacteria? ☑

Non-Communicable Diseases (p.65-67) ☑

26) Describe how smoking can increase the risk of a heart attack or stroke. ☑
27) Give a risk factor related to lifestyle for the development of liver disease. ☑
28) Write the equation for finding the body mass index of an individual. ☑
29) Give three examples of lifestyle changes that can help to prevent cardiovascular disease. ☑

Photosynthesis

You don't know <u>photosynthesis</u> 'til you know its <u>equation</u>. It's in a nice <u>green box</u> so you can't possibly miss it.

Plants are Able to Make Their Own Food by Photosynthesis

1) During photosynthesis, <u>photosynthetic organisms</u>, such as <u>green plants</u> and <u>algae</u>, use <u>energy</u> from the Sun to make <u>glucose</u>.

2) Some of the glucose is used to make <u>larger</u>, <u>complex molecules</u> that the plants or algae need to <u>grow</u>. These make up the organism's <u>biomass</u> — the mass of <u>living material</u>.

3) The <u>energy stored</u> in the organisms' <u>biomass</u> then works its way through the <u>food chain</u> as animals <u>eat</u> them and each other. So photosynthetic organisms are the main producers of food for <u>nearly all life on Earth</u>.

4) Photosynthesis happens inside <u>chloroplasts</u> — they contain <u>chlorophyll</u> which <u>absorbs light</u>. Energy is <u>transferred</u> to the <u>chloroplasts</u> by <u>light</u>. This is the <u>equation</u> for photosynthesis:

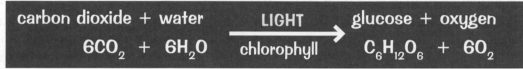

carbon dioxide + water $\xrightarrow[\text{chlorophyll}]{\text{LIGHT}}$ glucose + oxygen

$$6CO_2 + 6H_2O \xrightarrow[\text{chlorophyll}]{\text{LIGHT}} C_6H_{12}O_6 + 6O_2$$

5) Photosynthesis is an <u>endothermic</u> reaction — <u>energy</u> is <u>taken in</u> during the reaction.

6) The rate of photosynthesis is affected by the <u>light intensity</u>, the <u>concentration of CO₂</u> and the <u>temperature</u>. Any of these three factors can become the <u>limiting factor</u>. This just means that it's stopping photosynthesis from happening any <u>faster</u>. There's more about limiting factors on the next page.

You Can Investigate the Effect of Light Intensity on the Rate of Photosynthesis

<u>Canadian pondweed</u> (an aquatic plant) can be used to measure the effect of <u>light intensity</u> on the <u>rate of photosynthesis</u>. The rate at which the pondweed produces <u>oxygen</u> corresponds to the rate at which it's photosynthesising — the <u>faster</u> the rate of oxygen production, the <u>faster</u> the rate of photosynthesis. Here's how the experiment works:

PRACTICAL

1) The <u>apparatus</u> is <u>set up</u> according to the <u>diagram</u>. The gas syringe should be empty to start with. <u>Sodium hydrogencarbonate</u> may be added to the water to make sure the plant has enough <u>carbon dioxide</u> (sodium hydrogencarbonate releases CO₂ in solution).

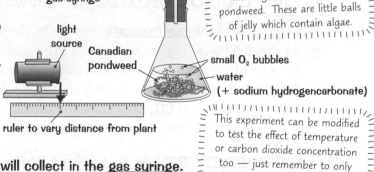

You can also do this experiment with algal balls, instead of pondweed. These are little balls of jelly which contain algae.

2) A source of <u>white light</u> is placed at a <u>specific distance</u> from the pondweed.

3) The pondweed is left to photosynthesise for a <u>set amount of time</u>.

This experiment can be modified to test the effect of temperature or carbon dioxide concentration too — just remember to only change one variable at a time.

4) As it photosynthesises, the oxygen released will collect in the <u>gas syringe</u>. This allows you to <u>accurately measure</u> the <u>volume</u> of oxygen produced.

5) The whole experiment is repeated with the <u>light source</u> at <u>different distances</u> from the pondweed. The <u>rate of oxygen production</u> at each distance can then be calculated (volume produced ÷ time taken).

6) For this experiment, any <u>variables</u> that could affect the results should be <u>controlled</u>, e.g. the <u>temperature</u> (which can be controlled by putting the conical flask in a <u>water bath</u>) and the <u>carbon dioxide concentration</u> (which can be controlled by adding a <u>set amount</u> of sodium hydrogencarbonate to a <u>set volume</u> of water).

I'm working on sunshine — woah oh...

You could also measure how much oxygen's produced by counting the bubbles — fun, but it's not as accurate.

Q1   Explain how photosynthesis contributes to a plant's biomass.   [2 marks]

Q2   State three limiting factors of photosynthesis.   [3 marks]

Limiting Factors in Photosynthesis

Remember, light intensity, CO_2 concentration and temperature are all <u>limiting factors</u> in photosynthesis.

Three Important Graphs for Rate of Photosynthesis

Not Enough LIGHT Slows Down the Rate of Photosynthesis

1) Light transfers the <u>energy</u> needed for photosynthesis.
2) At first, as the <u>light level</u> is raised, the rate of photosynthesis <u>increases steadily</u> (the rate is <u>directly proportional</u> to light intensity). But this is only true up to a <u>certain point</u>.
3) Beyond that, it <u>won't</u> make any difference — it'll be either the <u>temperature</u> or the <u>CO_2 level</u> which is the limiting factor.
4) In the lab you can investigate light intensity by <u>moving</u> a <u>lamp</u> closer to or further away from your plant (see previous page).

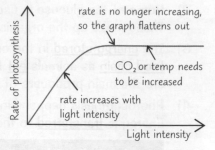

5) But if you just plot the rate of photosynthesis against "distance of lamp from the plant", you get a <u>weird-shaped graph</u>. To get a graph like the one above you either need to <u>measure</u> the light intensity at the plant using a <u>light meter</u> or do a bit of nifty maths with your results. Here's why:

The distance from the lamp and light intensity are <u>inversely proportional</u> to each other — this means as the <u>distance increases</u>, the <u>light intensity decreases</u>. However, light intensity decreases in proportion to the <u>square</u> of the distance. This is called the <u>inverse square law</u> and is written like this:

∝ is the 'proportional to' symbol.

$$\text{light intensity} \propto \frac{1}{\text{distance (d)}^2}$$

6) The inverse square law means that if you <u>halve</u> the <u>distance</u>, the <u>light intensity</u> will be <u>four times greater</u>. And if you <u>double</u> the distance, the light intensity will be <u>four times smaller</u>. (<u>Trebling</u> the distance would make it <u>six times smaller</u>.) You can use $1/d^2$ as a measure of light intensity:

E.g. at 20 cm, light intensity = $1/20^2$ = 1/400 = 0.0025 arbitrary units.
At 10 cm, light intensity = $1/10^2$ = 1/100 = 0.0100 arbitrary units.

<u>Halving</u> the distance has made the light intensity <u>four times</u> greater.

Too Little CARBON DIOXIDE Also Slows it Down

1) CO_2 is one of the <u>raw materials</u> needed for photosynthesis.
2) As with light intensity, increasing the <u>CO_2</u> concentration <u>increases</u> the rate of photosynthesis up to a point. After this the graph <u>flattens out</u>, showing that CO_2 is no longer the <u>limiting factor</u>.
3) As long as <u>light</u> and <u>CO_2</u> are in plentiful supply then the factor limiting photosynthesis must be <u>temperature</u>.

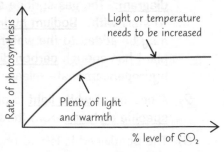

The TEMPERATURE has to be Just Right

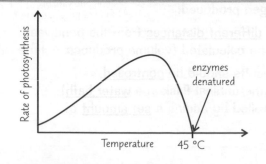

1) Usually, if the temperature is the <u>limiting factor</u> it's because it's <u>too low</u> — the <u>enzymes</u> needed for photosynthesis work more <u>slowly</u> at low temperatures.
2) But if the plant gets <u>too hot</u>, the enzymes it needs for photosynthesis and its other reactions will be <u>denatured</u> (see page 16).
3) This happens at about <u>45 °C</u> (pretty hot for outdoors, but <u>greenhouses</u> can get that hot if you're not careful).

Don't blame it on the sunshine, don't blame it on the CO_2...

...don't blame it on the temperature, blame it on the plant. Nothing like a song to help you revise.

Q1   Describe the relationship between increasing light intensity and the rate of photosynthesis.   [2 marks]

Transport in Plants

Plants need to get stuff from <u>A to B</u>. Flowering plants have <u>two types</u> of <u>transport vessel</u> — <u>xylem</u> and <u>phloem</u>. Both types of vessel go to <u>every part</u> of the plant, but they are totally <u>separate</u>.

Root Hairs Take In Minerals and Water

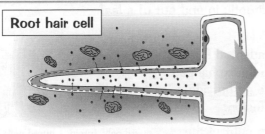

Root hair cell

1) The cells on the surface of plant roots grow into "<u>hairs</u>", which stick out into the soil.

2) Each branch of a root will be covered in <u>millions</u> of these microscopic hairs.

3) This gives the plant a <u>large surface area</u> for absorbing <u>water</u> and <u>mineral ions</u> from the soil.

4) The concentration of mineral ions is usually <u>higher</u> in the <u>root hair cells</u> than in the <u>soil</u> around them, so mineral ions are absorbed by <u>active transport</u> (see page 21). Water is absorbed by <u>osmosis</u>.

Phloem Tubes Transport Food

1) Phloem tubes are made of columns of <u>elongated</u> living cells with small <u>pores</u> in the <u>end walls</u> to allow stuff to flow through.

2) They transport <u>food substances</u> (mainly <u>sucrose</u>) made in the leaves to the rest of the plant for <u>immediate use</u> (e.g. in growing regions) or for <u>storage</u>.

3) This process is called <u>translocation</u> and it requires <u>energy</u> from respiration (see page 92). The transport goes in <u>both directions</u>.

Food (mainly dissolved sucrose)

Xylem Tubes Take Water UP

1) Xylem tubes are made of <u>dead cells</u> joined end to end with <u>no</u> end walls between them and a hole down the middle. They're strengthened with a material called <u>lignin</u>.

2) They carry <u>water</u> and <u>mineral ions</u> from the <u>roots</u> to the <u>stem</u> and <u>leaves</u>.

3) The movement of water <u>from</u> the <u>roots</u>, <u>through</u> the <u>xylem</u> and <u>out</u> of the <u>leaves</u> is called the <u>transpiration stream</u> (see below).

Water and minerals

Transpiration is the Loss of Water from the Plant

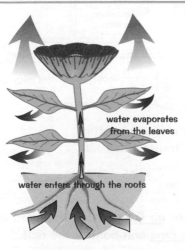

water evaporates from the leaves

water enters through the roots

1) Transpiration is caused by the <u>evaporation</u> and <u>diffusion</u> (see p.21) of water from a plant's surface. Most transpiration happens at the <u>leaves</u>.

2) The loss of water creates a slight <u>shortage</u> of water in the leaf, and so more water is drawn up from the rest of the plant through the <u>xylem vessels</u> to replace it.

3) This in turn means more water is drawn up from the <u>roots</u>, and so there's a constant <u>transpiration stream</u> of water through the plant.

4) The transpiration stream carries <u>mineral ions</u> that are dissolved in the water along with it.

Don't let revision stress you out — just go with the phloem...

Ph<u>loe</u>m transports substances in <u>both</u> directions, but xylem only transports things upwards — <u>xy</u> to the sky.

Q1   Explain how water moves through a plant in the transpiration stream.   [3 marks]

Stomata and Transpiration

Sorry, more on <u>transpiration</u>. But first, you need to learn about <u>stomata</u>...

Stomata are Needed for Gas Exchange

Stomata are <u>tiny pores</u> on the surface of a plant. They're mostly found on the lower surface of <u>leaves</u>. Stomata allow CO_2 and <u>oxygen</u> to <u>diffuse</u> directly in and out of a leaf. They also allow <u>water vapour</u> to escape during <u>transpiration</u>.

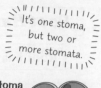
It's one stoma, but two or more stomata.

Transpiration is really just a <u>side-effect</u> of the way leaves are adapted for <u>photosynthesis</u>. They have to have <u>stomata</u> so that gases can be exchanged easily. Because there's more water <u>inside</u> the plant than in the <u>air outside</u>, the water escapes from the leaves through the stomata by diffusion.

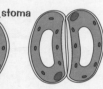
guard cells   stoma

guard cells turgid — stoma <u>open</u>

guard cells flaccid — stoma <u>closed</u>

Stomata are surrounded by <u>guard cells</u>, which <u>change shape</u> to control the size of the pore — when the guard cells are <u>turgid</u> (swollen with water) the stomata are <u>open</u> and when the guard cells are <u>flaccid</u> (low on water and limp) the stomata are <u>closed</u>.

Transpiration Rate is Affected by Environmental Factors

The faster the transpiration rate, the faster the water uptake by the plant.

1) <u>LIGHT INTENSITY</u> — the <u>brighter</u> the light, the <u>greater</u> the transpiration rate. <u>Stomata</u> begin to <u>close</u> as it gets darker. Photosynthesis can't happen in the dark, so they don't need to be open to let CO_2 in. When the stomata are closed, very little water can escape.

2) <u>TEMPERATURE</u> — the <u>warmer</u> it is, the <u>faster</u> transpiration happens. When it's warm the water particles have <u>more energy</u> to evaporate and diffuse out of the stomata.

3) <u>AIR FLOW</u> — the <u>better</u> the air flow around a leaf, e.g. stronger wind, the <u>greater</u> the transpiration rate. If air flow around a leaf is <u>poor</u>, the water vapour just <u>surrounds the leaf</u> and doesn't move away. This means there's a <u>high concentration</u> of water particles outside the leaf as well as inside it, so <u>diffusion</u> doesn't happen as quickly. If there's <u>good</u> air flow, the water vapour is <u>swept away</u>, maintaining a <u>low concentration</u> of water in the air outside the leaf. Diffusion then happens quickly, from an area of higher concentration to an area of lower concentration.

You Can Estimate Transpiration Rate

You can use a special piece of apparatus called a <u>potometer</u> to <u>estimate transpiration rate</u>. It actually <u>measures water uptake</u> by a plant, but it's <u>assumed</u> that water uptake by the plant is <u>directly related</u> to water loss from the leaves (transpiration). Here's what you do:

1) Set up the apparatus as in the diagram, and then record the <u>starting position</u> of the air bubble.

2) Start a stopwatch and record the <u>distance moved</u> by the bubble per unit time, e.g. per hour. Calculating the <u>speed</u> of <u>air bubble movement</u> gives an <u>estimate</u> of the <u>transpiration rate</u>.

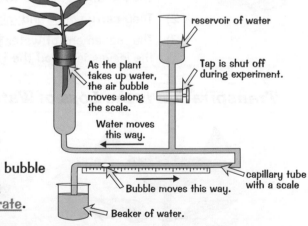
reservoir of water

As the plant takes up water, the air bubble moves along the scale.

Tap is shut off during experiment.

Water moves this way.

Bubble moves this way.

capillary tube with a scale

Beaker of water.

EXAMPLE: A potometer was used to estimate the transpiration rate of a plant cutting. The bubble moved 25 mm in 10 minutes. Estimate the transpiration rate.

To estimate the <u>rate of transpiration</u>, divide the <u>distance</u> the bubble moved by the <u>time taken</u>.

$$\frac{\text{distance moved}}{\text{time taken}} = \frac{25 \text{ mm}}{10 \text{ min}} = 2.5 \text{ mm min}^{-1}$$

You can use a potometer to estimate how <u>light intensity</u>, <u>temperature</u> or <u>air flow</u> around the plant affect the transpiration rate. Just remember to <u>only change one variable at a time</u> and control the rest.

I say stomaaarta, you say stomaaayta...

Sunny, warm and windy — the perfect conditions for transpiration and for hanging out your washing.

Q1   Explain how low light intensity affects the rate of water uptake by a plant.   [3 marks]

Adaptations of Leaves and Plants

A nice big diagram for you to learn here. Ah well. At least it means there aren't quite as many words...

Leaves are Adapted for Photosynthesis and Gas Exchange

The diagram below shows the structure of a typical leaf. You need to know how it's adapted for efficient photosynthesis and gas exchange.

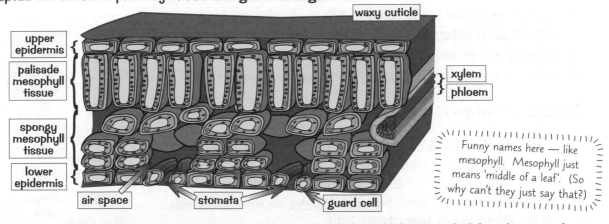

Funny names here — like mesophyll. Mesophyll just means 'middle of a leaf'. (So why can't they just say that?)

1) Leaves are broad, so there's a large surface area exposed to light, which is needed for photosynthesis.
2) The palisade layer has lots of chloroplasts. This means that they're near the top of the leaf where they can get the most light.
3) The upper epidermis is transparent so that light can pass through it to the palisade layer.
4) The xylem and phloem form a network of vascular bundles, which provide the leaf with water for photosynthesis and take away the glucose produced. They also help support the structure.
5) The epidermal tissues are covered with a waxy cuticle, which helps to reduce water loss by evaporation.
6) The tissues of leaves are also adapted for efficient gas exchange. E.g. the lower epidermis has lots of stomata, which let CO_2 diffuse directly into the leaf. Also, the spongy mesophyll tissue contains air spaces which increase the rate of diffusion of gases into and out of the leaf's cells.

Some Plants are Adapted to Live in Extreme Environments

Adaptations are features that help an organism to survive in its environment.

Some plants are adapted to live in extreme environments, e.g. places that are very hot or very dry (like deserts). Adaptations tend to affect the size and shape of the plant's leaves, its cuticle, and the number and position of its stomata. For example, plants living in deserts (like cacti) tend to have the following adaptations, which help them to conserve water:

1) Small leaves, or spines instead of leaves — this reduces the surface area for water loss by evaporation. Spines also help to stop animals eating the plant to get water.
2) Curled leaves, or hairs on the surface of leaves — this reduces air flow close to the leaf, trapping water vapour near the surface and reducing diffusion from the leaf to the air. (Spines also reduce air flow near the surface of the plant and so do a similar job.)

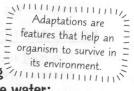

3) Thick waxy cuticles — again to reduce water loss by evaporation.
4) A thick, fleshy stem, which stores water.
5) Fewer stomata or stomata that only open at night — to reduce water loss by evaporation.
6) Stomata sunken in pits — this makes the stomata lower than the surface of the leaf, which reduces air flow close to the stomata. This reduces water loss in the same way as curled leaves or hairs.

My kitchen's an extreme environment for house plants...

...mainly because I always forget to water them. Hot deserts aren't the only extreme environment plants are adapted to living in. E.g. Arctic plants have adapted to carry out photosynthesis even when the temperature is really low. They have small leaves to reduce water loss too, and grow close to the ground to prevent wind damage.

Q1 Give three reasons why cacti have spines instead of leaves. [3 marks]

Plant Hormones

Plants produce chemicals called <u>hormones</u>, which regulate the plant's <u>growth</u> and <u>development</u>. Fancy.

Auxins are Plant Growth Hormones

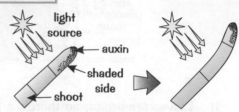

1) <u>Auxins</u> are <u>plant hormones</u> which control <u>growth</u> at the <u>tips</u> of <u>shoots</u> and <u>roots</u>. They move through the plant in <u>solution</u> (dissolved in water).

2) Auxin is produced in the <u>tips</u> and <u>diffuses backwards</u> to stimulate the <u>cell elongation process</u> which occurs in the cells <u>just behind</u> the tips.

3) Auxin <u>promotes</u> growth in the <u>shoot</u>, but actually <u>inhibits</u> growth in the <u>root</u>.

4) Auxins are involved in the <u>growth</u> responses of plants to <u>light</u> (phototropism) and <u>gravity</u> (gravitropism).

Auxins Change the Direction of Root and Shoot Growth

SHOOTS ARE POSITIVELY PHOTOTROPIC (grow towards light)

1) When a <u>shoot tip</u> is exposed to <u>light</u>, it accumulates <u>more auxin</u> on the side that's in the <u>shade</u> than the side that's in the <u>light</u>.

2) This makes the cells grow (elongate) <u>faster</u> on the <u>shaded side</u>, so the shoot bends <u>towards</u> the light.

By bending towards the light, the shoot will be able to <u>absorb more light</u> for <u>photosynthesis</u>, which enables the plant to <u>grow</u>. Handy. Shoots growing completely in the <u>dark</u> will be <u>tall</u> and <u>spindly</u> — the auxin in the tips makes them <u>elongate quickly</u> on <u>all sides</u>. A <u>taller shoot</u> has a better chance of <u>finding light</u>.

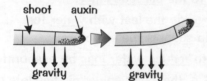

SHOOTS ARE NEGATIVELY GRAVITROPIC (grow away from gravity)

1) When a <u>shoot</u> is growing sideways, <u>gravity</u> produces an unequal distribution of auxin in the tip, with <u>more auxin</u> on the <u>lower side</u>.

2) This causes the lower side to grow <u>faster</u>, bending the shoot <u>upwards</u>.

ROOTS ARE POSITIVELY GRAVITROPIC (grow towards gravity)

1) A <u>root</u> growing sideways will also have more auxin on its <u>lower side</u>.

2) But in a root the <u>extra</u> auxin <u>inhibits</u> growth. This means the cells on <u>top</u> elongate faster, and the root bends <u>downwards</u>.

ROOTS ARE NEGATIVELY PHOTOTROPIC (grow away from light)

1) If a <u>root</u> starts being exposed to some <u>light</u>, <u>more auxin</u> accumulates on the more <u>shaded</u> side.

2) The auxin <u>inhibits</u> cell elongation on the shaded side, so the root bends <u>downwards</u>, back into the ground.

Roots that are underground <u>aren't exposed</u> to light. They grow downwards due to <u>positive gravitropism</u>.

You can do a Practical to Investigate Plant Growth Responses

For example, you can investigate the effect of <u>light</u> on the <u>growth</u> of cress seeds like this...

1) Put some <u>cress seeds</u> in a <u>Petri dish</u> lined with <u>moist filter paper</u>.

2) Surround the Petri dish with <u>black card</u>. (You might want to make a <u>box</u> out of black card and put the dish in that.) Cut a <u>hole</u> in <u>one side</u> of the card only.

3) Shine a <u>light</u> into the box <u>through</u> the hole.

4) Leave your cress seeds alone for <u>one week</u> until you can <u>observe</u> their <u>response</u> — you should find the seedlings <u>grow towards the light</u>. You can even measure the <u>angle</u> they're growing at.

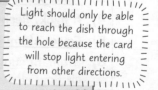
Light should only be able to reach the dish through the hole because the card will stop light entering from other directions.

A plant auxin to a bar — 'ouch'...

Quite a bit to learn on this page — cover it up and scribble it all down till you're confident you know it all.

Q1   Name a part of a plant that is positively gravitropic. [1 mark]

Commercial Uses of Plant Hormones

Plant hormones are <u>pretty useful</u> — people use them to do all kinds of things...

Plant Hormones Have Many Commercial Uses

1) As Selective Weedkillers

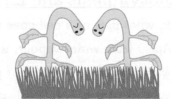

1) Most <u>weeds</u> growing in fields of crops or in a lawn are <u>broad-leaved</u>, in contrast to <u>grasses</u> and <u>cereals</u> which have very <u>narrow leaves</u>.

2) <u>Selective weedkillers</u> have been developed from <u>auxins</u>, which only affect the <u>broad-leaved plants</u>.

3) They totally <u>disrupt</u> their normal growth patterns, which soon <u>kills</u> them, whilst leaving the grass and crops <u>untouched</u>.

2) Growing from Cuttings with Rooting Powder

1) A <u>cutting</u> is part of a plant that has been <u>cut off it</u>, like the end of a branch with a few leaves on it.

2) Normally, if you stick cuttings in the soil they <u>won't grow</u>, but if you add <u>rooting powder</u>, which contains <u>auxins</u>, they will <u>produce roots</u> rapidly and start growing as <u>new plants</u>.

3) This enables growers to produce lots of <u>clones</u> (exact copies) of a really good plant <u>very quickly</u>.

3) Controlling Flower and Fruit Formation

1) <u>Gibberellins</u> are plant hormones that stimulate <u>seed germination</u> (growth of a seed into a plant), <u>stem growth</u> and <u>flowering</u>. They can be used to make plants flower <u>earlier</u> than they would usually do so, or under <u>conditions</u> in which they wouldn't usually flower (e.g. when it's <u>warmer</u> than usual).

2) They can also be used to <u>reduce flower formation</u>, which can <u>improve fruit quality</u>. (Fruit grows from pollinated flowers, see below.) E.g. <u>apricot trees</u> often produce too many flowers. This causes too many fruits to form — the tree can't support them all and they grow quite small. Fewer flowers means fewer fruits, which are able to grow nice and big.

4) Producing Seedless Fruit

1) Fruit (with seeds in the middle) normally only grows on flowering plants which have been <u>pollinated by insects</u>. If the flower <u>doesn't</u> get pollinated, the fruit and seeds <u>don't grow</u>.

2) If <u>plant hormones</u> such as <u>gibberellins</u> are applied to the <u>unpollinated flowers</u> of some types of plant, the <u>fruit will grow</u> but the <u>seeds won't</u>. Some <u>seedless citrus fruits</u> can be grown this way.

5) Controlling the Ripening of Fruits

1) The <u>ripening</u> of fruits can be controlled either while they are still on the plant, or during <u>transport</u> to the shops. This allows the fruit to be picked while it's still <u>unripe</u> (and therefore firmer and <u>less easily damaged</u>).

2) A <u>ripening hormone</u> called <u>ethene</u> is then added and the fruit will ripen on the way to the supermarket and be <u>perfect</u> just as it reaches the shelves.

6) Controlling Seed Germination

1) Lots of seeds <u>won't germinate</u> until they've been through <u>certain conditions</u> (e.g. a period of <u>cold</u> or of <u>dryness</u>).

2) <u>Seeds</u> can be treated with <u>gibberellins</u> to make them germinate at <u>times of year</u> that they <u>wouldn't</u> normally. It also helps to make sure <u>all</u> the seeds in a batch germinate at the <u>same time</u>.

You will germinate when I SAY you can — and NOT BEFORE...

Make sure you learn the effects of auxins, gibberellins and ethene and how we use them to our advantage.

Q1   State one way in which gibberellins can be used commercially.   [1 mark]

Revision Questions for Topic 6

Plants, plants and more plants — that pretty much sums up Topic 6 for you.

• Try these questions and tick off each one when you get it right.

• When you've done all the questions under a heading and are completely happy, tick it off.

Photosynthesis and Limiting Factors (p.69-70) ☑

1) In what part of a cell does photosynthesis take place?

2) Apart from water vapour, what gas is needed for photosynthesis?

3) Name the two products of photosynthesis.

4) Why is photosynthesis described as an endothermic reaction?

5) Describe how you could investigate the effect of light intensity on the rate of photosynthesis.

6) Describe the relationship between light intensity and distance from a light source.

7) What effect would a low carbon dioxide concentration have on the rate of photosynthesis?

8) What effect would a temperature above 45 °C usually have on the rate of photosynthesis? Why?

Transport in Plants and Transpiration (p.71-72) ☑

9) How are root hair cells adapted to their function?

10) By what process do phloem tubes transport sucrose around a plant?

11) Describe the structure of xylem vessels.

12) a) What are stomata?
   b) What is the role of stomata in transpiration?

13) Give three factors that affect the rate of transpiration.

14) Describe how you'd use a potometer to estimate the rate of transpiration.

Adaptations of Leaves and Plants (p.73) ☑

15) Give three ways in which a typical leaf is adapted to absorb the maximum amount of light for photosynthesis.

16) Give two ways in which a leaf is adapted for efficient gas exchange.

17) How do curled leaves help a plant living in dry conditions?

Plant Hormones (p.74-75) ☑

18) What are auxins?

19) Shoots are positively phototropic. What does this mean?

20) Roots are positively gravitropic. Explain the role of auxin in this response.

21) Explain how selective weedkillers work.

22) List three things that gibberellins stimulate in plants.

23) Describe a commercial use of the plant hormone ethene.

Hormones

Way back in Topic 2 you learnt how information is passed around the body via <u>neurones</u>. Well the body also uses <u>hormones</u> as a way to communicate, which is what this page is all about. Enjoy.

Hormones Are Chemical Messengers Sent in the Blood

1) <u>Hormones</u> are <u>chemicals</u> released directly into the <u>blood</u>. They are carried in the blood to other parts of the body, but only affect particular cells in particular organs (called <u>target organs</u>). Hormones control things in organs and cells that need <u>constant adjustment</u>.

2) Hormones are produced in (and secreted by) various <u>glands</u>, called <u>endocrine glands</u>. These glands make up your <u>endocrine system</u>.

3) These are the endocrine glands you need to know:

THE PITUITARY GLAND

The pituitary gland produces <u>many hormones</u> that regulate <u>body conditions</u>. It is sometimes called the '<u>master gland</u>' because these hormones act on <u>other glands</u>, directing them to <u>release hormones</u> that bring about <u>change</u>.

OVARIES — females only

Produce <u>oestrogen</u>, which is involved in the <u>menstrual cycle</u> (see page 79).

TESTES — males only

Produce <u>testosterone</u>, which controls <u>puberty</u> and <u>sperm production</u> in males.

THYROID GLAND

This produces <u>thyroxine</u>, which is involved in regulating things like the <u>rate of metabolism</u>, <u>heart rate</u> and <u>temperature</u> (see next page).

ADRENAL GLANDS

These produce <u>adrenaline</u>, which is used to prepare the body for a '<u>fight or flight</u>' response (see next page).

THE PANCREAS

This produces <u>insulin</u>, which is used to regulate the <u>blood glucose level</u> (see page 81).

Hormones and Neurones Have Differences

<u>NEURONES</u>:
Very <u>FAST</u> action.
Act for a very <u>SHORT TIME</u>.
Act on a very <u>PRECISE AREA</u>.

<u>HORMONES</u>:
<u>SLOWER</u> action.
Act for a <u>LONG TIME</u>.
Act in a more <u>GENERAL</u> way.

So if you're not sure whether a response is nervous or hormonal, have a think...

1) If the response is <u>really quick</u>, it's <u>probably nervous</u>. Some information needs to be passed to effectors really quickly (e.g. pain signals, or information from your eyes telling you about the lion heading your way), so it's no good using hormones to carry the message — they're too slow.

2) But if a response <u>lasts for a long time</u>, it's <u>probably hormonal</u>. For example, when you get a shock, the hormone adrenaline is released into the body (causing the 'fight or flight' response, where your body is hyped up ready for action). You can tell it's a hormonal response (even though it kicks in pretty quickly) because you feel a bit wobbly for a while afterwards.

Nerves, hormones — no wonder revision makes me tense...

Hormones control various organs and cells in the body, though they tend to control things that aren't immediately life-threatening (so things like sexual development, blood glucose level, water content, etc.).

Q1   Name the endocrine glands that only males have.   [1 mark]

Adrenaline and Thyroxine

On the previous page you learnt what <u>hormones</u> are. Now it's time to look at a <u>couple of examples</u>...

Adrenaline Prepares You for 'Fight or Flight'

1) <u>Adrenaline</u> is a hormone released by the <u>adrenal glands</u> (which are located just above the kidneys — see previous page).

2) Adrenaline prepares the body for '<u>fight or flight</u>' — in other words, <u>standing</u> your <u>ground</u> in the face of a <u>threat</u> (e.g. a predator) or bravely <u>running away</u>. It does this by activating processes that increase the supply of <u>oxygen and glucose</u> to cells. For example:

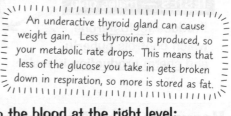

- Adrenaline <u>binds</u> to specific <u>receptors</u> in the <u>heart</u>. This causes the heart muscle to <u>contract</u> more frequently and with <u>more force</u>, so heart rate and blood pressure <u>increase</u>.

- This increases <u>blood flow</u> to the <u>muscles</u>, so the cells receive more <u>oxygen</u> and <u>glucose</u> for increased <u>respiration</u>.

- Adrenaline also binds to receptors in the <u>liver</u>. This causes the liver to <u>break down</u> its <u>glycogen</u> stores (see. p.81) to release <u>glucose</u>.

- This increases the <u>blood glucose level</u>, so there's more glucose in the blood to be transported to the cells.

3) When your brain detects a <u>stressful situation</u>, it sends <u>nervous impulses</u> to the <u>adrenal glands</u>, which respond by secreting <u>adrenaline</u>. This gets the body ready for <u>action</u>.

Hormone Release can be Affected by Negative Feedback

Your body can <u>control</u> the levels of hormones (and other substances) in the blood using <u>negative feedback</u> <u>systems</u>. When the body detects that the level of a substance has gone <u>above or below</u> the <u>normal level</u>, it <u>triggers a response</u> to bring the level <u>back to normal</u> again. Here's an example of just that:

Thyroxine Regulates Metabolism

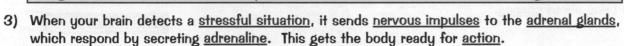

1) <u>Thyroxine</u> is a hormone released by the <u>thyroid gland</u>.

2) It plays an important role in regulating <u>metabolic rate</u> — the speed at which chemical reactions in the body occur.

An underactive thyroid gland can cause weight gain. Less thyroxine is produced, so your metabolic rate drops. This means that less of the glucose you take in gets broken down in respiration, so more is stored as fat.

3) A <u>negative feedback system</u> keeps the amount of thyroxine in the blood at the right level:

- When the blood thyroxine level is <u>lower than normal</u>, the <u>hypothalamus</u> (a structure in the brain) is stimulated to release <u>thyrotropin releasing hormone</u> (<u>TRH</u>).

- TRH stimulates the <u>pituitary gland</u> to release <u>thyroid stimulating hormone</u> (<u>TSH</u>).

- TSH stimulates the <u>thyroid gland</u> to release <u>thyroxine</u>, so the blood thyroxine level <u>rises</u> back towards normal.

- When the blood thyroxine level becomes <u>higher than</u> <u>normal</u>, the release of <u>TRH</u> from the hypothalamus is inhibited, which reduces the production of <u>TSH</u>, so the blood thyroxine level <u>falls</u>.

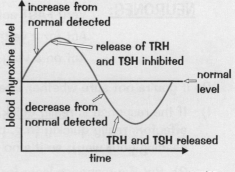

A higher than normal thyroxine level also directly inhibits the secretion of TSH from the pituitary gland.

Negative feedback sucks, especially from your science teacher...

You can think about negative feedback working like a thermostat — if the temperature gets too low, the thermostat will turn the heating on, then if the temperature gets too high, it'll turn the heating off again.

Q1   Name the gland that releases thyroxine.   [1 mark]

Q2   Describe how release of TRH from the hypothalamus affects the blood thyroxine level.   [2 marks]

The Menstrual Cycle

You need to know all about the <u>hormones</u> that control the <u>menstrual cycle</u> — lucky you...

The Menstrual Cycle Has Four Stages

The menstrual cycle is the <u>monthly sequence of events</u> in which the female body releases an <u>egg</u> and prepares the <u>uterus</u> (womb) in case the egg is <u>fertilised</u>. This is what happens at <u>each stage</u>:

<u>Stage 1</u> <u>Day 1 is when menstruation starts</u>.
The lining of the uterus breaks down and is released.

<u>Stage 2</u> <u>The uterus lining is repaired</u>, from day 4 to
day 14, until it becomes a thick spongy layer full of blood vessels ready for a fertilised egg to implant there.

<u>Stage 3</u> <u>An egg develops and is released</u> from the ovary (<u>ovulation</u>) at about day 14.

<u>Stage 4</u> <u>The lining is then maintained</u> for about 14 days, until day 28. If no fertilised egg has landed on the uterus wall by day 28, the spongy lining starts to break down again and the whole cycle starts over.

> The fancy name for the lining of the uterus is the 'endometrium'.

The Menstrual Cycle is Controlled by Four Hormones

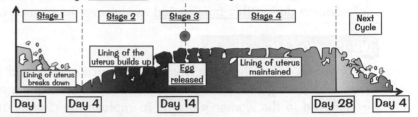

① FSH (follicle-stimulating hormone)
1) Released by the <u>pituitary gland</u>.
2) Causes a <u>follicle</u> (an <u>egg</u> and its surrounding cells) to <u>mature</u> in one of the ovaries.
3) Stimulates <u>oestrogen</u> production.

② Oestrogen
1) Released by the <u>ovaries</u>.
2) Causes the lining of the uterus to <u>thicken</u> and <u>grow</u>.
3) A high level stimulates an <u>LH surge</u> (a rapid increase).

③ LH (luteinising hormone)
1) Released by the <u>pituitary gland</u>.
2) The LH surge stimulates <u>ovulation</u> at day 14 — the follicle ruptures and the <u>egg is released</u>.
3) Stimulates the <u>remains</u> of the <u>follicle</u> to develop into a structure called a <u>corpus luteum</u> — which secretes <u>progesterone</u>.

④ Progesterone
1) Released by the <u>corpus luteum</u> after <u>ovulation</u>.
2) <u>Maintains</u> the lining of the uterus.
3) <u>Inhibits</u> the release of <u>FSH</u> and <u>LH</u>.
4) When the level of progesterone <u>falls</u>, and there's a low oestrogen level, the uterus lining <u>breaks down</u>.
5) A <u>low</u> progesterone level allows <u>FSH</u> to <u>increase</u>... and then the whole cycle starts again.

If a fertilised egg implants in the uterus (i.e. the woman becomes <u>pregnant</u>) then the level of <u>progesterone</u> will <u>stay high</u> to maintain the lining of the uterus during pregnancy.

What do you call a fish with no eye — FSH...

OK, this stuff is pretty tricky. Try scribbling down everything on the page until you can get it all without peeking.

Q1   Explain the role of LH in the menstrual cycle.   [3 marks]

Controlling Fertility

Hormones can be used artificially to help infertile women have babies and to help fertile women not have babies.

Hormones can be Used to Treat Infertility

If a person is infertile, it means they can't reproduce naturally. There are methods an infertile couple can use to become pregnant, many of which involve hormones. You need to learn these two examples:

Clomifene therapy

Some women are infertile because they don't ovulate or they don't ovulate regularly. These women can take a drug called clomifene. This works by causing more FSH and LH to be released by the body, which stimulate egg maturation and ovulation — see previous page. By knowing when the woman will be ovulating, the couple can have intercourse during this time period to improve the chance of becoming pregnant.

IVF ("in vitro fertilisation")

IVF involves collecting eggs from the woman's ovaries and fertilising them in a lab using the man's sperm. These are then grown into embryos. Once the embryos are tiny balls of cells, one or two of them are transferred to the woman's uterus to improve the chance of pregnancy. FSH and LH are given before egg collection to stimulate egg production (so more than one egg can be collected).

IVF is an example of Assisted Reproductive Technology (ART) — a fertility treatment that involves eggs being handled (and usually fertilised) outside of the body.

Contraceptives are Used to Prevent Pregnancy

1) Hormones can also be used as contraceptives. For example, oestrogen can be used to prevent the release of an egg. This may seem kind of strange (since naturally oestrogen helps stimulate the release of eggs). But if oestrogen is taken every day to keep the level of it permanently high, it inhibits the production of FSH, and after a while egg development and production stop and stay stopped.

2) Progesterone can also be used to reduce fertility. It works in several different ways — one of which is by stimulating the production of thick cervical mucus, which prevents any sperm getting through the entrance to the uterus (the cervix) and reaching an egg.

3) Some hormonal contraceptives contain both oestrogen and progesterone — for example, the combined pill (which is an oral contraceptive) and the contraceptive patch (which is worn on the skin).

4) The mini-pill (another oral contraceptive) and the contraceptive injection both contain progesterone only.

5) Pregnancy can also be prevented by barrier methods of contraception — these put a barrier between the sperm and egg so they don't meet. Examples include condoms (both male and female) and diaphragms (flexible, dome-shaped devices that fit over the opening of the uterus and are inserted before sex).

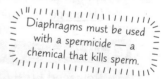
Diaphragms must be used with a spermicide — a chemical that kills sperm.

Hormonal and Barrier Contraceptive Methods Have Pros and Cons

I've got this barrier thing sorted...

1) Generally, when used correctly, hormonal methods are more effective at preventing pregnancy than barrier methods. Also, hormonal methods mean the couple don't have to stop and think about contraception each time they have intercourse (as they would if they relied on barrier methods).

2) However, hormonal methods can have unpleasant side-effects, such as headaches, acne and mood changes. Also, hormonal methods don't protect against sexually transmitted infections — condoms are the only form of contraception that do this.

IVF... FSH... LH... ART — I feel like I'm at the opticians...

Make sure you understand how and why hormones are used in fertility treatments and contraceptive methods.

Q1   Describe how hormones are used in IVF.   [3 marks]

Homeostasis — Control of Blood Glucose

Homeostasis means maintaining the right conditions inside your body, so that everything works properly. Ace.

Homeostasis is Maintaining a Constant Internal Environment

1) Conditions in your body need to be kept steady — this is really important because your cells need the right conditions in order to function properly, including the right conditions for enzyme action (see p.16). It can be dangerous for your health if conditions vary too much from normal levels.

2) To maintain a constant internal environment, your body needs to respond to both internal and external changes, whilst balancing inputs (stuff going into your body) with outputs (stuff leaving).

3) Examples of homeostasis in action include:

- Osmoregulation (regulating water content) — you need to keep a balance between the water you gain (in drink, food, and from respiration) and the water you pee, sweat and breathe out. See pages 84-85.

- Thermoregulation (regulating body temperature) — you need to reduce your body temperature when you're hot, but increase it when the environment is cold. See p.83.

- Blood glucose regulation — you need to make sure the amount of glucose in your blood doesn't get too high or too low (see below).

4) Negative feedback systems (see p.78) help to keep conditions in your body steady. This means that if a condition changes away from the normal level, a response is triggered that counteracts the change. E.g. a rise in blood glucose level causes a response that lowers blood glucose level (and vice versa).

Insulin and Glucagon Control Blood Glucose Concentration

1) Eating foods containing carbohydrate puts glucose into the blood from the small intestine.

2) The normal metabolism of cells removes glucose from the blood.

3) Vigorous exercise removes much more glucose from the blood.

4) Excess glucose can be stored as glycogen in the liver and in the muscles.

5) When these stores are full then the excess glucose is stored as lipid (fat) in the tissues.

6) Changes in blood glucose are monitored and controlled by the pancreas, using the hormones insulin and glucagon, as shown:

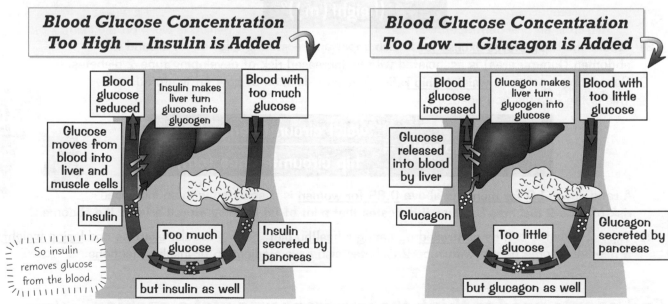

Learn about homeostasis — and keep your cool...

Homeostasis is really important for keeping processes in your body ticking over nicely. Make sure you learn the definition of homeostasis and can explain how blood glucose concentration is regulated by insulin and glucagon.

Q1   Explain how blood glucose concentration is returned to normal when it has become too high.   [3 marks]

Diabetes

Diabetes is an example of when homeostasis doesn't work. Make sure you fully understand how insulin affects blood glucose concentration (on the previous page) before you try getting your head around diabetes.

Type 1 Diabetes — Caused by a Lack of Insulin

1) Type 1 diabetes is a condition where the pancreas produces little or no insulin. The result is that a person's blood glucose can rise to a level that can kill them.

Remember, insulin reduces blood glucose level.

2) A person with type 1 diabetes will need to be treated with insulin therapy — this usually involves injecting insulin into the blood. This is often done at mealtimes to make sure that the glucose is removed from the blood quickly once the food has been digested. This stops the level of glucose in the blood from getting too high and is a very effective treatment. Insulin is usually injected into subcutaneous tissue (fatty tissue just under the skin). The amount of insulin that needs to be injected depends on the person's diet and how active they are.

Injecting too much insulin could result in a dangerously low blood glucose level.

3) As well as insulin therapy, people with type 1 diabetes also need to think about:

> • Limiting the intake of foods rich in simple carbohydrates, i.e. sugars (which cause the blood glucose level to rise rapidly).
>
> • Taking regular exercise — this helps to remove excess glucose from the blood.

Type 2 Diabetes — a Person is Resistant to Insulin

1) Type 2 diabetes is a condition where the pancreas doesn't produce enough insulin or when a person becomes resistant to insulin (their body's cells don't respond properly to the hormone). In both of these cases, blood glucose level rises.

2) There is a correlation (see p.10) between obesity and type 2 diabetes — this means that obese people have an increased risk of developing type 2 diabetes. People are classified as obese if they have a body mass index (BMI) of over 30. BMI is worked out using this formula:

$$BMI = \frac{weight\ (kg)}{(height\ (m))^2}$$

See page 66 for more on calculating BMI and waist-to-hip ratios.

3) Where the body stores excess fat is also important — storing a lot of fat around the abdomen (tummy area) is associated with an increased risk of developing type 2 diabetes. Calculating a person's waist-to-hip ratio gives an indication of how fat is stored. This is the formula you need:

$$Waist\text{-}to\text{-}hip\ ratio = \frac{waist\ circumference\ (cm)}{hip\ circumference\ (cm)}$$

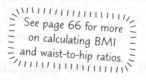

A ratio above 1.0 for men and above 0.85 for women is associated with an increased risk of type 2 diabetes because it indicates that a lot of fat is being stored around the abdomen.

4) Type 2 diabetes can be controlled by eating a healthy diet, getting regular exercise and losing weight if needed. Some people with type 2 diabetes also have medication or insulin injections.

And people used to think the pancreas was just a cushion... (true)

Don't forget that there are two types of diabetes. Make sure you know how each one is caused and what the different treatments are. Remember as well that obesity is a big risk factor for developing type 2 diabetes.

Q1 Describe the cause of type 1 diabetes. [1 mark]

Q2 Give two measures of obesity that can help to assess a person's risk of developing type 2 diabetes. [2 marks]

Thermoregulation

Thermoregulation is the process your body uses to keep its internal temperature steady. So next time you go all red and sweaty in P.E., just be grateful your body's thermoregulating as it should.

Body Temperature is Controlled by the Hypothalamus

1) All enzymes have an optimum temperature — this is the temperature at which they work best.

2) The enzymes in the human body work best at about 37 °C. Below this temperature enzyme activity slows down and above this temperature enzymes may start to denature so they can't work at all.

3) Homeostasis maintains our core body temperature at a steady 37 °C. Any change in body temperature triggers a response that counteracts it, e.g. a rise in body temperature triggers a response to bring it back down again.

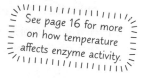
See page 16 for more on how temperature affects enzyme activity.

4) The thermoregulatory centre in the hypothalamus (a structure in the brain) acts as your own personal thermostat.

5) It contains receptors that are sensitive to the blood temperature in the brain. It also receives impulses from receptors in the skin (nerve endings) that provide information about the external temperature. These receptors are located in the epidermis (the outer layer of the skin) and in the dermis (a deeper layer of skin just below the epidermis).

6) When the hypothalamus detects a change, it causes a response in the skin:

When You're Too Hot...

1) Erector muscles relax, so hairs lie flat.

2) Lots of sweat (containing water and salts) is produced in sweat glands in the dermis. The sweat is released onto the surface of the skin through pores in the epidermis. When the sweat evaporates it transfers energy from your skin to the environment, cooling you down.

3) Blood vessels close to the surface of the skin dilate (widen). This is called vasodilation. It allows more blood to flow near the surface, so it can transfer more energy into the surroundings, which cools you down.

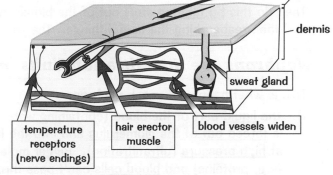

epidermis

dermis

sweat gland

temperature receptors (nerve endings)

hair erector muscle

blood vessels widen

When You're Too Cold...

1) Erector muscles contract. Hairs stand on end to trap an insulating layer of air near the surface of the skin, which helps keep you warm.

2) Very little sweat is produced.

3) Blood vessels near the surface of the skin constrict (vasoconstriction). This means less blood flows near the surface, so less energy is transferred to the surroundings.

4) When you're cold you also shiver (your muscles contract automatically). This increases your rate of respiration, which transfers more energy to warm the body.

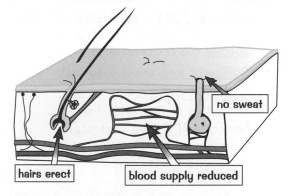

no sweat

hairs erect

blood supply reduced

Shiver me timbers — it's a wee bit nippy in here...

People who are exposed to extreme cold without protection can get frostbite — the blood supply to the fingers and toes is cut off to reduce the amount of energy lost (but this kills the cells, and the digits go black). Yuk.

Q1 Explain how blood flow through the skin is affected when a person is too cold. [2 marks]

Topic 7 — Animal Coordination, Control and Homeostasis

Osmoregulation and The Kidneys

The <u>kidneys</u> play a big part in this whole homeostasis thing too. They're important for <u>osmoregulation</u> (regulating <u>water content</u> in the body).

Regulating Water Content is Really Important

1) It's really important that the <u>water content</u> of the <u>blood</u> is <u>controlled</u> to keep <u>cells functioning normally</u>.

2) If the concentration of water in the blood is <u>too high</u> then water will move <u>into</u> the body cells by <u>osmosis</u> (see p.21). If too much water moves into the cells then the cells may <u>burst</u>.

Animal cells burst when they contain too much water because they don't have a rigid cell wall (unlike plant cells).

3) If the concentration of water in the blood is <u>too low</u> then water will move <u>out of</u> the cells into the blood by osmosis. This causes the cells to <u>shrink</u>.

4) The <u>kidneys</u> help to regulate water content by controlling how much water is <u>reabsorbed</u> and how much is <u>lost in urine</u>.

The Kidneys are Part of the Urinary System

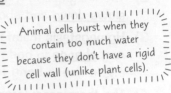

Kidneys have <u>three main roles</u>:

1) <u>Removal of urea</u> from the blood. Urea is produced in the <u>liver</u> from the breakdown of <u>excess amino acids</u>.

2) <u>Adjustment of ion levels</u> in the blood.

3) <u>Adjustment of water content</u> of the blood.

They do this by <u>filtering</u> stuff out of the blood under <u>high pressure</u>, and then <u>reabsorbing</u> the useful things. The end product is <u>urine</u>.

You need to be able to describe the structure of the urinary system.

renal vein — renal artery — left kidney — ureter — bladder — urethra

Nephrons are the Filtration Units in the Kidneys

This is what happens in each <u>nephron</u>:

1) The <u>liquid</u> part of the blood (containing water, urea, ions and glucose) is <u>forced out</u> of the <u>glomerulus</u> and into the <u>Bowman's capsule</u> at <u>high pressure</u> (<u>ultrafiltration</u>). <u>Bigger</u> molecules (e.g. proteins) and <u>blood cells</u> can't pass through the membranes and are <u>not forced out</u>.

2) As the liquid flows along the nephron, <u>useful</u> substances are <u>reabsorbed</u>:

   • <u>All</u> the <u>glucose</u> is <u>selectively</u> reabsorbed — it's moved back into the blood <u>against</u> the concentration gradient.

   • <u>Sufficient ions</u> are reabsorbed.

   • <u>Sufficient water</u> is reabsorbed, according to the level of the hormone <u>ADH</u> (see next page).

   Animals living in drought conditions have longer loops of Henle to reabsorb more water.

3) Whatever isn't reabsorbed (e.g. urea, excess water, excess ions) continues <u>out</u> of the <u>nephron</u> via the <u>collecting duct</u>. It then passes into the <u>ureter</u> and down to the <u>bladder</u> as <u>urine</u>. Urine is released through the <u>urethra</u>.

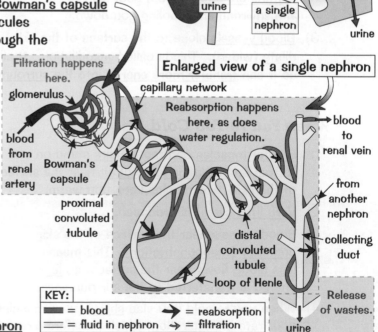

Filtration happens here. glomerulus — capillary network — blood from renal artery — Bowman's capsule — proximal convoluted tubule — Reabsorption happens here, as does water regulation. — blood to renal vein — from another nephron — distal convoluted tubule — collecting duct — loop of Henle — Release of wastes. — urine

Enlarged view of a single nephron

a single nephron — urine

KEY:
■ = blood   → = reabsorption
▭ = fluid in nephron   ⇢ = filtration

Learn this lot or else urine trouble come exam time...

The kidneys are really important for osmoregulation, but the brain is involved too (as you'll soon find out).

Q1   State the function of the glomerulus and the Bowman's capsule in a nephron.   [1 mark]

More on The Kidneys

Your kidneys have a clever way of regulating water content. But problems occur when the kidneys don't work.

Water Content is Controlled by a Negative Feedback System

1) The amount of water reabsorbed in the kidney nephrons is controlled by anti-diuretic hormone (ADH).

2) The brain monitors the water content of the blood and instructs the pituitary gland to release ADH into the blood according to how much is needed. ADH makes the collecting ducts of the nephrons more permeable so that more water is reabsorbed back into the blood. This stops the body from becoming dehydrated.

3) The whole process of water content regulation is controlled by a negative feedback system:

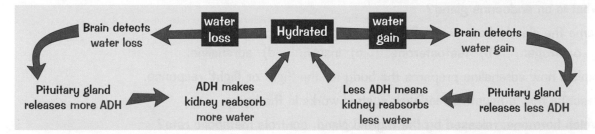

E.g. if the amount of sodium ions in the blood increases, the concentration of water in the blood will fall. The brain will detect that the blood needs more water, so it will release more ADH. More water will be reabsorbed from the collecting ducts so the water content of the blood will rise.

Dialysis Filters the Blood Mechanically

1) Patients who have kidney failure can't filter their blood properly — but a dialysis machine can be used to filter their blood for them.

2) Dialysis has to be done regularly to keep dissolved substances at the right concentrations, and to remove waste.

3) Dialysis fluid has the same concentration of salts and glucose as blood plasma (which means those aren't removed from the blood).

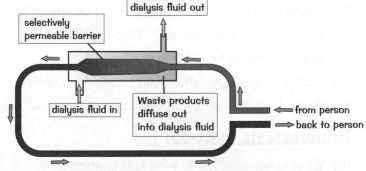

4) The barrier is permeable to things like ions and waste substances, but not big molecules like proteins (just like membranes in the kidney). So the waste substances (e.g. urea), plus excess ions and water from the blood, move across the membrane into the dialysis fluid. Cells and proteins stay in the blood.

Kidney Transplants Cure Kidney Disease But Can Be Rejected

At the moment, the only cure for kidney disease is to have a kidney transplant. Healthy kidneys are usually transplanted from people who have died suddenly, say in a car accident, and who are on the organ donor register or carry a donor card (provided their relatives give the go-ahead).

The donor kidney can be rejected by the patient's immune system — treated like a foreign body and attacked by antibodies. To help prevent this happening, precautions are taken:

1) A donor with a tissue type that closely matches the patient is chosen.

2) The patient is treated with drugs that suppress the immune system, so that their immune system won't attack the transplanted kidney.

Reabsorb the facts and excrete the rest...

Donor kidneys are ideally matched by blood type (and a few other things) to the recipient, which make them less likely to be rejected. However, it means a potentially long waiting time for a suitable kidney.

Q1 What is the purpose of the selectively permeable membrane in a dialysis machine? [2 marks]

Revision Questions for Topic 7

Congratulations, you've made it to the end of <u>Topic 7</u> — now for some questions to make sure you've been paying attention...

- Try these questions and <u>tick off each one</u> when you <u>get it right</u>.
- When you've done <u>all the questions</u> under a heading and are <u>completely happy</u>, tick it off.

<u>Hormones (p.77-78)</u> ☑

1) What is a hormone? ☑
2) How do hormones travel to target organs? ☑
3) What is an endocrine gland? ☑
4) Name the gland where each of the following hormones is produced:
   a) oestrogen,   b) testosterone,   c) insulin,   d) adrenaline. ☑
5) Explain how adrenaline prepares the body for the 'fight or flight' response. ☑
6) Describe how a negative feedback system works in the body. ☑
7) Which hormone, released by the thyroid gland, controls metabolic rate? ☑

<u>The Menstrual Cycle and Fertility (p.79-80)</u> ☑

8) Draw a timeline of the 28 day menstrual cycle.
   Label the four stages of the cycle and label when the egg is released. ☑
9) Describe two effects of FSH on the body. ☑
10) Describe two effects of oestrogen on the body. ☑
11) Which hormone is secreted by a corpus luteum? ☑
12) What is clomifene therapy? Who might use it? ☑
13) Briefly describe how IVF is carried out. ☑
14) Explain how progesterone can be used in contraception to prevent pregnancy. ☑
15) Write down two pros and two cons of hormonal contraceptives. ☑

<u>Homeostasis (p.81-85)</u> ☑

16) What is homeostasis? Why is it important? ☑
17) Describe the roles of insulin and glucagon in controlling a person's blood glucose concentration. ☑
18) Explain how type 1 and type 2 diabetes can be treated. ☑
19) What is thermoregulation? Why is it important for enzymes in the body? ☑
20) Explain how changes in the skin help to control body temperature when you're too hot. ☑
21) What is osmoregulation? ☑
22) Describe what might happen to body cells if the concentration of water in the blood is too low. ☑
23) Excess amino acids are broken down in the liver.
    Name the waste product of this process, which must be removed in urine. ☑
24) List the main structures in the urinary system. ☑
25) Sketch a nephron and label all the parts. ☑
26) Describe how urine is formed. ☑
27) Describe how the brain responds when it detects a fall in the water content of the blood. ☑
28) Give two treatments for kidney failure and briefly describe each one. ☑

Exchange of Materials

Like all organisms, animals need to <u>exchange</u> things with their environment — but being <u>multicellular</u> makes things a little bit complicated...

Organisms Exchange Substances with their Environment

1) All organisms must <u>take in</u> substances that they <u>need</u> from the environment and <u>get rid</u> of any <u>waste products</u>. For example:
   - Cells need <u>oxygen</u> for <u>aerobic respiration</u> (see page 92), which produces <u>carbon dioxide</u> as a waste product. These two <u>gases</u> move between <u>cells</u> and the <u>environment</u> by <u>diffusion</u> (see next page).
   - <u>Water</u> is taken up by cells by <u>osmosis</u>. In animals, dissolved <u>food molecules</u> (the products of digestion, e.g. glucose, amino acids) and <u>mineral ions</u> diffuse along with it.
   - <u>Urea</u> (a waste product produced by animals from proteins, see p.84) diffuses from <u>cells</u> to the <u>blood plasma</u> for removal from the body by the kidneys.

   There's more on diffusion and osmosis on page 21.

2) How <u>easy</u> it is for an organism to exchange substances with its environment depends on the organism's <u>surface area to volume ratio</u> (<u>SA : V</u>).

You Can Compare Surface Area to Volume Ratios

A ratio shows <u>how big</u> one value is <u>compared</u> to another. The <u>larger</u> an organism is, the <u>smaller</u> its surface area is compared to its volume. You can show this by calculating <u>surface area to volume ratios</u>:

A hippo can be represented by a 2 cm × 4 cm × 4 cm block.

The <u>area</u> of a surface is found by the equation: LENGTH × WIDTH
So the hippo's <u>total surface area</u> is:

$$(4 \times 4) \times 2 \text{ (top and bottom surfaces of block)}$$
$$+ (4 \times 2) \times 4 \text{ (four sides of the block)}$$
$$= 64 \text{ cm}^2.$$

The <u>volume</u> of a block is found by the equation: LENGTH × WIDTH × HEIGHT
So the hippo's <u>volume</u> is $4 \times 4 \times 2 = 32 \text{ cm}^3$.

The surface area to volume ratio of the hippo can be written as <u>64 : 32</u>.
To get the ratio in the form <u>n : 1</u>, <u>divide both sides</u> of the ratio by the <u>volume</u>.
So the surface area to volume ratio of the hippo is <u>2 : 1</u>.

A mouse can be represented by a 1 cm × 1 cm × 1 cm block.
Its <u>surface area</u> is $(1 \times 1) \times 6 = 6 \text{ cm}^2$.
Its <u>volume</u> is $1 \times 1 \times 1 = 1 \text{ cm}^3$.
So the surface area to volume ratio of the mouse is <u>6 : 1</u>.

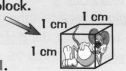

The cube mouse's surface area is <u>six</u> times its volume, but the cube hippo's surface area is only <u>twice</u> its volume. So the <u>mouse</u> has a <u>larger</u> surface area compared to its volume.

Multicellular Organisms Need Exchange Surfaces

1) In <u>single-celled organisms</u>, gases and dissolved substances can diffuse <u>directly into</u> (or out of) the cell across the cell membrane — it's because they have a <u>large surface area</u> compared to their <u>volume</u>, so <u>enough substances</u> can be exchanged across the membrane to supply the volume of the cell.

2) <u>Multicellular organisms</u> (such as <u>animals</u>) have a <u>smaller surface area</u> compared to their <u>volume</u>. This makes it difficult to exchange <u>enough substances</u> to supply their <u>entire volume</u> across their <u>outside surface</u> alone. So they need some sort of <u>exchange surface</u> for efficient diffusion and a <u>mass transport system</u> to move substances between the exchange surface and the rest of the body.

3) The exchange surfaces have to allow <u>enough</u> of the necessary substances to pass through, so they are <u>adapted</u> to maximise effectiveness (see next page).

Not that I'm endorsing putting animals in boxes...

Have a go at this question to make sure you understand how to calculate surface area to volume ratios.

Q1   A bacterial cell can be represented by a 1 μm × 1 μm × 4 μm block. Calculate the cell's surface area to volume ratio. Give your ratio in its simplest whole number form.   [3 marks]

Diffusion and the Alveoli

The alveoli are an <u>exchange surface</u> found in the lungs of mammals. They're <u>well-adapted</u> for the <u>efficient exchange</u> of two important <u>gases</u> — oxygen and carbon dioxide.

The Rate of Diffusion Depends on Three Main Things

Gases are exchanged in the lungs by <u>diffusion</u>. (There's more on diffusion on page 21.)
The <u>rate of diffusion</u> of any substance is affected by these <u>three factors</u>:

1) <u>Distance</u> — substances diffuse <u>more quickly</u> when they haven't <u>as far</u> to move. Pretty obvious.

2) <u>Concentration difference</u> (<u>gradient</u>) — substances diffuse faster if there's a <u>big difference</u> in concentration between the area they are diffusing <u>from</u> and the area they are diffusing <u>to</u>. If there are lots more particles on one side, there are more there to move across.

3) <u>Surface area</u> — the <u>more surface</u> there is available for molecules to move across, the <u>faster</u> they can get from one side to the other.

Gas Exchange in Mammals Happens in the Alveoli

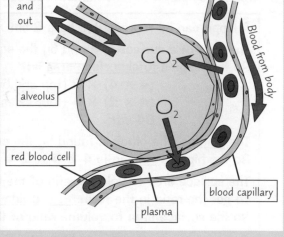

Remember — one alveolus, many alveoli.

1) The job of the lungs is to transfer <u>oxygen</u> (O_2) to the <u>blood</u> and to <u>remove</u> waste <u>carbon dioxide</u> (CO_2) from it.

2) To do this, the lungs contain millions of little air sacs called <u>alveoli</u> where <u>gas exchange</u> takes place.

3) Blood <u>arriving</u> at the alveoli has just returned to the lungs from the <u>rest of the body</u>, so it contains <u>lots of CO_2</u> and <u>not much O_2</u>. This maximises the <u>concentration gradient</u> for the diffusion of both gases.

4) O_2 <u>diffuses out</u> of the <u>air</u> in the <u>alveoli</u> (where the concentration of O_2 is <u>high</u>) and into the <u>blood</u> (where the concentration of O_2 is <u>low</u>). CO_2 diffuses in the <u>opposite direction</u> to be breathed out.

5) The alveoli are specialised to maximise the <u>diffusion</u> of O_2 and CO_2. They have:
   - A moist lining for <u>dissolving</u> gases.
   - A good <u>blood supply</u> to maintain the concentration gradients of O_2 and CO_2.
   - <u>Very thin</u> walls — minimising the <u>distance</u> that gases have to move.
   - An enormous <u>surface area</u> (about 75 m^2 in humans).

O_2 and CO_2 diffuse across the membranes of the cells that make up the walls of the capillary and alveolus. These membranes are partially permeable — see page 21.

Fick's Law Describes the Rate of Diffusion

The relationship between the <u>rate of diffusion</u> and the <u>factors</u> that affect it is described by <u>Fick's Law</u>. It states that:

$$\text{rate of diffusion} \propto \frac{\text{surface area} \times \text{concentration difference}}{\text{thickness of membrane}}$$

'$\propto$' means '<u>is proportional to</u>'. Essentially, what this means is that the <u>rate of diffusion</u> will <u>DOUBLE</u> if:

1) the <u>surface area</u> or the <u>difference</u> in concentration <u>DOUBLES</u>, OR

2) the <u>thickness</u> of the membrane <u>HALVES</u>.

Al Veoli — the Italian gas man...

Without gas exchange surfaces like the alveoli, multicellular organisms wouldn't be able to absorb oxygen quickly enough to supply all of their cells. Have a go at this question and see what you've learnt.

Q1   Give one way in which the alveoli are adapted for gas exchange.   [1 mark]

Circulatory System — Blood

Blood is a tissue. One of its jobs is to act as a huge transport system. There are four main things in blood...

Red Blood Cells Carry Oxygen

1) The job of red blood cells (also called erythrocytes) is to carry oxygen from the lungs to all the cells in the body.
2) They have a biconcave disc shape (in other words, they look a bit like a jam doughnut that's being pressed in at the top and bottom) to give a large surface area for absorbing oxygen.

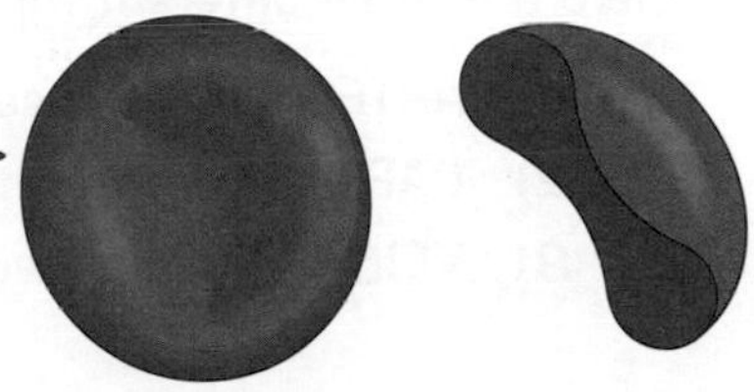

3) They don't have a nucleus — this allows more room to carry oxygen.
4) They contain a red pigment called haemoglobin, which contains iron.
5) In the lungs, haemoglobin binds to oxygen to become oxyhaemoglobin. In body tissues, the reverse happens — oxyhaemoglobin splits up into haemoglobin and oxygen, to release oxygen to the cells.

The more red blood cells you've got, the more oxygen can get to your cells. At high altitudes there's less oxygen in the air — so people who live there produce more red blood cells to compensate.

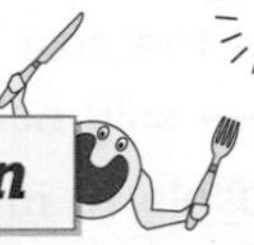

White Blood Cells Defend Against Infection

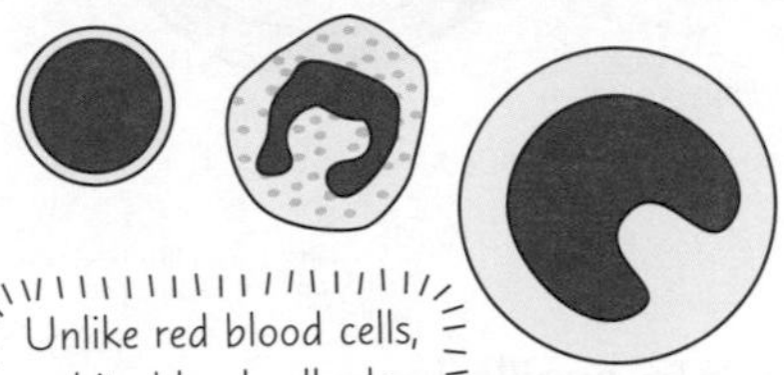

Unlike red blood cells, white blood cells do have a nucleus.

1) Phagocytes are white blood cells that can change shape to engulf (gobble up) unwelcome microorganisms — this is called phagocytosis.
2) Lymphocytes are white blood cells that produce antibodies against microorganisms (see p.58). Some also produce antitoxins to neutralise any toxins produced by the microorganisms.
3) When you have an infection, your white blood cells multiply to fight it off — so a blood test will show a high white blood cell count.

Platelets Help Blood Clot

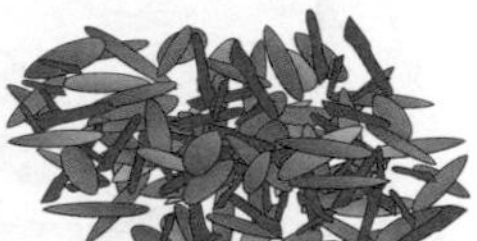

1) These are small fragments of cells. They have no nucleus.
2) They help the blood to clot at a wound — to stop all your blood pouring out and to stop microorganisms getting in. (So platelets kinda float about waiting for accidents to happen.)
3) Lack of platelets can cause excessive bleeding and bruising.

Plasma is the Liquid That Carries Everything in Blood

This is a pale straw-coloured liquid which carries just about everything:

1) Red and white blood cells and platelets.
2) Nutrients like glucose and amino acids. These are the soluble products of digestion which are absorbed from the gut and taken to the cells of the body.
3) Carbon dioxide from the organs to the lungs.
4) Urea from the liver to the kidneys.

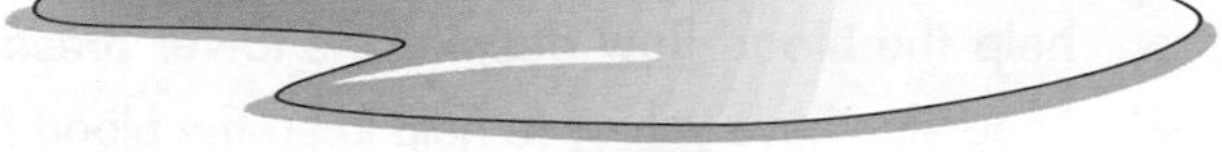

5) Hormones.
6) Proteins.
7) Antibodies and antitoxins produced by the white blood cells.

Platelets — ideal for small dinners...

When you're ill the doctor often takes a blood sample for analysis. Blood tests can be used to diagnose loads of things — not just disorders of the blood. This is because the blood transports so many chemicals produced by so many organs... and it's easier to take blood than, say, a piece of muscle.

Q1 Describe the purpose of platelets in blood. [1 mark]

Q2 Outline three ways in which red blood cells are adapted to carry oxygen. [3 marks]

Circulatory System — Blood Vessels

Want to know more about the <u>circulatory system</u>... Good. Because here's another page.

Blood Vessels are Designed for Their Function

There are three different types of blood vessel:

1) ARTERIES — these carry the blood <u>away</u> from the heart.

2) CAPILLARIES — these are involved in the <u>exchange of materials</u> at the tissues.

3) VEINS — these carry the blood <u>to</u> the heart.

Arteries Carry Blood Under Pressure

1) The heart pumps the blood out at <u>high pressure</u> so the artery walls are <u>strong</u> and <u>elastic</u>.

2) The walls are <u>thick</u> compared to the size of the hole down the middle (the "<u>lumen</u>" — silly name!).

3) They contain thick layers of <u>muscle</u> to make them <u>strong</u>, and <u>elastic fibres</u> to allow them to stretch and <u>spring back</u>.

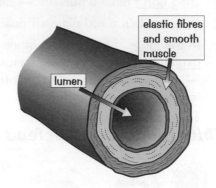

elastic fibres and smooth muscle

lumen

Capillaries are Really Small

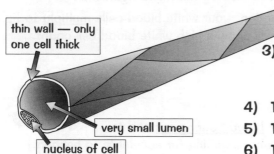

thin wall — only one cell thick

very small lumen

nucleus of cell

1) Arteries branch into <u>capillaries</u>.

2) Capillaries are really <u>tiny</u> — too small to see.

3) They are very <u>narrow</u>, so they can squeeze into the gaps between cells. This means they can carry the blood <u>really close</u> to <u>every cell</u> in the body to <u>exchange substances</u> with them.

4) They have <u>permeable walls</u>, so substances can <u>diffuse in</u> and <u>out</u>.

5) They supply <u>food</u> and <u>oxygen</u>, and take away <u>waste</u> like CO_2.

6) Their walls are usually <u>only one cell thick</u>. This <u>increases</u> the rate of diffusion by <u>decreasing</u> the <u>distance</u> over which it occurs.

Veins Take Blood Back to the Heart

1) Capillaries eventually <u>join up</u> to form <u>veins</u>.

2) The blood is at <u>lower pressure</u> in the veins so the walls don't need to be as <u>thick</u> as artery walls.

3) They have a <u>bigger lumen</u> than arteries to help the blood <u>flow</u> despite the lower pressure.

4) They also have <u>valves</u> to help keep the blood flowing in the <u>right direction</u>.

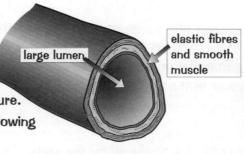

large lumen

elastic fibres and smooth muscle

valve

Learn this page — don't struggle in vein...

Here's an interesting fact for you — your body contains about 60 000 miles of blood vessels. That's about six times the distance from London to Sydney in Australia. Of course, capillaries are really tiny, which is how they can be such a big length — they can only be seen with a microscope.

Q1   Explain how veins are adapted to carry blood back to the heart.   [2 marks]

Q2   Explain the advantage of capillary walls being only one cell thick.   [1 mark]

Circulatory System — The Heart

The heart basically just <u>pushes</u> the blood around — it's kind of a bully...

Mammals Have a Double Circulatory System

1) This means that the heart pumps blood around the body in <u>two circuits</u>. In the first circuit, the heart pumps <u>deoxygenated blood</u> to the <u>lungs</u> to <u>take in oxygen</u>. Oxygenated blood then returns to the heart. In the <u>second circuit</u>, the heart pumps <u>oxygenated blood</u> around all the <u>other organs</u> of the body to deliver oxygen to the body cells. Deoxygenated blood then returns to the heart.

2) <u>Fish</u> have a <u>single circulatory system</u> — deoxygenated blood from the fish's body travels to the heart, which then pumps it <u>right round</u> the body again in a <u>single circuit</u> (via the gills where it picks up oxygen).

Lungs

Heart   Rest of body

The Heart Pumps Blood Through the Blood Vessels

The mammalian heart has <u>four chambers</u> and <u>four major blood vessels</u>.

A fish's heart only has two chambers.

Blue = deoxygenated blood.
Red = oxygenated blood.

1) The <u>right atrium</u> of the heart receives <u>deoxygenated</u> blood from the <u>body</u> (through the <u>vena cava</u>).

2) The deoxygenated blood moves through to the <u>right ventricle</u>, which pumps it to the lungs (via the <u>pulmonary artery</u>).

3) The <u>left atrium</u> receives <u>oxygenated</u> blood from the <u>lungs</u> (through the <u>pulmonary vein</u>).

4) The oxygenated blood then moves through to the <u>left ventricle</u>, which pumps it out round the <u>whole body</u> (via the <u>aorta</u>).

to the lungs
to the body
pulmonary artery
vena cava
aorta
pulmonary vein
Right Side
right atrium
left atrium
Left Side
semi-lunar valves
tricuspid valve
right ventricle   *left ventricle*
bicuspid valve

(This is the left and right side of the person whose heart it is.)

The <u>left</u> ventricle has a much <u>thicker wall</u> than the <u>right</u> ventricle. It needs more <u>muscle</u> because it has to pump blood around the <u>whole body</u> at high pressure, whereas the right ventricle only has to pump it to the <u>lungs</u>. <u>Valves</u> prevent the <u>backflow</u> of blood in the heart.

You Can Calculate How Much Blood is Pumped Every Minute

1) <u>Cardiac output</u> is the <u>total volume</u> of blood pumped by a ventricle every <u>minute</u>. You can calculate it using this equation:

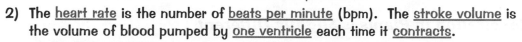

cardiac output = heart rate × stroke volume

in cm³ min⁻¹   in beats per minute   in cm³

2) The <u>heart rate</u> is the number of <u>beats per minute</u> (bpm). The <u>stroke volume</u> is the volume of blood pumped by <u>one ventricle</u> each time it <u>contracts</u>.

3) You might be asked to find the <u>stroke volume</u> or the <u>heart rate</u> in the exam <u>instead</u> of the cardiac output — if so, you can just <u>rearrange</u> the equation above. You can use this <u>formula triangle</u> to help you:

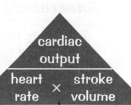

cardiac output
heart rate × stroke volume

Just cover up the thing you want to find with your finger and write down what's left showing.

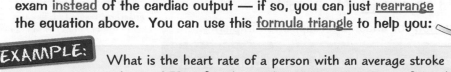

EXAMPLE: What is the heart rate of a person with an average stroke volume of 72 cm³ and a cardiac output of 5420 cm³ min⁻¹?

Heart rate (bpm) = cardiac output (cm³ min⁻¹) ÷ stroke volume (cm³)

= 5420 ÷ 72 = 75 bpm

Are you pumped after this page? I know I am...

Make sure you learn the diagram of the heart and all its labels. It won't be fun, but it'll help you in the exam.

Q1   Calculate the stroke volume for a heart rate of 67 bpm and a cardiac output of 4221 cm³ min⁻¹.   [2 marks]

Respiration

You need <u>energy</u> to keep your body going. Energy comes from <u>food</u>, and it's <u>released</u> by <u>respiration</u>.

Cellular Respiration Releases Energy

1) Respiration is <u>NOT</u> breathing in and breathing out, as you might think.

2) <u>Respiration</u> actually goes on in <u>every cell</u> of all living organisms — and it happens <u>continuously</u>.

3) It's the process of <u>transferring</u> (releasing) <u>energy</u> from the breakdown of <u>organic compounds</u> (usually <u>glucose</u>).

4) Because energy is transferred <u>to the environment</u>, respiration is an <u>exothermic reaction</u>. Some of this energy is transferred by <u>heat</u>.

5) There are <u>two types</u> of respiration, <u>aerobic</u> and <u>anaerobic</u>.

Organic compounds are compounds containing carbon. They include carbohydrates, lipids and proteins.

The <u>energy</u> is then used for things like:
- <u>metabolic processes</u> — such as making larger molecules from smaller ones (e.g. proteins from amino acids),
- <u>contracting muscles</u> (in animals),
- <u>maintaining</u> a steady <u>body temperature</u> (in mammals and birds).

Aerobic Respiration Needs Plenty of Oxygen

1) <u>Aerobic respiration</u> is what happens when there's <u>plenty of oxygen</u> available.

2) <u>Aerobic</u> just means "<u>with oxygen</u>" and it's the most efficient way to transfer <u>energy</u> from <u>glucose</u>.

3) This type of respiration goes on <u>all the time</u> in <u>plants</u> and <u>animals</u>. Here's the equation:

$$glucose + oxygen \longrightarrow carbon\ dioxide + water$$
$$C_6H_{12}O_6 + 6O_2 \longrightarrow 6CO_2 + 6H_2O$$

This is the reverse of the photosynthesis equation (see page 69).

Anaerobic Respiration Doesn't Use Oxygen At All

1) When you do really <u>vigorous exercise</u> your body can't supply enough <u>oxygen</u> to your muscles for aerobic respiration — even though your <u>heart rate</u> and <u>breathing rate</u> increase as much as they can. Your muscles have to start <u>respiring anaerobically</u> as well.

2) <u>An</u>aerobic just means "<u>without</u> oxygen". It transfers much <u>less energy</u> than aerobic respiration so it's much less <u>efficient</u>. In anaerobic respiration, the glucose is only <u>partially</u> broken down, and <u>lactic acid</u> is also produced.

3) The <u>lactic acid</u> builds up in the muscles — it gets <u>painful</u> and leads to <u>cramp</u>.

4) This is the word equation for anaerobic respiration in <u>animals</u>:

$$glucose \longrightarrow lactic\ acid$$

Anaerobic Respiration in Plants is Slightly Different

1) <u>Plants</u> can respire <u>without oxygen</u> too, but they produce <u>ethanol</u> (alcohol) and CO_2 <u>instead</u> of lactic acid.

2) This is <u>the word equation</u> for anaerobic respiration in <u>plants</u>:

Fungi such as yeast also do anaerobic respiration like this.

$$glucose \longrightarrow ethanol + carbon\ dioxide$$

I reckon aerobics classes should be called anaerobics instead...

You need to be able to compare anaerobic and aerobic respiration for your exam. Remember, anaerobic respiration has different products to aerobic respiration and transfers much less energy, as well as taking place without oxygen. Both aerobic and anaerobic respiration are exothermic though — don't forget that.

Q1   After five minutes of intense sprinting, a student got cramp in his leg.
      Explain what caused this.

[3 marks]

Topic 8 — Exchange and Transport in Animals

Investigating Respiration — PRACTICAL

You need to know how to <u>investigate</u> the <u>rate of respiration</u> in <u>small organisms</u> — so we've concocted a lovely little page all about it. Time to get hands on with some little critters.

You Can Measure the Rate of Respiration Using a Respirometer

In <u>aerobic respiration</u>, organisms <u>use up oxygen</u> from the air. By measuring the amount of <u>oxygen consumed</u> by organisms in a <u>given time</u>, you can calculate their <u>rate of respiration</u>. Here's an experiment which uses <u>woodlice</u>, a <u>water bath</u> and a piece of equipment called a <u>respirometer</u>. It allows you to measure the effect of <u>temperature</u> on the <u>rate of respiration</u> of the woodlice. (You could use <u>germinating peas</u> or <u>beans</u> instead of woodlice. Germinating seeds respire to provide energy for growth.)

1) Firstly, some <u>soda lime granules</u> are added to <u>two</u> test tubes. Soda lime <u>absorbs</u> the CO_2 produced by the <u>respiring</u> woodlice in the experiment.

Soda lime is corrosive. Wear safety goggles and gloves when handling it to protect your eyes and skin.

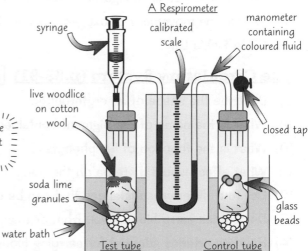

A Respirometer — syringe, calibrated scale, manometer containing coloured fluid, live woodlice on cotton wool, closed tap, soda lime granules, water bath, glass beads, Test tube, Control tube

2) A ball of <u>cotton wool</u> is placed above the <u>soda lime</u> in each tube. <u>Woodlice</u> are placed on top of the cotton wool in one tube. <u>Glass beads</u> with the <u>same mass</u> as the woodlice are used in the <u>control tube</u>. (There's more on controls on page 5.)

3) The <u>respirometer</u> is then set up as shown in the <u>diagram</u>.

Make sure the woodlice don't come into contact with the soda lime.

4) The <u>syringe</u> is used to set the fluid in the <u>manometer</u> to a <u>known level</u>.

5) The apparatus is then <u>left</u> for a set period of time in a <u>water bath</u> set to <u>15 °C</u>.

6) During this time, there'll be a <u>decrease</u> in the <u>volume</u> of the air in the <u>test tube</u> containing the <u>woodlice</u>. This is because the woodlice <u>use up oxygen</u> in the tube as they respire. (The CO_2 they produce is <u>absorbed</u> by the soda lime so it doesn't affect the experiment.)

7) The decrease in volume <u>reduces the pressure</u> in the tube, causing the <u>coloured liquid</u> in the manometer to move <u>towards</u> the <u>test tube</u> containing the <u>woodlice</u>.

You can also use cotton wool soaked in a few drops of potassium hydroxide solution to absorb the CO_2.

8) The <u>distance moved</u> by the liquid in a <u>given time</u> is measured. This value can then be used to calculate the <u>volume of oxygen taken in</u> by the woodlice <u>per minute</u>. This gives you the <u>rate of respiration</u> in, e.g. $cm^3 \ min^{-1}$.

9) <u>Repeat</u> steps 1-8 with the water bath set at <u>different temperatures</u>, e.g. <u>20 °C</u> and <u>25 °C</u>. This will allow you to see how <u>changing the temperature</u> affects the rate of respiration.

Any <u>live animals</u> you use in this experiment should be treated <u>ethically</u>. E.g. it's important not to <u>leave</u> the woodlice in the respirometer for <u>too long</u>, or they may <u>run out</u> of oxygen and <u>die</u>. There's more on the ethical treatment of organisms in experiments on page 108.

My rate of respiration has increased after all that...

Controls are mega important in experiments — they check that the thing you're observing (e.g. respiring woodlice) is what's affecting the results and nothing else. So you should make sure everything else is kept exactly the same.

Q1 A student is carrying out an experiment to measure the effect of temperature on the rate of respiration in germinating beans.
   a) What could the student use as her control? [1 mark]
   b) What could she use to keep the beans at different temperatures? [1 mark]

Revision Questions for Topic 8

So there you have it — all you need to know about exchange and transport. Now it's time to test yourself...
- Try these questions and <u>tick off each one</u> when you <u>get it right</u>.
- When you've done <u>all the questions</u> under a heading and are <u>completely happy</u>, tick it off.

Exchange of Materials (p.87) ☑

1) Name three substances that animals have to exchange with their environment. ☑
2) Why do multicellular organisms need specialised exchange surfaces? ☑
3) Why do multicellular organisms need mass transport systems? ☑

Diffusion and the Alveoli (p.88) ☑

4) What three factors affect the rate of diffusion across a membrane? ☑
5) Where does gas exchange take place within the lungs? ☑
6) Explain the movement of oxygen between the alveoli and the blood. ☑
7) State Fick's Law. ☑

The Circulatory System (p.89-91) ☑

8) Describe the shape of an erythrocyte. ☑
9) What is the name of the pigment contained within red blood cells and what does it do? ☑
10) What is the function of lymphocytes? ☑
11) What effect would there be on the body if there weren't enough platelets? ☑
12) List four different substances that can be carried in the plasma. ☑
13) Do arteries carry blood away from or towards the heart? ☑
14) How are arteries adapted for carrying blood at high pressure? ☑
15) Why are the walls of capillaries so thin? ☑
16) What is the function of the valves found within veins? ☑
17) Write the name of the blood vessel that:
    a) carries blood into the right atrium.
    b) carries blood towards the lungs.
    c) carries blood into the left atrium. ☑
18) What is the equation for cardiac output? ☑
19) How would you calculate the heart rate of an individual if you were
    given values for their cardiac output and stroke volume? ☑

Respiration (p.92-93) ☑

20) What is the purpose of cellular respiration? ☑
21) Is respiration exothermic or endothermic? Explain your answer. ☑
22) What is the equation for the aerobic respiration of glucose? ☑
23) Under what circumstances do muscles perform anaerobic respiration? ☑
24) When using a respirometer to measure the oxygen consumption of respiring organisms,
    what is the purpose of the soda lime in the respirometer? ☑

Ecosystems and Interactions Between Organisms

It's tough in the wild — organisms <u>depend on each other</u> for survival. Everybody needs good neighbours...

Ecosystems are Organised into Different Levels

Ecosystems have <u>different levels</u> of <u>organisation</u>:

1) <u>Individual</u> — A <u>single</u> organism.
2) <u>Population</u> — <u>All</u> the organisms of <u>one species</u> in a <u>habitat</u>.
3) <u>Community</u> — All the organisms of <u>different species</u> living in a habitat.
4) <u>Ecosystem</u> — A community of <u>organisms</u> along with all the <u>non-living</u> (<u>abiotic</u>) <u>conditions</u> (see below).

> A habitat is the place where an organism lives, e.g. a rocky shore or a field.
> A species is a group of similar organisms that can reproduce to give fertile offspring.

Organisms in a Community Are Interdependent

1) Organisms <u>depend</u> on each other for things like <u>food</u> and <u>shelter</u> in order to <u>survive</u> and <u>reproduce</u>. This is known as <u>interdependence</u>. It means that a <u>change</u> in the population of <u>one species</u> can have huge <u>knock on effects</u> for <u>other species</u> in the same community.

2) <u>Mutualism</u> is a relationship between two organisms, from which <u>both</u> organisms <u>benefit</u>. E.g. <u>bees</u> and <u>flowering plants</u> have a mutualistic relationship. When bees visit flowers to get nectar, <u>pollen</u> is transferred to their bodies. The bees then spread the pollen to <u>other plants</u> when they land on their flowers. The bees get <u>food</u> and the plants get <u>help reproducing</u>. Wahey — everyone's a winner.

3) <u>Parasites</u> live very closely with a <u>host species</u> (e.g. in or on them). The parasite takes what it needs to survive, but the host <u>doesn't</u> benefit. E.g. <u>fleas</u> are <u>parasites</u> of <u>mammals</u> such as <u>dogs</u>. Fleas feed on their host's blood, but don't offer anything in return.

Environmental Changes Affect Communities in Different Ways

The <u>environment</u> in which plants and animals live <u>changes all the time</u>. These changes are probably caused by <u>abiotic</u> (non-living) and <u>biotic</u> (living) factors and affect communities in different ways — for some species <u>population size</u> may <u>increase</u>, for others it may <u>decrease</u>, or the <u>distribution</u> of populations (where they live) may change. Here are some <u>examples</u> of the effects of changes in <u>abiotic</u> and <u>biotic</u> factors:

Abiotic Factors Affect Communities...

1) <u>Temperature</u> — e.g. the distribution of <u>bird species</u> in Germany is probably changing because of a rise in average temperature. For instance, the <u>European Bee-Eater bird</u> is a <u>Mediterranean</u> species but it's now present in parts of <u>Germany</u>.

2) <u>Amount of water</u> — e.g. <u>daisies</u> grow best in soils that are <u>slightly damp</u>. If the soil becomes <u>waterlogged</u> or <u>too dry</u>, the population of daisies will <u>decrease</u>.

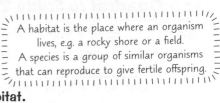

3) <u>Light intensity</u> — e.g. as trees grow and provide more <u>shade</u>, <u>grasses</u> may be replaced by <u>fungi</u> (or <u>mosses</u>, etc.) which are better able to <u>cope</u> with the <u>lower light intensity</u>.

4) <u>Levels of pollutants</u> — e.g. <u>lichen</u> are unable to survive if the concentration of <u>sulfur dioxide</u> (an <u>air pollutant</u>) is too <u>high</u> (see page 105).

... and so do Biotic Factors

1) <u>Competition</u> — organisms <u>compete with other species</u> (and members of their own species) for the <u>same resources</u>. E.g. red and grey <u>squirrels</u> live in the same habitat and eat the same food. Competition with the grey squirrels for these resources in some areas means there's not enough food for the reds — the <u>population</u> of red squirrels is <u>decreasing</u>, partly as a result of this.

2) <u>Predation</u> — e.g. if the <u>number of lions</u> (predators) <u>decreases</u> then the number of <u>gazelles</u> (their prey) might <u>increase</u> because <u>fewer</u> of them will be <u>eaten</u> by the lions.

Revision — an abiotic factor causing stress in my community...

Organisms like everything to be just right — temperature, light, food... I'd never get away with being that fussy.

Q1   Give two abiotic factors that could affect the community in an ecosystem.   [2 marks]

Investigating Ecosystems

Studying <u>ecology</u> gives you the chance to <u>rummage around</u> in bushes and get your hands <u>dirty</u>. It's proper fun.

Use a Quadrat to Study The Distribution of Small Organisms

A <u>quadrat</u> is a <u>square</u> frame enclosing a <u>known area</u>, e.g. 1 m². To compare <u>how common</u> an organism is in <u>two sample areas</u> just follow these simple steps:

1) Place a <u>1 m² quadrat</u> on the ground at a <u>random point</u> within the <u>first</u> sample area. You could do this by dividing the sample area into a grid and using a random number generator to pick coordinates to place your quadrats at. This will help to make sure the results you get are <u>representative</u> of the <u>whole sample area</u>.

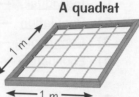
A quadrat
1 m
1 m

2) <u>Count</u> all the organisms you're interested in <u>within</u> the quadrat.

3) <u>Repeat</u> steps 1 and 2 lots of times.

4) <u>Work out</u> the <u>mean</u> number of organisms per quadrat within the first sample area.

5) <u>Repeat</u> steps 1 to 4 in the <u>second</u> sample area.

6) Finally <u>compare</u> the two means. E.g. you might find a mean of 2 daisies per m² in one area, and 22 daisies per m² (lots more) in another area.

$$\text{Mean} = \frac{\text{total number of organisms}}{\text{number of quadrats}}$$

Estimate Population Size by Scaling Up from a Small Sample Area

To work out the <u>population size</u> of an organism in one sample area you need to work out the <u>mean number of organisms per m²</u> (if your quadrat has an area of 1 m², this is the same as the mean number of organisms per quadrat, worked out above). Then just <u>multiply the mean</u> by the <u>total area</u> of the habitat:

EXAMPLE: Students used 0.5 m² quadrats to randomly sample daisies in a field. They found a mean of 10 daisies per quadrat. The field's area was 800 m². Estimate the population of daisies in the field.

1) Work out the <u>mean number of organisms per m²</u>. 1 ÷ 0.5 = 2   2 × 10 = 20 daisies per m²

2) Multiply the <u>mean per m²</u> by the <u>total area</u> (in m²) of the habitat. 20 × 800 = 16 000 daisies in the field

Use Belt Transects to Study Distribution Along a Gradient

PRACTICAL

Sometimes <u>abiotic factors</u> will <u>change across a habitat</u>. The change is known as a <u>gradient</u>. You can use quadrats to help find out how organisms (like plants) are <u>distributed along</u> a gradient. For example, how a species becomes <u>more or less common</u> as you move from an area of <u>shade</u> (near a hedge at the edge of a field) to an area of full sun (the middle of the field). The quadrats are laid out along a <u>line</u>, forming a <u>belt transect</u>. Here's what you do:

1) <u>Mark out a line</u> in the area you want to study, e.g. from the hedge to the middle of the field.

2) Then <u>collect data</u> along the line using <u>quadrats</u> placed <u>next to</u> each other. If your transect is <u>quite long</u>, you could place the quadrats at <u>regular intervals</u> (e.g. every 2 metres) instead. Collect data by <u>counting</u> all the organisms of the species you're interested in, or by <u>estimating percentage cover</u>. This means estimating the <u>percentage area</u> of a quadrat covered by a particular type of organism.

tape measure

quadrat 1

3) You could also <u>record</u> other data, such as the <u>mean height</u> of the plants you're counting or the <u>abiotic factors</u> in each quadrat (e.g. you could use a <u>light meter</u> to measure the light intensity).

4) <u>Repeat</u> steps 1 and 2 several times, then find the <u>mean</u> number of organisms or mean percentage cover for <u>each quadrat</u>.

Make sure you can correctly identify the organisms you're investigating. If necessary, use books or information from the internet to help you.

5) Plot graphs to see if the <u>changing abiotic factor</u> is <u>correlated</u> with a change in the <u>distribution</u> of the species you're studying.

Drat, drat, and double drat — my favourite use of quadrats...

Unless you're doing a transect, it's key that you put your quadrat down in a random place before you start counting.

Q1   Describe how quadrats could be used to investigate the distribution of organisms along a gradient. [3 marks]

Ecosystems and Energy Transfers

This page might not be the most interesting page, but at least you're not getting <u>eaten</u> by a <u>load</u> of <u>rabbits</u>...

Some Energy Passes Along The Food Chain — But Most Doesn't

1) The <u>Sun</u> is the <u>source of energy</u> for nearly <u>all life on Earth</u>.

2) <u>Plants</u> convert <u>a small %</u> of the light energy that falls on them <u>into glucose</u>. They use some of the glucose <u>immediately</u> in <u>respiration</u> and <u>store</u> some of the rest as <u>biomass</u> (the mass of living material that makes up an organism).

3) The <u>rabbit</u> then <u>eats</u> the <u>plant</u>. It <u>uses</u> some of the energy it gets from the plant, and some of the rest is <u>stored</u> in its body as <u>biomass</u>. Then the <u>fox eats</u> the <u>rabbit</u> and gets some of the energy stored in the rabbit's biomass. This is a simple <u>food chain</u>.

4) Energy is used by organisms at each stage to <u>stay alive</u>, i.e. in <u>respiration</u>, which transfers energy for <u>all life processes</u>, including <u>movement</u>. A lot of energy is <u>transferred to the surroundings</u> by <u>heat</u>.

Each stage of a food chain is called a trophic level.

5) This energy <u>isn't stored</u> as biomass, so it <u>isn't transferred</u> to the organisms in the next <u>trophic level</u>. (It's 'lost' to the food chain.)

6) Energy that does get stored as biomass <u>doesn't all get transferred</u> to the next trophic level either. That's because <u>not all</u> of an organism <u>gets eaten</u> (e.g. bones) and because not all of the bits that do get eaten can be digested — <u>undigested material</u> is <u>lost</u> from the food chain in <u>faeces</u>.

7) This explains why you hardly ever get <u>food chains</u> with more than about <u>five trophic levels</u>. So much energy is lost at each stage that there's not enough left to support more organisms after four or five stages. You also tend to get <u>fewer organisms</u> at each trophic level (although this <u>isn't always</u> the case).

ENERGY TRANSFERRED BY HEAT

materials lost in animals' waste

Pyramids of Biomass Show Weight

1) A <u>pyramid of biomass</u> shows how much the creatures at each level of a food chain would <u>weigh</u> if you <u>put them together</u>. Since biomass is a <u>store</u> of <u>energy</u> (see above), a pyramid of biomass also shows <u>how much energy</u> there is at <u>each stage</u> in the <u>food chain</u>.

2) The pyramid of biomass below shows the <u>food chain</u> of a mini meadow ecosystem. The dandelions are the <u>producer</u> (starting point) — they make their own food using energy from the Sun. They're eaten by the rabbits (primary consumers), which are eaten by the fox (secondary consumer)... and so on.

3) If you weighed them, all the <u>dandelions</u> would have a <u>big biomass</u> and the <u>hundreds of fleas</u> would have <u>a very small biomass</u>.

4) Each time you go <u>up</u> one <u>trophic level</u>, the <u>mass</u> of organisms goes <u>down</u>. This is because most of the <u>biomass</u> (or <u>energy</u>) is <u>lost</u> (as shown above) and so <u>does not</u> become biomass in the <u>next level up</u>. This gives rise to the <u>pyramid shape</u> that <u>almost every</u> pyramid of biomass has.

You need to be able to <u>construct</u> pyramids of biomass. Luckily it's pretty <u>simple</u> — they'll give you <u>all</u> the <u>information</u> you need to do it in the exam. If you do get asked to draw a pyramid of biomass, remember that the first level is always the <u>producer</u>, the second level is the <u>primary consumer</u>, the third level is the <u>secondary consumer</u>, and so on. Make sure you draw each bar to a sensible <u>scale</u>, e.g. 5 small squares on a grid = 1 kg.

Fleas | 0.002 kg (not even slightly to scale...)
Fox 4 kg
Rabbits 40 kg
Dandelions 1000 kg

Pyramids of Biomass — the eighth wonder of the world...

Pyramids of biomass are a way of describing food chains quantitatively (rather than just saying 'foxes eat rabbits', you say what mass of foxes eats what mass of rabbits, etc.). Don't forget that there's energy in that biomass too.

Q1 Give two reasons why much of the energy in one trophic level is not passed on to the next. [2 marks]

More on Ecosystems and Energy Transfers

If you like <u>food chains</u>, <u>numbers</u> and <u>formulas</u>, then this page might just be the most <u>exciting</u> thing you've ever seen. If not, just power through and make sure you've got it all in your head.

You Need to be Able to Interpret Data on Energy Transfers

The diagram below shows an example of a <u>food chain</u>.

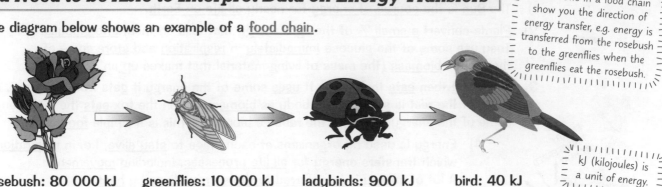

The arrows in a food chain show you the direction of energy transfer, e.g. energy is transferred from the rosebush to the greenflies when the greenflies eat the rosebush.

rosebush: 80 000 kJ   greenflies: 10 000 kJ   ladybirds: 900 kJ   bird: 40 kJ

kJ (kilojoules) is a unit of energy.

1) The numbers show the <u>amount of energy</u> transferred to the <u>next level</u>. So <u>80 000 kJ</u> is the amount of energy transferred to the <u>greenflies</u>, and <u>10 000 kJ</u> is the amount transferred to the <u>ladybirds</u>.

2) You can work out how much energy has been <u>lost</u> at each level by <u>taking away</u> the energy that is transferred to the <u>next</u> level from the energy that was available at the <u>previous</u> level.

EXAMPLE:

Calculate the energy lost between the first and second trophic levels.

energy lost = energy available at previous level − energy transferred to next level
= 80 000 kJ − 10 000 kJ
= 70 000 kJ lost

3) You can also calculate the <u>efficiency of energy transfer</u> between levels using this handy formula:

$$\text{efficiency} = \frac{\text{energy transferred to next level}}{\text{energy available at previous level}} \times 100$$

Here's an example:

EXAMPLE:

Calculate the efficiency of energy transfer between the first and second trophic levels.

$$\text{efficiency} = \frac{\text{energy transferred to next level}}{\text{energy available at previous level}} \times 100 = \frac{10\ 000}{80\ 000} \times 100$$

= 12.5% efficient — Efficiency is usually pretty low (around 10%).

4) You can also calculate the <u>biomass</u> lost between trophic levels or the efficiency of biomass transfer using the formulae above — just substitute the word 'energy' for 'biomass'.

I could do with an extra energy transfer today...

Hmmm maths... thankfully it's not as scary as it looks. As long as you understand the examples above and have a good crack at the question below, I'm sure you'll be as happy as a greenfly in a garden centre. Hooray.

Q1 The diagram below shows a food chain.

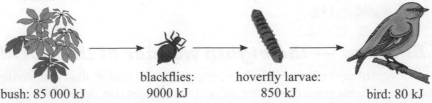

bush: 85 000 kJ   blackflies: 9000 kJ   hoverfly larvae: 850 kJ   bird: 80 kJ

Calculate the efficiency of energy transfer between the second and third trophic levels.   [2 marks]

Human Impacts on Biodiversity

However you look at it, we humans have a huge impact on the environment around us, including on biodiversity.

Human Activities Affect Biodiversity

Biodiversity is the variety of living organisms in an ecosystem. Human interactions within ecosystems often affect biodiversity. Sometimes we have a positive impact on biodiversity (e.g. by carrying out conservation schemes or reforestation, see next page), but we often have a negative effect. Here are some examples:

Fertilisers can Leach into Water and Cause Eutrophication

Nitrates are put onto fields as fertilisers (see p.104). If too much fertiliser is applied and it rains afterwards, nitrates easily find their way into rivers and lakes. The result is eutrophication — an excess of nutrients in water — which can lead to the death of many of the species present in the water, reducing the biodiversity of the habitat:

Pollution by sewage can cause eutrophication in the same way that fertilisers do.

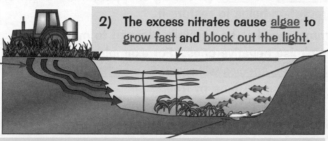

1) Fertilisers enter the water, adding excess nitrates (more than plants in the water can take in).

2) The excess nitrates cause algae to grow fast and block out the light.

3) Plants can't photosynthesise due to lack of light and start to die and decompose.

4) With more food available, microorganisms that feed on decomposing plants increase in number and use up oxygen in the water.

5) Organisms that need oxygen for aerobic respiration (e.g. fish) die.

Fish can be Farmed in Holding Nets in Open Water

Fish farms in areas of open water (e.g. lakes or the sea) can reduce biodiversity in the surrounding area. Here's how:

1) Food is added to the nets to feed the fish, which produce huge amounts of waste. Both the food and the waste can leak into the open water, causing eutrophication and the death of wild species.

2) Fish farms in open water often act as a breeding ground for large numbers of parasites. These parasites can get out of the farm and infect wild animals, sometimes killing them.

3) Predators (e.g. sea lions) are attracted to the nets and can become trapped in them and die.

4) Sometimes farmed fish can escape into the wild, which can cause problems for wild populations of indigenous species (see below).

Sometimes fish are farmed in large tanks rather than in open water nets. These farms are low in biodiversity because often only one species is farmed, the tanks are often kept free of plants and predators, and any parasites and microorganisms are usually killed.

The Introduction of Non-Indigenous Species Can Reduce Biodiversity

1) A non-indigenous species is one that doesn't naturally occur in an area. They can be introduced intentionally (e.g. for food or hunting) or unintentionally (e.g. as a stowaway in international cargo). The introduction of a non-indigenous species may cause problems for indigenous (native) species.

2) Non-indigenous species compete with indigenous species for resources like food and shelter. Sometimes, they are better at getting these resources and out-compete the indigenous species, which decrease in number and eventually die out. For example, signal crayfish were introduced to the UK for food, but they prey on and out-compete many indigenous river species, reducing biodiversity.

3) Non-indigenous species sometimes also bring new diseases to a habitat. These often infect and kill lots of indigenous species, reducing the habitat's biodiversity.

My dirty gym kit definitely increases the biodiversity of my bag...

OK, there's a lot of negativity on this page, but you need to know it all for your exam. Best get cracking.

Q1   Suggest how introducing a non-indigenous species could reduce the biodiversity of an area.   [2 marks]

Conservation and Biodiversity

Trying to conserve biodiversity can be tricky, given all the challenges that face different ecosystems (many of which are a result of human activities). There are benefits of doing this though, so it's pretty worthwhile...

There Are Lots of Ways to Conserve and Maintain Biodiversity

Lots of human activities can reduce biodiversity (see previous page). However, there are plenty of things that we can do to increase biodiversity. Here are a couple of examples...

Reforestation Can Increase Biodiversity in Deforested Areas

1) Reforestation is when land where a forest previously stood is replanted to form a new forest.

2) Forests generally have a high biodiversity because they contain a wide variety of trees and plants, and these provide food and shelter for lots of different animal species. Deforestation reduces this biodiversity by removing the trees (either by chopping them down or burning them). Reforestation helps to restore it.

3) Reforestation programmes need to be carefully planned to maximise positive effects and minimise negative ones. For example, replanting a forest with a variety of tree species will result in a higher biodiversity than replanting using only a single type of tree.

Conservation Schemes Protect At-Risk Species

1) Conservation schemes can help to protect biodiversity by preventing species from dying out.

2) Conservation methods include:

- Protecting a species' natural habitat (so that individuals have a place to live).
- Protecting species in safe areas outside of their natural habitat (e.g. animals can be protected in zoos) and introducing captive breeding programmes to increase numbers.
- The use of seed banks to store and distribute the seeds of rare and endangered plants.

Maintaining Biodiversity Has Many Benefits

There are lots of benefits to both wildlife and humans of maintaining biodiversity on a local and global scale.

1) Protecting the human food supply — over-fishing has greatly reduced fish stocks in the world's oceans. Conservation programmes can ensure that future generations will have fish to eat.

2) Ensuring minimal damage to food chains — if one species becomes extinct it will affect all the organisms that feed on and are eaten by that species, so the whole food chain is affected. This means conserving one species may help others to survive.

3) Providing future medicines — many of the medicines we use today come from plants. Undiscovered plant species may contain new medicinal chemicals. If these plants are allowed to become extinct, e.g. through rainforest destruction, we could miss out on valuable medicines.

4) Cultural aspects — individual species may be important in a nation's or an area's cultural heritage, e.g. the bald eagle is being conserved in the USA as it is regarded as a national symbol.

5) Ecotourism — people are drawn to visit beautiful, unspoilt landscapes with a variety of animal and plant species. Ecotourism (environmentally-friendly tourism) helps bring money into biodiverse areas where conservation work is taking place.

6) Providing new jobs — things such as ecotourism, conservation schemes and reforestation schemes provide employment opportunities for local people.

If a reforested area is cut down again, is that redeforestation...

Well who knew protecting biodiversity had so many advantages. That's the last time I vacuum up a spider...

Q1   Explain how reforestation affects biodiversity.   [3 marks]

Food Security

As the <u>population</u> of planet Earth increases, growing <u>enough food for everyone</u> isn't going to get any easier...

Not Everyone Has 'Food Security'

1) The world's <u>population</u> is <u>rising very quickly</u> and it's not slowing down.

2) This means that global <u>food production</u> must <u>increase</u> too, so that we all have access to <u>enough food</u> that is <u>safe for us to eat</u> and has the right balance of <u>nutrition</u> — this is known as '<u>food security</u>'.

3) As the world's <u>population</u> continues to <u>grow</u> we need to <u>produce more food</u>, so that each person still has the <u>same amount</u> of food to eat.

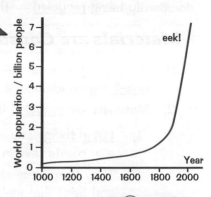

Biological Factors Affect the Level of Food Security

The <u>increasing human population</u> is a <u>biological factor</u> affecting food security. So are:

Increasing consumption of meat and fish, and increasing animal farming

1) As people become <u>wealthier</u>, their diets are likely to change to include a <u>wider variety of foods</u>, including <u>more meat and fish</u> (which are <u>expensive</u> to buy). This can be <u>bad news</u> for food security.

2) There's <u>less energy</u> and <u>less biomass</u> every time you move up a stage in a food chain, so for a given area of land, you can produce <u>a lot more food</u> for humans by <u>growing crops</u> rather than by having <u>grazing animals</u>. Plus, animals and fish being reared to be eaten are often <u>fed crops</u> that would otherwise be eaten by <u>humans</u> (e.g. corn).

3) There's also a risk of <u>over-fishing</u> wild fish, so that there won't be enough available to catch in the future.

Environmental changes caused by human activity

1) Burning <u>fossil fuels</u> (coal, oil and natural gas) releases lots of <u>carbon dioxide</u>, which is a <u>greenhouse gas</u>. Greenhouse gases naturally <u>trap energy</u> in the atmosphere — this helps to keep the Earth <u>warm</u>. But <u>increasing levels</u> of greenhouse gases are causing the <u>global temperature</u> to <u>rise</u>. This is <u>global warming</u>.

2) Global warming is a type of <u>climate change</u> and it causes other forms of climate change, e.g. changing rainfall patterns. Climate change may affect the <u>growth of crops</u>, which could <u>reduce yields</u>.

3) <u>Other changes</u> caused by humans, such as <u>soil pollution</u>, could also reduce our ability to grow crops.

Yield means 'the amount of useful product made'.

Sustainability

1) <u>Sustainability</u> means meeting the needs of <u>today's</u> population <u>without</u> affecting the ability of <u>future</u> generations to meet their needs. We must think about sustainability when addressing <u>food security</u>.

2) For example, <u>diesel</u> and <u>petrol</u> are made from crude oil — a non-renewable fossil fuel that will eventually run out. There's currently an increase in the <u>growth</u> of <u>crops</u> to make <u>biofuels</u>, e.g. <u>bioethanol</u>, which is made by fermenting the sugar in corn and sugar cane. Biofuels are <u>renewable alternatives</u> to fossil fuels — but they <u>take up land</u> that could be used for <u>food crops</u>. We need to <u>balance our need</u> for this land to make biofuels with the need to grow more food <u>now</u> and in the <u>future</u>.

3) Also, the high <u>input costs</u> of farming (e.g. the price of fertilisers, fuel and machinery) may make it <u>too expensive</u> for farmers in some areas to <u>continue farming</u> and <u>maintain food production</u> in the future.

New pests and pathogens

1) <u>Pests</u> (e.g. some insects) and <u>pathogens</u> (e.g. bacteria, fungi) can <u>cause damage</u> to crops and livestock.

2) When <u>new</u> pests and pathogens emerge, they can have a <u>negative impact</u> on yields. E.g. if a new disease spreads to a crop, lots of the population <u>may not be resistant</u> to the disease. This means a <u>large number</u> of the crop plants will be <u>damaged</u>, <u>reducing</u> the <u>yield</u> and the amount that <u>can be sold as food</u>.

Food insecurity — potatoes with a lack of self-confidence...

Increasing the level of food security across the globe is a pretty big deal. If we don't, it's bad news for everyone.

Q1   Describe how the outbreak of a new crop pathogen could reduce the level of food security.   [2 marks]

The Carbon Cycle

Recycling may be a buzz word for us but it's old school for nature. All the nutrients in our environment are constantly being recycled — there's a nice balance between what goes in and what goes out again.

Materials are Constantly Recycled in an Ecosystem

1) An ecosystem is all the organisms living in an area, as well as all the non-living conditions, e.g. soil quality, availability of water, temperature.

There's more on ecosystems on page 95.

2) Materials are recycled through both the living (biotic) and non-living (abiotic) components of ecosystems:

> 1) Living things are made of elements they take from the environment, e.g. plants take in carbon and oxygen from the air and nitrogen from the soil.
>
> 2) They turn these elements into the complex compounds (carbohydrates, proteins and fats) that make up living organisms. Elements are passed along food chains when animals eat the plants and each other.
>
> 3) The elements are recycled — waste products and dead organisms are broken down by decomposers (usually microorganisms) and the elements in them are returned to the soil or air, ready to be taken in by new plants and put back into the food chain.

The Carbon Cycle Shows How Carbon is Recycled

Carbon is an important element in the materials that living things are made from.
But there's only a fixed amount of carbon in the world. This means it's constantly recycled:

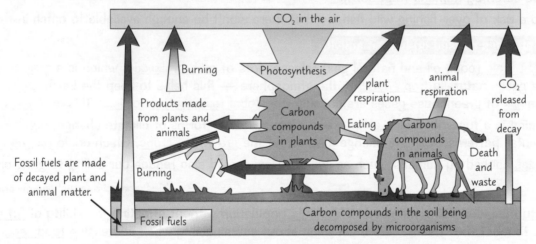

CO_2 in the air

Burning

Photosynthesis

plant respiration

animal respiration

CO_2 released from decay

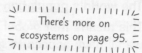

CO_2 = carbon dioxide

Products made from plants and animals

Carbon compounds in plants

Eating

Carbon compounds in animals

Death and waste

Fossil fuels are made of decayed plant and animal matter.

Burning

Fossil fuels

Carbon compounds in the soil being decomposed by microorganisms

This diagram isn't half as bad as it looks. Learn these important points:

1) There's only one arrow going down from CO_2 in the air. The whole thing is 'powered' by photosynthesis. Green plants use the carbon from CO_2 to make carbohydrates, fats and proteins.

2) Eating passes the carbon compounds in the plant along to animals in a food chain (see p.97).

3) Both plant and animal respiration while the organisms are alive releases CO_2 back into the air.

4) Plants and animals eventually die and decompose, or are killed and turned into useful products.

5) When plants and animals decompose they're broken down by microorganisms, such as bacteria and fungi. These decomposers release CO_2 back into the air by respiration, as they break down the material.

6) Some useful plant and animal products, e.g. wood and fossil fuels, are burned (combustion). This also releases CO_2 back into the air.

7) Decomposition of materials means that habitats can be maintained for the organisms that live there, e.g. nutrients are returned to the soil and waste material, such as dead leaves, doesn't just pile up.

Carbon cycle — isn't that what Wiggo rides...

Carbon atoms are very important — they're found in plants, animals, your petrol tank and on your burnt toast.

Q1   Describe the role of microorganisms in the carbon cycle.   [3 marks]

The Water Cycle

Next time you get soaked on your way to school and moan about the rain, think back to this page and spare a thought for the water cycle — the underrated natural phenomenon that helps keep us all alive.

The Water Cycle Means Water is Endlessly Recycled

The water here on planet Earth is constantly recycled. Strange but true...

1) Energy from the Sun makes water evaporate from the land and sea, turning it into water vapour. Water also evaporates from plants — this is known as transpiration (see pages 71-72).

2) The warm water vapour is carried upwards (as warm air rises). When it gets higher up it cools and condenses to form clouds.

3) Water falls from the clouds as precipitation (usually rain, but sometimes snow or hail) onto land, where it provides fresh water for plants and animals.

4) It then drains into the sea and the whole process starts again.

If it wasn't for the water cycle constantly recycling water, we'd quickly run out of the stuff. That would be reeeeeally bad news because all living things on our planet need water to survive.

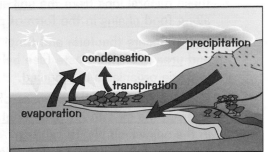

A Drought Occurs When There Isn't Enough Precipitation

Droughts can cause big problems, partly because we rely on precipitation to get fresh water for drinking (sea water is too salty). Luckily, in times of drought, there are methods we can use to produce potable water (water that's suitable for drinking). One of these methods is called desalination.

Desalination Can Be Used to Produce Potable Water From Salt Water

Desalination removes salts (mineral ions) from salt water (e.g. sea water). There are a few different methods of desalination. One really simple method is thermal desalination. This is where salt water is boiled in a large enclosed vessel, so that the water evaporates. The steam rises to the top of the vessel, but the salts stay at the bottom. The steam then travels down a pipe from the top of the vessel and condenses back into pure water.

Reverse Osmosis Is a Widely Used Modern Method of Desalination

1) Osmosis is the net movement of water across a partially permeable membrane, from an area of HIGHER water concentration to an area of LOWER water concentration (see page 21).

2) The higher the salt concentration in a solution, the lower the water concentration, so you could also say that osmosis is the net movement of water from an area of LOWER salt concentration to an area of HIGHER salt concentration.

3) Reverse osmosis reverses this process to get rid of impurities in water. Here's how:

Reverse osmosis — net movement of water molecules

pure water | salt water | Pressure

Normal osmosis

1) Salt water is first treated to remove solids, before being fed at a very high pressure into a vessel containing a partially permeable membrane.

2) The pressure causes the water molecules to move in the opposite direction to osmosis — from a higher salt concentration to a lower salt concentration.

3) As the water is forced through the membrane, the salts are left behind, removing them from the water.

Come on out, it's only a little water cycle, it won't hurt you...

Make sure you really understand the water cycle and how desalination produces fresh water before you turn over.

Q1   Explain how water from the sea can eventually fall as rain.   [4 marks]

The Nitrogen Cycle

Just like carbon and water, nitrogen is constantly being recycled.

Nitrogen is Recycled in the Nitrogen Cycle

1) The atmosphere contains 78% nitrogen gas, N_2. This is very unreactive and so it can't be used directly by plants or animals. Nitrogen is needed for making proteins for growth, so living organisms have to get it somehow.

2) Nitrogen in the air has to be turned into mineral ions such as nitrates before plants can use it. Plants absorb these mineral ions from the soil and use the nitrogen in them to make proteins. Nitrogen is then passed along food chains in the form of proteins, as animals eat plants (and each other).

3) Decomposers (bacteria and fungi in the soil) break down proteins in rotting plants and animals, and urea in animal waste (see below). This returns the nitrogen to the soil — so the nitrogen in these organisms is recycled.

4) Nitrogen fixation is the process of turning N_2 from the air into nitrogen-containing ions in the soil which plants can use.
There are two main ways that this happens:

   a) Lightning — there's so much energy in a bolt of lightning that it's enough to make nitrogen react with oxygen in the air to give nitrates.

   b) Nitrogen-fixing bacteria in roots and soil (see below).

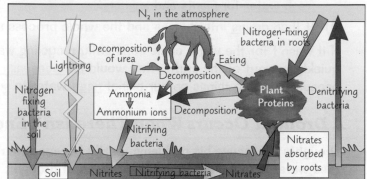

5) There are four different types of bacteria involved in the nitrogen cycle:

   a) DECOMPOSERS — decompose proteins and urea and turn them into ammonia. Ammonia forms ammonium ions in solution that plants can use.

   b) NITRIFYING BACTERIA — turn ammonia in decaying matter into nitrites and then into nitrates. Different species of nitrifying bacteria are responsible for producing nitrites and nitrates.

   c) NITROGEN-FIXING BACTERIA — turn atmospheric N_2 into ammonia, which forms ammonium ions.

   d) DENITRIFYING BACTERIA — turn nitrates back into N_2 gas. This is of no benefit to living organisms. Denitryfying bacteria are often found in waterlogged soils.

6) Some nitrogen-fixing bacteria live in the soil. Others live in nodules on the roots of legume plants (e.g. peas and beans). When these plants decompose, the nitrogen stored in them and in their nodules is returned to the soil. Nitrogen ions can also leak out of the nodules during plant growth. The plants have a mutualistic relationship (see page 95) with the bacteria — the bacteria get food (sugars) from the plant, and the plant gets nitrogen ions from the bacteria to make into proteins.

Farmers Can Increase the Amount of Nitrates in the Soil

Like all plants, crops take up nitrates from the soil as they grow. But crops are harvested, rather than being left to die and decompose, so the nitrogen they contain isn't returned to the soil. Over time, the nitrogen content of the soil decreases, leading to poor crop growth and deficiency diseases. So farmers have ways of increasing the amount of nitrates in the soil to help their crops grow better:

1) CROP ROTATION — This is where, instead of growing the same crop in a field year after year, different crops are grown each year in a cycle. The cycle usually includes a nitrogen-fixing crop (e.g. peas or beans), which helps to put nitrates back into the soil for another crop to use the following year.

2) FERTILISERS — Spreading animal manure or compost on fields recycles the nutrients left in plant and animal waste and returns them to the soil through decomposition. Artificial fertilisers containing nitrates (and other mineral ions needed by plants) can also be used, but these can be expensive.

It's the cyyyycle, the cyycle of liiiiife...

Bacteria do a lot of the hard work in the nitrogen cycle. Aided by a bolt or two of lightning. Naturally.

Q1   Describe how the nitrogen compounds in dead leaves are turned into nitrates in the soil.   [3 marks]

Topic 9 — Ecosystems and Material Cycles

Indicator Species

The <u>presence</u> or <u>absence</u> of certain organisms in an area can be <u>monitored</u> and used as an <u>indicator</u> of pollution.

Indicator Species Are Used to Show the Level of...

Some <u>organisms</u> are very <u>sensitive to changes</u> in their environment and so can be studied to see the effect of human activities — these organisms are known as <u>indicator species</u>.

1) Water Pollution

1) If <u>raw sewage</u> or <u>fertilisers</u> containing <u>nitrates</u> are released into a <u>river</u>, the <u>microorganisms</u> in the water increase in number and use up the <u>oxygen</u> (see page 99).

2) Some invertebrate animals, like <u>stonefly larvae</u> and <u>freshwater shrimps</u> are <u>good indicators</u> for water pollution because they're <u>very sensitive</u> to the concentration of <u>dissolved oxygen</u> in the water. If you find stonefly larvae in a river, it <u>indicates</u> that the <u>water is clean</u>.

3) Other <u>invertebrate</u> species have adapted to live in <u>polluted conditions</u> — so if you see a lot of them you know there's a problem. E.g. <u>blood worms</u> and <u>sludgeworms</u> indicate a <u>very high level of water pollution</u>.

2) Air Pollution

1) <u>Air pollution</u> can be monitored by looking at particular types of <u>lichen</u> that are very sensitive to the concentration of <u>sulfur dioxide</u> in the atmosphere. (Sulfur dioxide is a pollutant released from <u>car exhausts</u>, power stations, etc.) The number and type of lichen at a particular location will indicate <u>how clean</u> the air is. E.g. the air is <u>clean</u> if there are <u>lots of lichen</u> — especially <u>bushy lichen</u>, which need cleaner air than crusty lichen.

Bushy lichen   Crusty lichen

2) <u>Blackspot fungus</u> is found on <u>rose leaves</u>. It is also sensitive to the level of sulfur dioxide in the air, so its presence will indicate <u>clean air</u>.

3) You might get some data on indicator species in the exam, e.g. data showing there are <u>more</u> lichen species <u>further away</u> from a city centre. This is probably because outside the city centre, there is <u>less pollution</u> and the air contains <u>less sulfur dioxide</u> and other pollutants.

The Use of Indicator Species Isn't Without Flaws

There are a couple of ways of using <u>indicator species</u> to <u>measure pollution</u>:

1) You could do a simple survey to see if a species is <u>present</u> or <u>absent</u> from an area. This is a <u>quick</u> way of telling whether an area is polluted or not, but it's no good for telling <u>how polluted</u> an area is.

2) Counting the number of times an indicator species <u>occurs</u> in an area will give you a <u>numerical</u> value, allowing you to see roughly <u>how polluted</u> one area is in <u>comparison</u> with another.

Using indicator species is a <u>simple</u> and <u>cost-effective</u> way of saying whether or not an area is polluted. But indicator species can't give <u>accurate</u> figures for <u>exactly</u> how much pollution is present. There may also be <u>factors other than pollution</u> playing a role in the <u>presence</u> or <u>absence</u> of a species in an environment. Sometimes, it's better to use <u>non-living indicators</u>. For example:

1) <u>Dissolved oxygen meters</u> and <u>chemical tests</u> are used to accurately measure the concentration of dissolved oxygen in water, to show how the level of <u>water pollution</u> is changing.

2) <u>Electronic meters</u> and various <u>laboratory tests</u> are also used to accurately measure the concentration of <u>sulfur dioxide</u> in air, to show how <u>air pollution</u> is changing.

Teenagers are an indicator species — not found in clean rooms...

Don't forget that the absence of an indicator species could mean the opposite of what they indicate.
E.g. the absence of stonefly larvae could indicate polluted water. Nice and simple, innit?

Q1   A gardener finds blackspot fungus on the leaves of her rose plant.
Explain what this indicates about the local air quality.   [2 marks]

Decomposition

Decomposition is <u>really</u> important. Without it there'd be piles of <u>dead stuff</u> everywhere. Let's <u>break it down</u>...

Things Decompose Because of Microorganisms

1) <u>Living things</u> (and the <u>waste</u> they produce) are made of <u>elements</u> taken from the world around them. When living things <u>die</u> or release <u>waste</u>, decomposition returns these elements to the <u>soil</u> or <u>air</u>.

2) Nearly all <u>decomposition</u> is done by <u>microorganisms</u> like <u>soil bacteria</u> and <u>fungi</u> (known as <u>decomposers</u>).

3) The <u>rate of decay</u> depends on <u>three</u> main things:

    1) <u>TEMPERATURE</u> — A <u>warm</u> temperature <u>speeds up</u> the rate of <u>enzyme-controlled reactions</u> in microbes, so decay happens <u>faster</u>. Enzymes <u>denature</u> if the temperature gets too high (see p.16).

    2) <u>WATER CONTENT</u> — Decay takes place <u>faster</u> in <u>moist environments</u> because the organisms involved in decay need <u>water</u> to <u>survive</u> and carry out <u>biological processes</u>.

    3) <u>OXYGEN AVAILABILITY</u> — The rate of decomposition is <u>faster</u> where there is <u>plenty of oxygen</u> available. Many microorganisms need <u>oxygen</u> for <u>aerobic respiration</u> (see page 92). Some decomposers don't need oxygen to respire, but these decomposers work <u>slower</u> anyway.

Food Preservation Methods Reduce the Rate of Decay

To preserve food, we use methods that <u>slow decomposition</u> by making the oxygen availability, water content and temperature <u>less suitable</u> for microorganisms' <u>survival</u> and <u>reproduction</u>. For example:

- Storing foods in a <u>fridge</u> or <u>freezer</u> lowers the temperature of the food. This <u>slows down</u> the decomposers' <u>rate of reproduction</u> (or <u>stops</u> it altogether in the case of freezing).

- Storing food in <u>airtight cans</u> stops microorganisms <u>getting in</u>. Once the food is in, the cans are <u>sealed</u>, and <u>sterilised</u> (by exposing them to a <u>high pressure</u> and <u>temperature</u>) to <u>kill</u> any microorganisms present.

- <u>Drying</u> food <u>removes</u> the <u>water</u> that microorganisms need to <u>survive</u> and <u>reproduce</u>, as does adding <u>salt</u> or <u>sugar</u>, which causes the microorganisms to <u>lose water</u> by <u>osmosis</u> (see p.21).

Ideal Conditions Are Maintained to Make Compost

Compost is <u>decomposed organic matter</u> (e.g. food waste) that is used as a <u>fertiliser</u> for crops and garden plants. It's produced quickest in <u>warm</u>, <u>moist</u> conditions when there's <u>plenty</u> of <u>oxygen</u> available. <u>Compost bins</u> create the <u>ideal conditions</u> for decomposers. For example, some have <u>mesh sides</u> to increase the <u>oxygen availability</u>. The decomposing material is kept <u>moist</u> and <u>heat</u> is generated by the decomposers themselves. Some compost bins are <u>insulated</u> to increase the <u>temperature</u> further.

You can Calculate the Rate of Decomposition

EXAMPLE: A block of cheese was left out of the fridge. The graph below shows the amount of mould that formed on the cheese. Moulds are fungi that decompose the cheese.

Calculate the average rate at which the cheese decomposed during the first week, giving your answer as units of mould day⁻¹.

1) Draw a <u>line</u> on your graph at <u>7 days</u> and <u>read off</u> the <u>amount</u> of mould that had formed.

2) <u>Divide</u> the amount of mould by the number of days. $\frac{25}{7}$

3) <u>Calculate</u> the answer and don't forget to give the <u>units</u>. = 3.6 units of mould day⁻¹

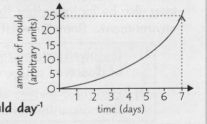

You might get asked to calculate the <u>change</u> in the <u>rate of decomposition</u> during two different time periods. To do this, just <u>subtract</u> the <u>lower</u> rate from the <u>higher</u> rate.

G, G, G, E♭, F, F, F, D — sorry, just decomposing Beethoven's 5th...

So if you want your strawberries to stay fresh, put them in the fridge... or eat them all in one go with lots of cream.

Q1   Name three things that affect the rate of decay.   [3 marks]

Topic 9 — Ecosystems and Material Cycles

Revision Questions for Topic 9

Well, that was a bit of a mucky topic if you ask me. All that <u>fieldwork</u>, <u>farming</u>, <u>bacteria</u> and <u>decomposition</u> — I feel like I need a hot bath now to freshen up a bit. Anyway, there's no lounging about in the bath for you...

- Try these questions and <u>tick off each one</u> when you <u>get it right</u>.
- When you've done <u>all the questions</u> under a heading and are <u>completely happy</u>, tick it off.

Ecosystems (p.95-98) ☑

1) Define the following terms: a) population, b) community. ☑
2) What does it mean if two species are interdependent? ☑
3) Give an example of a mutualistic relationship. ☑
4) Give two biotic factors and explain how each one could affect a community. ☑
5) Briefly describe how you could use quadrats to investigate the population size of a species. ☑
6) What is a belt transect? ☑
7) Explain why food chains rarely have more than five trophic levels. ☑
8) What does each bar on a pyramid of biomass represent? ☑
9) True or false? Producers always go at the top of a pyramid of biomass. ☑
10) What is the formula for calculating the efficiency of energy transfer between levels of a food chain? ☑

Biodiversity and Food Security (p.99-101) ☑

11) How can fertilisers lead to eutrophication? ☑
12) Give four ways in which fish farms can reduce biodiversity. ☑
13) What is a non-indigenous species? ☑
14) Give three examples of conservation schemes. ☑
15) Give three benefits of maintaining biodiversity. ☑
16) What is meant by the term 'food security'? ☑
17) Give five biological factors that affect food security. ☑

The Carbon, Water and Nitrogen Cycles (p.102-104) ☑

18) Name the process that removes carbon from the air in the carbon cycle. ☑
19) Name two processes that put carbon back into the air. ☑
20) Produce a labelled diagram of the water cycle. ☑
21) Why is the ability to produce potable water important in times of drought? ☑
22) What does desalination mean? ☑
23) Name a common method of desalination. ☑
24) Describe the role of nitrogen-fixing bacteria in the nitrogen cycle. ☑
25) What is crop rotation? Why is it beneficial to farmers? ☑

Indicator Species and Decomposition (p.105-106) ☑

26) Name two indicator species found in clean water. ☑
27) Explain how lichen are used as an indicator species. ☑
28) Explain how water content affects the rate of decay. ☑
29) Explain why cold conditions can help to preserve food. ☑
30) Give three ways to increase the rate of decomposition of compost. ☑

Safety, Ethics and Heating

There are lots of things to <u>think about</u> when you're doing an experiment, not just what you're having for tea.

Make Sure You're Working Safely in the Lab

1) <u>Before</u> you start any experiment, make sure you know about any <u>safety precautions</u> to do with your <u>method</u> or the <u>chemicals</u> you're using. You need to <u>follow</u> any instructions that your teacher gives you <u>carefully</u>. The chemicals you're using may be <u>hazardous</u> — for example, they might be <u>flammable</u> (<u>catch fire easily</u>), or they might <u>irritate</u> or <u>burn</u> your <u>skin</u> if it comes into contact with them.

2) Make sure that you're wearing <u>sensible clothing</u> when you're in the lab (e.g. open shoes won't protect your feet from spillages). When you're doing an experiment, you should wear a <u>lab coat</u> to protect your skin and clothing. Depending on the experiment, you may need to also wear <u>safety goggles</u> and <u>gloves</u>.

3) You also need to be aware of <u>general safety</u> in the lab, e.g. keep anything <u>flammable</u> away from lit Bunsen burners, don't directly touch any <u>hot equipment</u>, handle <u>glassware</u> (including microscope slides) carefully to <u>avoid breakages</u>, etc.

You Need to Think About Ethical Issues In Your Experiments

Any <u>organisms</u> involved in your investigations need to be treated <u>safely</u> and <u>ethically</u>. <u>Animals</u> need to be treated <u>humanely</u> — they should be <u>handled carefully</u> and any wild animals captured for studying should be <u>returned to their original habitat</u>. Any animals kept in the lab should also be <u>cared for</u> in a humane way, e.g. they should not be kept in conditions that are <u>too hot</u>. If you are carrying out an experiment involving other <u>students</u>, they should not be forced to participate <u>against their will</u> or feel <u>pressured</u> to take part.

Bunsen Burners Have a Naked Flame

Bunsen burners are good for <u>heating things quickly</u>. But you need to make sure you're using them <u>safely</u>:

- You should always use a Bunsen burner on a <u>heat-proof mat</u>.
- If your Bunsen burner is alight but not heating anything, make sure you <u>close</u> the hole so that the flame becomes <u>yellow</u> and <u>clearly visible</u>.
- Use the <u>blue</u> flame to heat things. If you're heating a vessel <u>in</u> the flame, hold it at the <u>top</u> (e.g. with <u>tongs</u>) and point the opening <u>away from</u> yourself (and others).
- If you're heating something <u>over</u> the flame (e.g. a beaker of water), you should put a <u>tripod and gauze</u> over the Bunsen burner before you light it, and place the vessel on this.
- Whenever you use a Bunsen burner, you should wear <u>safety goggles</u> to protect your eyes.

Heat-proof mat

Hole is closed

to gas

The Temperature of an Electric Water Bath Can Be Set

1) A <u>water bath</u> is a container filled with water that can be heated to a <u>specific temperature</u>. A <u>simple</u> water bath can be made by heating a <u>beaker of water</u> over a <u>Bunsen burner</u> and monitoring the temperature with a <u>thermometer</u> (see p.17). However, it can be hard to keep the temperature of the water <u>constant</u>.

2) An <u>electric water bath</u> will <u>monitor</u> and <u>adjust</u> the temperature for you. It's a much easier way of keeping the temperature of a reaction mixture constant. Here's how you use one:

- <u>Set</u> the temperature on the water bath, and allow the water to <u>heat up</u>.
- To make sure it's reached the right temperature, use a <u>thermometer</u>.
- Place the vessel containing your substance in the water bath using <u>test tube holders</u> or <u>tongs</u>. The level of the water outside the vessel should be <u>just above</u> the level of the substance inside the vessel.
- The substance will then be warmed to the <u>same temperature</u> as the water. As the substance in the vessel is surrounded by water, the heating is very <u>even</u>.

water bath
rack
vessel
temperature display
temperature control

Naked flames — ooo er...

Working safely and ethically is a really big part of carrying out an experiment. You need to be thinking about these things before you so much as pick up a test tube, or cut up a plant.

Measuring Substances

Get your lab coats on, it's time to find out about some of the skills you'll need in <u>experiments</u>...

Use the Right Apparatus to Take Accurate Readings

1) Length

1) <u>Length</u> can be <u>measured</u> in different <u>units</u> (e.g. mm, cm, m). Smaller units have a higher degree of <u>accuracy</u>. For example, it's more <u>accurate</u> to measure the length of a potato cylinder to the nearest <u>mm</u> than the nearest <u>cm</u>.

2) You'll need to decide on the <u>appropriate level of accuracy</u> for your experiment. For example, the length of a <u>leaf</u> would be better measured in <u>millimetres</u>, but the length of a <u>transect line</u> would be better measured in <u>metres</u>.

3) It is also important to <u>choose</u> the <u>right equipment</u> when measuring length — a <u>ruler</u> would probably be best for small things, but a <u>metre rule</u> or <u>tape measure</u> would be better for larger distances.

How big?

2) Area

In biology, you might need to measure the <u>area</u> of something (e.g. part of a habitat, a living thing). Living things are usually quite <u>complex shapes</u>, but you can make their area easier to work out by comparing them to a <u>simpler shape</u> and working out the area of that (e.g. <u>inhibition zones</u> on agar plates spread with bacteria are roughly <u>circular</u> — see p.64). To find the area of something:

1) First, you'll need to take <u>accurate measurements</u> of its dimensions.

> If you want to <u>measure</u> the area of a <u>field</u> (see page 96) that is <u>rectangular</u>, you'll need to use a <u>tape measure</u> or a <u>trundle wheel</u> to measure the <u>length</u> and <u>width</u> of the field. Record your readings in metres.

2) Then you can <u>calculate</u> its <u>area</u>.

> Area of a <u>rectangle</u> = <u>length</u> × <u>width</u>.
> So, if your field is 30 m by 55 m, the <u>area</u> would be 30 × 55 = <u>1650 m²</u>.

Don't forget the units of area are always something squared, e.g. mm².

Here are some examples of other area formulas that may come in useful:

- Area of a triangle = ½ × base × height
- Area of a circle = πr^2

3) Mass

To weigh a substance, start by putting the <u>container</u> you are weighing your substance into on a <u>balance</u>. Set the balance to exactly <u>zero</u> and then weigh out the correct amount of your substance. Easy peasy.

4) Time

1) If your experiment involves <u>timing</u> something (e.g. how long a reaction takes to happen) or taking measurements at <u>regular intervals</u>, it's probably best to use a <u>stopwatch</u>.

2) Using a <u>stopwatch</u> that measures to the nearest <u>0.1 s</u> will make your results more <u>accurate</u>.

3) Always make sure you <u>start</u> and <u>stop</u> the stopwatch at exactly the right time. For example, if you're investigating the rate of a reaction, you should start timing at the <u>exact moment</u> you mix the reagents and start the reaction.

4) It's a good idea to get the <u>same person</u> to do the timing so the results are as <u>precise</u> as possible.

5) Temperature

You can use a <u>thermometer</u> to measure temperature. Make sure that the <u>bulb</u> of the thermometer is <u>completely submerged</u> in the substance you're measuring and that you wait for the temperature to <u>stabilise</u> before you take your initial reading. Read off the <u>scale</u> on the thermometer at <u>eye level</u> to make sure your reading is correct.

When you're reading off a scale, write down the value of the graduation that the amount is closest to. If it's exactly halfway between two values, round up.

Practical Skills

Measuring Substances

6) Volume of a Liquid

There's more than one way to measure the volume of a <u>liquid</u>. Whichever method you use, always read the volume from the <u>bottom of the meniscus</u> (the curved upper surface of the liquid) when it's at <u>eye level</u>.

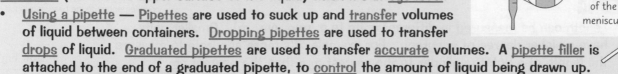

Read volume from here — the bottom of the meniscus.

- <u>Using a pipette</u> — <u>Pipettes</u> are used to suck up and <u>transfer</u> volumes of liquid between containers. <u>Dropping pipettes</u> are used to transfer <u>drops</u> of liquid. <u>Graduated pipettes</u> are used to transfer <u>accurate</u> volumes. A <u>pipette filler</u> is attached to the end of a graduated pipette, to <u>control</u> the amount of liquid being drawn up.
- <u>Using a measuring cylinder</u> — <u>Measuring cylinders</u> come in all different <u>sizes</u>. Make sure you choose one that's the right size for the measurement you want to make. It's no good using a huge 1 dm³ cylinder to measure out 2 cm³ of a liquid — the graduations will be too big, and you'll end up with <u>massive errors</u>. It'd be much better to use one that measures up to 10 cm³.

7) Volume of a Gas

1) To accurately measure the <u>volume</u> of gas, you should use a <u>gas syringe</u>.

2) Alternatively, you can use an <u>upturned measuring cylinder</u> filled with <u>water</u>. The gas will <u>displace</u> the water so you can <u>read the volume</u> off the <u>scale</u>.

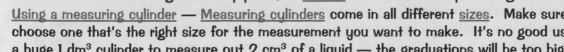

gas syringe

3) You could also <u>count the bubbles</u> of gas released. But the bubbles could be <u>different sizes</u> and if they're produced quickly you might <u>miss some</u> — so this method is <u>less accurate</u>.

4) When you're measuring a gas, you need to make sure that the equipment is set up so that none of the gas can <u>escape</u>, otherwise your results won't be <u>accurate</u>.

8) pH

The method you should use to measure pH depends on what your experiment is.

1) <u>Indicators</u> are dyes that <u>change colour</u> depending on whether they're in an <u>acid</u> or an <u>alkali</u>. You use them by adding a couple of drops of the indicator to the solution you're interested in. <u>Universal indicator</u> is a <u>mixture</u> of indicators that changes colour <u>gradually</u> as pH changes. It's useful for <u>estimating</u> the pH of a solution based on its colour.

2) <u>Indicator paper</u> is useful if you don't want to colour the entire solution that you're testing. It <u>changes colour</u> depending on the pH of the solution it touches. You can also hold a piece of <u>damp indicator paper</u> in a <u>gas sample</u> to test its pH.

Blue litmus paper turns <u>red</u> in acidic conditions and red litmus paper turns <u>blue</u> in alkaline conditions.

3) <u>pH meters</u> have a <u>digital display</u> that gives an <u>accurate value</u> for the pH of a solution.

9) Continuous Sampling

1) <u>Continuous sampling</u> is when <u>lots of samples</u> are taken at <u>regular intervals</u> over a particular time period. This means you can see what is happening <u>during the experiment</u>, not just the outcome of it.

2) Using a <u>data logger</u> connected to a computer is an <u>example</u> of continuous sampling. Data loggers can be used to measure a range of variables, including <u>temperature</u>, <u>pH</u> and <u>O₂ concentration</u>.

Make Sure You Can Draw Diagrams of Your Equipment

When you're writing out a <u>method</u> for your experiment, it's always a good idea to draw a <u>labelled diagram</u> showing how your apparatus will be <u>set up</u>. The easiest way to do this is to use a scientific drawing, where each piece of apparatus is drawn as if you're looking at its <u>cross-section</u> (with no shading or colouring). E.g.

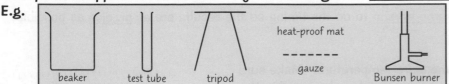

beaker   test tube   tripod   heat-proof mat   gauze   Bunsen burner

The pieces of glassware are drawn without tops so they aren't sealed. If you want to draw a closed system, remember to draw a bung in the top.

Experimentus apparatus...

Wizardry won't help you here, unfortunately. It's best you just get your head down and learn this stuff.

Answers

p.12 — Cells
Q1 a) Contains genetic material that controls the activities of the cell *[1 mark]*.
b) Where most of the reactions for respiration take place *[1 mark]*.
c) Involved in translation of genetic material in the synthesis of proteins *[1 mark]*.

p.13 — Specialised Cells
Q1 a) To transport the male's DNA to the female's egg *[1 mark]*.
b) Any two from: they have a long tail *[1 mark]* to allow the sperm cell to swim to the egg cell *[1 mark]*. / They contain lots of mitochondria *[1 mark]* to provide energy for swimming *[1 mark]* that can digest the membrane of the egg cell to deliver the DNA into the egg cell *[1 mark]*. They have a haploid nucleus *[1 mark]* so that when the sperm cell and egg cell combine at fertilisation, the resulting cell has the right number of chromosomes *[1 mark]*.

p.14 — Microscopy
Q1 Select the lowest-powered objective lens *[1 mark]* and move the stage up so the slide is just underneath the objective lens *[1 mark]*. Looking through the lens, move the stage downwards until the specimen is nearly in focus *[1 mark]*. Adjust the height of the stage with the fine adjustment knob until the image is in focus *[1 mark]*.

p.15 — More Microscopy
Q1 real size = image size ÷ magnification
= 7 × 10^{-1} mm (or 0.7 mm) ÷ 400 *[1 mark]*
= 0.00175 mm *[1 mark]*
× 1000 = 1.75 µm *[1 mark]*

p.16 — Enzymes
Q1 If the pH is too high or too low, it can interfere with the bonds holding the enzyme together. This changes the shape of the active site *[1 mark]* and denatures the enzyme *[1 mark]*.

p.17 — More on Enzymes
Q1 33 ÷ 60 = 0.55 cm^3 s^{-1} *[1 mark]*

p.18 — Enzymes in Breakdown and Synthesis
Q1 a) simple sugars *[1 mark]*
b) amino acids *[1 mark]*

p.19 — Testing for Biological Molecules
Q1 Proteins are present *[1 mark]*.

p.20 — Energy in Food
Q1 To minimise the energy transferred to the environment *[1 mark]*.

p.21 — Diffusion, Osmosis and Active Transport
Q1 E.g. active transport requires energy and diffusion is passive *[1 mark]*. Active transport moves substances against a concentration gradient whereas diffusion is the movement of substances down a concentration gradient *[1 mark]*.

p.22 — Investigating Osmosis
Q1 percentage change $= \frac{11.4 - 13.3}{13.3} \times 100$
= -14.3% *[2 marks for correct answer, 1 mark for correct answer without minus sign]*

p.24 — Mitosis
Q1 The cell grows and increases the amount of subcellular structures it has *[1 mark]*. It also duplicates its DNA *[1 mark]*.

p.25 — Cell Division and Growth
Q1 a) cell elongation *[1 mark]*
b) Cell elongation makes a plant's cells expand so the cells get bigger (and the plant grows) *[1 mark]*.

p.26 — Stem Cells
Q1 The tips of plant shoots contain meristem tissue *[1 mark]*. Meristems produce unspecialised cells that are able to divide and form any cell type in the plant *[1 mark]*. This means the plant is able to produce all the different specialised cells it needs in order to grow into a new plant *[1 mark]*.

p.27 — The Brain and Spinal Cord
Q1 a) E.g. it controls unconscious activities. / It controls breathing. / It controls heart rate. *[1 mark]*
b) E.g. it is responsible for muscle coordination / balance *[1 mark]*.

p.28 — The Nervous System
Q1 A sensory neurone has one long dendron and one short axon *[1 mark]* with a cell body in the middle *[1 mark]*. The function of a sensory neurone is to carry nerve impulses from receptor cells to the CNS *[1 mark]*.

p.29 — Synapses and Reflexes
Q1 Impulses are sent from receptors in his hand along a sensory neurone to the CNS *[1 mark]*. The impulse is transferred across a synapse to a relay neurone *[1 mark]* via the release of neurotransmitters *[1 mark]*. It is then transferred across another synapse to a motor neurone *[1 mark]* and travels along the motor neurone to the effector (a muscle in his arm) *[1 mark]*.

p.30 — The Eye
Q1 The lens may be the wrong shape / the eyeball may be too short *[1 mark]*, meaning that light from near objects is brought into focus behind the retina *[1 mark]*.

p.32 — Sexual Reproduction and Meiosis
Q1 24 chromosomes *[1 mark]*
Q2 When the cell divides, some of the chromosomes from the organism's father and some of the chromosomes from the organism's mother go into each new cell *[1 mark]*. The mixing up of the chromosomes/genes creates genetic variation *[1 mark]*.

p.33 — Asexual and Sexual Reproduction
Q1 E.g. reproducing asexually can produce lots of offspring very quickly so the strawberry plant could colonise an area very rapidly *[1 mark]*. It also means that the strawberry plant can take advantage of good conditions for growth without needing a mate *[1 mark]*. However, asexual reproduction produces genetically identical organisms *[1 mark]*. This means that if environmental conditions change, making it difficult for the strawberry plant to survive, the whole population of strawberry plants could be affected *[1 mark]*.

p.34 — DNA
Q1 A and T *[1 mark]*.
C and G *[1 mark]*.
Q2 The salt helps the DNA to stick together *[1 mark]*.

p.35 — Protein Synthesis
Q1 The order of bases in a gene determines the order of amino acids in a protein *[1 mark]*. Each gene contains a different order of bases, which the gene can code for a particular protein *[1 mark]*.
Q2 A genetic variant could alter the sequence of amino acids coded for by a gene *[1 mark]*, which could affect the shape of the protein, decreasing its activity *[1 mark]*.

p.36 — More on Protein Synthesis
Q1 RNA polymerase binds to a region of non-coding DNA in front of the gene to be transcribed *[1 mark]*. The two strands of DNA unzip and the RNA polymerase moves along the coding DNA *[1 mark]*. As the RNA polymerase moves along, it joins together RNA molecules that are complementary to the base sequence of the coding DNA *[1 mark]*.

p.37 — The Work of Mendel
Q1 Scientists of the time didn't have the background knowledge to properly understand Mendel's findings because they didn't know about genes, DNA and chromosomes *[1 mark]*.

p.38 — Genetic Diagrams
Q1 Your genotype is the combination of alleles you have *[1 mark]*. Your phenotype is the characteristics you have *[1 mark]*.

p.39 — More Genetic Diagrams
Q1 Ff and ff *[1 mark]*.

p.40 — Sex-Linked Genetic Disorders
Q1 a) 1 in 4/25% *[1 mark]*.
(There's a 50% chance of the couple having a boy and a 50% chance of that boy having haemophilia. You can draw a genetic diagram if it helps:

	X^H	Y
X^H	X^{H}X^H	X^{H}Y
X^h	X^{H}X^h	(X^{h}Y)

The circled offspring is a boy with haemophilia.)
b) 0% *[1 mark]*

p.41 — Inheritance of Blood Groups
Q1 The mother must have the genotype I^{A}O *[1 mark]* and the father must have the genotype I^{B}O *[1 mark]* to produce a child with the genotype I^{O}I^O and blood group O *[1 mark]*.

p.42 — Variation
Q1 It results in new combinations of alleles in offspring *[1 mark]*.

p.43 — The Human Genome Project
Q1 A person's genes can be used to help predict what diseases they're most at risk of developing *[1 mark]*. This means that they could be given lifestyle and diet advice to help prevent them from getting the diseases *[1 mark]*.

p.45 — Natural Selection and Evidence for Evolution
Q1 Arranging fossils in chronological/date order shows gradual changes/development in organisms *[1 mark]*.

p.46 — Darwin and Wallace
Q1 Wallace provided evidence for natural selection *[1 mark]* and worked with Darwin to develop the theory *[1 mark]*.

p.47 — Fossil Evidence for Human Evolution
Q1 Any three from: e.g. Lucy's feet were more arched than Ardi's / had no ape-like big toe unlike Ardi's. / Lucy's arms and legs were more human-like than Ardi's. / Lucy had a bigger brain than Ardi. / The structure of Lucy's leg bones and feet suggest she was more efficient at walking upright than Ardi. *[1 mark for each correct statement. Maximum 3 marks.]*

p.48 — More Evidence for Evolution
Q1 a) That they belong to a more recent species, like *Homo neanderthalis* / *Homo sapiens* *[1 mark]*.
b) E.g. using stratigraphy. / Using carbon-14 dating to date any carbon-containing material found with the tools. *[1 mark]*

p.49 — Classification

Q1 E.g. RNA/DNA sequencing showed that Archaea and Bacteria were less closely related than first thought *[1 mark]*.

p.50 — Selective Breeding

Q1 E.g. selective breeding reduces the gene pool *[1 mark]*. This can cause an increased chance of organisms inheriting harmful genetic defects *[1 mark]*. There is also an increased chance that a population could be wiped out by a new disease *[1 mark]*.

p.51 — Tissue Culture

Q1 E.g. remove pieces of tissue from fast-growing regions/the shoot tips of the tree *[1 mark]*. Place the tissue in a growth medium containing nutrients and growth hormones *[1 mark]*, under aseptic conditions *[1 mark]*. Once the tissue has grown roots and shoots, place the young plant in compost to allow it to grow further *[1 mark]*.

p.52 — Genetic Engineering

Q1 It can improve the yield of the crop *[1 mark]*, because herbicide-resistant crops can be sprayed with herbicides to kill weeds without the crop being damaged *[1 mark]*.

p.53 — GMOs and Human Population Growth

Q1 E.g. use of GM crops with improved yields *[1 mark]*, use of fertilisers on poor soils *[1 mark]*, use of biological pest control methods *[1 mark]*.

p.55 — Health and Disease

Q1 The Ebola virus is spread via bodily fluids *[1 mark]*. Its spread can be prevented by isolating infected individuals *[1 mark]* and sterilising any areas where the virus may be present *[1 mark]*.

p.56 — Viruses and STIs

Q1 The virus attaches to a specific host cell and injects its genetic material into the cell *[1 mark]*. It then uses enzymes/proteins in the host cell to replicate its genetic material and make components of new viruses *[1 mark]*. The viral components assemble *[1 mark]* and the host cell splits open and releases them *[1 mark]*.

p.57 — Plant Diseases

Q1 E.g. leaves/stems have a waxy cuticle *[1 mark]*. Cells are surrounded by a cellulose cell wall *[1 mark]*.

p.58 — Fighting Disease

Q1 They have cells that produce mucus to trap pathogens *[1 mark]*. They have cells with cilia *[1 mark]*, which waft the mucus up to the back of the throat where it can be swallowed *[1 mark]*.

Q2 A type of white blood cell that is involved in the specific immune response/produces antibodies *[1 mark]*.

p.59 — Memory Lymphocytes and Immunisation

Q1 Memory lymphocytes are produced in response to a foreign antigen and remain in the body for a long time *[1 mark]*. So when the pathogen enters the body again, there are more cells that recognise it and can produce antibodies against it *[1 mark]*.

p.60 — Monoclonal Antibodies

Q1 A (mouse) B-lymphocyte *[1 mark]* and a tumour cell/myeloma cell *[1 mark]*.

p.61 — More on Monoclonal Antibodies

Q1 Cancer cells have proteins on their surface that aren't found on normal body cells, called tumour markers *[1 mark]*. You can make monoclonal antibodies that will bind to these tumour markers *[1 mark]*. An anti-cancer drug can be attached to these monoclonal antibodies *[1 mark]*. The antibodies target the cancer cells and the drug kills them, but leave the normal body cells unaffected *[1 mark]*.

p.62 — Antibiotics and Other Medicines

Q1 In a double-blind trial, patients are randomly put into two groups — some receive the drug and some receive a placebo *[1 mark]*. Neither the patient nor the doctor knows whether the patient is getting the drug or a placebo until all of the results have been gathered *[1 mark]*.

p.64 — Investigating Antibiotics and Antiseptics

Q1 a) A *[1 mark]*

b) diameter = 13 mm
radius = 13 ÷ 2 = 6.5 mm *[1 mark]*
$\pi r^2 = \pi \times 6.5^2 = 132.7...$
= 133 mm^2 *[1 mark]*

c) E.g. a paper disc that has not been soaked in antiseptic *[1 mark]*.

d) To show that any difference in the growth of the bacteria is only due to the effect of the antiseptic *[1 mark]*.

p.65 — Non-Communicable Diseases

Q1 E.g. smoking / diet high in saturated fat / drinking too much alcohol / not enough exercise / obesity *[1 mark]*.

p.66 — Measures of Obesity

Q1 a) Beginning: 76.0 kg ÷ 1.58 m^2
= 30.4 kg m^{-2} *[1 mark]*
End: 73.0 kg ÷ 1.58 m^2 = 29.2 kg m^{-2} *[1 mark]*

b) Before: moderately obese *[1 mark]*
After: overweight *[1 mark]*

p.67 — Treatments for Cardiovascular Disease

Q1 E.g. having heart surgery is a major procedure with a risk of bleeding, blood clots and infection *[1 mark]*. If making lifestyle changes or taking medicines are an option, then these are much less risky *[1 mark]*.

p. 69 — Photosynthesis

Q1 Photosynthesis produces glucose *[1 mark]*, which is used to make larger, complex molecules that make up the mass of the plant's living material/the plant's biomass *[1 mark]*.

Q2 Temperature, light intensity and carbon dioxide concentration *[1 mark for each]*.

p.70 — Limiting Factors in Photosynthesis

Q1 The rate of photosynthesis increases with increasing light intensity/is directly proportional to light intensity *[1 mark]* up to a point at which the rate levels off *[1 mark]*.

p.71 — Transport in Plants

Q1 Water is lost from a plant's leaves by evaporation and diffusion *[1 mark]*. This creates a slight shortage of water in the leaves, so more water is drawn up through the xylem vessels to replace it *[1 mark]*. This in turn means there's more water drawn up from the roots, so there's a constant transpiration stream through the plant *[1 mark]*.

p.72 — Stomata and Transpiration

Q1 In low light conditions, the stomata begin to close *[1 mark]*. This means that very little water can escape *[1 mark]*, so the rate of transpiration and therefore the rate of water uptake by the plant decreases *[1 mark]*.

p.73 — Adaptations of Leaves and Plants

Q1 Spines provide a smaller surface area than broad leaves, so less water is lost through evaporation *[1 mark]*. Spines help to stop animals eating the cacti to get water *[1 mark]*. Spines help to reduce air flow near the surface of the plant, so less water is lost through evaporation *[1 mark]*.

p.74 — Plant Hormones

Q1 the roots *[1 mark]*

p.75 — Commercial Uses of Plant Hormones

Q1 Any one from: e.g. they can be used to control flower/fruit formation. / They can be used to produce seedless fruits. / They can be used to control seed germination. *[1 mark]*

p. 77 — Hormones

Q1 testes *[1 mark]*

p.78 — Adrenaline and Thyroxine

Q1 thyroid gland *[1 mark]*

Q2 TRH stimulates the pituitary gland to release thyroid stimulating hormone/TSH *[1 mark]*. TSH stimulates the thyroid gland to release thyroxine, so the blood thyroxine level rises *[1 mark]*.

p.79 — The Menstrual Cycle

Q1 LH stimulates the release of an egg/ovulation *[1 mark]*. It also stimulates the remains of the follicle to develop into a corpus luteum *[1 mark]*, which secretes progesterone *[1 mark]*.

p.80 — Controlling Fertility

Q1 FSH *[1 mark]* and LH *[1 mark]* are given before egg collection to stimulate egg production *[1 mark]*.

p.81 — Homeostasis — Control of Blood Glucose

Q1 Insulin *[1 mark]* is secreted by the pancreas into the bloodstream *[1 mark]*. The insulin causes glucose to move into the liver and muscle cells, so the concentration in the blood returns to normal *[1 mark]*.

p.82 — Diabetes

Q1 Type 1 diabetes is caused when the pancreas produces little or no insulin *[1 mark]*.

Q2 E.g. body mass index/BMI *[1 mark]*, waist-to-hip ratio *[1 mark]*.

p.83 — Thermoregulation

Q1 Less blood flows near the surface of the skin *[1 mark]* because vasoconstriction occurs in the blood vessels near the surface *[1 mark]*.

p.84 — Osmoregulation and The Kidneys

Q1 They filter the blood *[1 mark]*.

p.85 — More on The Kidneys

Q1 It allows ions and waste substances to diffuse out of the blood into the dialysis fluid *[1 mark]*, but not large molecules like proteins (so they won't be lost from the blood) *[1 mark]*.

p.87 — Exchange of Materials

Q1 Surface area:
(1 × 1) × 2 = 2
(4 × 1) × 4 = 16
2 + 16 = 18 µm^2 *[1 mark]*
Volume:
1 × 1 × 4 = 4 µm^3 *[1 mark]*
So the surface area to volume ratio is 18 : 4, which is 9 : 2 in its simplest form *[1 mark]*.
(In this question the ratio has been simplified down to the smallest whole numbers. It's not in the form n : 1 because then n would not be a whole number.)

p.88 — Diffusion and the Alveoli

Q1 Any one from: e.g. they have a large surface area. / They have a moist lining for dissolving gases. / They have very thin walls. / They have a good blood supply *[1 mark]*.

p.89 — Circulatory System — Blood

Q1 They help the blood to clot at a wound, to stop blood pouring out/microorganisms getting in *[1 mark]*.

Q2 They have a large surface area for absorbing oxygen *[1 mark]*. They don't have a nucleus, which allows more room for carrying oxygen *[1 mark]*. They contain haemoglobin, which can combine with oxygen in the lungs and release it in body tissues *[1 mark]*.

p.90 — Circulatory System — Blood Vessels

Q1 They have a big lumen to help the blood flow despite the low pressure *[1 mark]* and they have valves to keep the blood flowing in the right direction *[1 mark]*.

Q2 It increases the rate of diffusion of substances across them between the blood and cells *[1 mark]*.

p.91 — Circulatory System — The Heart

Q1 stroke volume = cardiac output ÷ heart rate
= 4221 cm³ min⁻¹ ÷ 67 bpm
= 63 cm³ *[2 marks for the correct answer, or 1 mark for the correct calculation]*

p.92 — Respiration

Q1 The leg muscles didn't get enough oxygen during the sprint, so began to use anaerobic respiration *[1 mark]*. This resulted in the production of lactic acid *[1 mark]*. The build up of lactic acid in the muscles caused cramp *[1 mark]*.

p.93 — Investigating Respiration

Q1 a) E.g. a test tube with glass beads that are the same mass as the germinating beans *[1 mark]*. (You could use boiled beans instead of glass beads.)

b) A series of water baths each set to a different temperature *[1 mark]*.

p.95 — Ecosystems and Interactions Between Organisms

Q1 Any two from: temperature / amount of water / light intensity / levels of pollutants *[1 mark for each correct answer, up to 2 marks]*

p.96 — Investigating Ecosystems

Q1 Quadrats could be placed in a line across the habitat, forming a belt transect *[1 mark]*. Data could then be collected from the quadrats *[1 mark]*. These two steps should be repeated in the same area and a mean should be calculated for each quadrat *[1 mark]*.

p.97 — Ecosystems and Energy Transfers

Q1 Any two from: e.g. organisms use it in respiration. / It is transferred to the surroundings by heat. / Organisms don't always eat every part of the organism they're consuming. / Some of the organism being eaten may be indigestible. *[1 mark for each correct answer, up to 2 marks]*

p.98 — More on Ecosystems and Energy Transfers

Q1 The hoverfly larvae are the third trophic level in this food chain. They transfer 850 kJ to the next trophic level. 9000 kJ was available at the second trophic level (the blackflies).

$$= \frac{850}{9000} \times 100$$

= 9.44%
[1 mark for 850 ÷ 9000, 1 mark for correct answer]

p.99 — Human Impacts on Biodiversity

Q1 Non-indigenous species may out-compete indigenous species for resources, so that the indigenous species decreases in number or dies out *[1 mark]*. Non-indigenous species can also bring new diseases to a habitat, which can infect and kill the indigenous species *[1 mark]*.

p.100 — Conservation and Biodiversity

Q1 Reforestation increases biodiversity in deforested areas *[1 mark]* because it increases the number of tree species in an area *[1 mark]*, which provide food and shelter for animal species *[1 mark]*.

p.101 — Food Security

Q1 E.g. the outbreak of a new crop pathogen could result in damage to crops, causing a reduction in yields *[1 mark]*. Less food means a lower level of food security *[1 mark]*.

p.102 — The Carbon Cycle

Q1 Microorganisms in the carbon cycle are decomposers *[1 mark]*. They break down dead organisms and waste products *[1 mark]* and release CO_2 through respiration as they do so *[1 mark]*.

p.103 — The Water Cycle

Q1 Energy from the Sun makes water from the sea evaporate, turning it into water vapour *[1 mark]*. The water vapour is carried upwards, as warm air rises *[1 mark]*. When it gets higher up, it cools and condenses to form clouds *[1 mark]*. Water then falls from the clouds as precipitation, usually as rain *[1 mark]*.

p.104 — The Nitrogen Cycle

Q1 Decomposers turn proteins in dead leaves into ammonia *[1 mark]*. Then nitrifying bacteria turn the ammonia into nitrites *[1 mark]* and then into nitrates *[1 mark]*.

p.105 — Indicator Species

Q1 The fungus is very sensitive to the level of sulfur dioxide in the air *[1 mark]* so its presence indicates that the air is clean *[1 mark]*.

p.106 — Decomposition

Q1 Temperature *[1 mark]*, water content *[1 mark]* and oxygen availability *[1 mark]*.

Index

A

abiotic factors 95
accuracy 6
acquired characteristics 42
active transport 21
ADH (anti-diuretic hormone) 85
adrenal glands 77, 78
adrenaline 78
aerobic respiration 92
AIDS 56
alcohol 65
alleles 38-42
alveoli 88
amino acids 18, 35
amylase 17
anaerobic respiration 92
animal cells 12
anomalous results 6
antibiotic resistance 45
antibiotics 62
   investigating 63, 64
antibodies 58-61, 89
antigens 58, 59
antiseptics 57
   investigating 63, 64
apparatus in experiments 108-110
Ardi (fossil) 47
arteries 90
aseptic techniques 63
asexual reproduction 24, 33
Assisted Reproductive
      Technology (ART) 80
autoclaves 63
auxins 74, 75

B

averages 7
axons 28

Bacillus thuringiensis (Bt) 53
bacteria 12, 49, 55
   cultures of 63, 64
bar charts 7
bases (DNA) 34, 35
belt transects 96
Benedict's reagent 19
biodiversity 99, 100
biofuels 101
biological molecules 18, 19
biological pest control 53
biomass 69, 97
biotic factors 95
biuret test (for proteins) 19
blood 89
   groups 41
   vessels 90
B-lymphocytes 58-60
BMI (body mass index) 66, 82
brain 27

C

calorimetry 20
cancer 25
   diagnosis and treatment 61
capillaries 90
carbohydrates 18
carbon cycle 102
cardiac output 91
cardiovascular disease 65, 67
cataracts 30

cell

   cycle 24
   division 24, 25
   membranes 12, 21
   structure 12
   walls 12
central nervous system 27-29
Chalara ash dieback 55
Chlamydia 56
chloroplasts 12, 69
cholera 55
chromosomes 24, 34
ciliated epithelial cells 13
circulatory system 89-91
classification 49
clinical testing 62
clomifene therapy 80
codominant alleles 41
colour blindness 30, 40
communicable diseases 55
communication of ideas 3
communities 95
competition 95
compost 106
conclusions 10
conservation 100
continuous sampling 110
contraceptives 80
control experiments 5
control variables 5
converting units 9, 15
correlations 8, 10
crop rotation 104
CT scanners 27

D

Darwin, Charles 46
data loggers 110
decomposition 102, 104, 106
   calculating the rate of 106
dependent variables 5
desalination 103
diabetes 82
dialysis 85
differentiation 25, 26
diffusion 21
   factors affecting rate 88
diploid cells 24, 32
disease 55
DNA 34-36
   extraction from fruit 34
dominant alleles 38
drug development and testing 62

E

Ebola 55
ecosystems 95
   investigating 96
effectors 28, 29
egg cells 13, 32
emulsion test (for lipids) 19
endocrine glands 77
energy (in food) 20
energy transfers (in ecosystems) 97, 98
enzymes 16-18
   investigating activity 17
erythrocytes 89
ethene 75
ethical issues 3, 108

eukaryotic cells 12
eutrophication 99
evaluations 11
evolution 45-48
exchange surfaces 87, 88
eyes 30

F

family pedigrees 39
fatty acids 18
fertilisation 32
fertilisers 53, 99, 104
Fick's Law 88
fight or flight response 78
fish farms 99
five kingdom classification 49
food
  chains 97, 98
  preservation 106
  security 53, 101
fossils 45, 47
FSH 79, 80
fungi 55, 102, 106

G

gametes 32
gas exchange
  humans 88
  plants 72, 73
genes 34, 35
genetically modified organisms
    (GMOs) 52, 53
genetic
  diagrams 38-41
  engineering 52
  variants 35
  variation 42
genomes 34
gibberellins 75
glucagon 81
glucose 69, 81, 92
glycerol 18
graphs 8
gravitropism 74
growth 25

H

haploid cells 13, 32
hazards 4
health 55
heart (structure of) 91
herd immunity 59
heterozygous organisms 38
HIV 56
homeostasis 81
homozygous organisms 38
hormones 77-81
human evolution 47, 48
Human Genome Project 43
human population growth 53, 101
hybridomas 60
hypothalamus 78, 83
hypotheses 2, 5

I

immune system 58, 59
immunisations 59
independent variables 5
indicator species 105
inhibition zones 63, 64
inoculating loops 63
insulin 81, 82
interdependence 95

interphase 24
inverse square law 70
iodine test (for starch) 17, 19
IVF 80

K

kidneys 84, 85

L

Leakey's fossils 47
leaves (adaptations of) 73
LH 79, 80
limiting factors (photosynthesis)
    69, 70
lipids 18, 19
liver disease 65
long-sightedness 30
Lucy (fossil) 47
lymphocytes 58-60, 89
lysogenic pathway 56
lysozymes 58
lytic pathway 56

M

magnification 15
malaria 55
malnutrition 65
mass transport systems 87
mean (average) 7
meiosis 32
memory lymphocytes 59
Mendel, Gregor 37
menstrual cycle 79
meristems 26
microscopes 14, 15
mitochondria 12
mitosis 24, 25
models 2
monoclonal antibodies 60, 61
monohybrid inheritance 38, 39
motor neurones 28, 29
mRNA 36
mutations 35, 42
mutualism 95
myelin sheaths 28

N

natural selection 45, 46
negative feedback 78, 81, 85
nephrons 84
nervous system 28
neurones 27-29
neurotransmitters 29
nitrogen cycle 104
non-coding DNA 35, 36
non-communicable diseases
    55, 65
non-indigenous species 99
nuclei 12
nucleotides 34

O

obesity 65, 66, 82
oestrogen 79, 80
osmoregulation 84, 85
osmosis 21
  investigating 22
ovaries 77, 79

P

pancreas 77, 81
parasitism 95

pathogens 55
  defences against 57, 58
peer review 2
pentadactyl limbs 48
percentile charts 25
PET scanners 27
phagocytes 89
phenotypes 38, 42
phloem 71, 73
photosynthesis 69, 70
  investigating rate 69
phototropism 74
pituitary gland 77-79, 85
plant
  cells 12
  defences against disease 57
  extracts 64
  hormones 74, 75
plasma 89
plasmids 12, 52
platelets 89
pollution 95, 105
populations 95, 96
precision 6
preclinical testing 62
predation 95
predictions 2, 5
pregnancy tests 60
progesterone 79, 80
prokaryotic cells 12
proteins 18, 19
protein synthesis 35, 36
protists 49, 55
Punnett squares 38
pyramids of biomass 97

Q

quadrats 96

R

random errors 6
random sampling 96
range (of data) 7
rates of reaction 10, 17
receptors 28, 29
recessive alleles 38
red blood cells 89
reducing sugars 19
reflexes 29
reforestation 100
relay neurones 28, 29
repeatability 5, 6
reproducibility 5, 6
resolution 6, 14
respiration 92
  investigating rate 93
reverse osmosis 103
ribosomes 12, 36
risk factors for disease 65
risks 4
RNA polymerase 36
root hair cells 71

S

safety in experiments 4, 108
sample size 5
scientific drawings 14, 110
secondary immune response 59
selective breeding 50
sensory neurones 28, 29
sex determination 39
sex-linked disorders 40

sexual reproduction 13, 32, 33
short-sightedness 30
significant figures 7
S.I. units 9
smoking 65
specialised cells 13, 26
specific immune response 58
sperm cells 13, 32
spinal cord 27
standard form 15
starch 17-19
stem cells 26
stimuli 28, 29
STIs 56
stomach ulcers 55
stomata 72, 73
stone tools 48
sub-cellular structures 12
surface area to volume ratios 87
sustainability 101
synapses 29
systematic errors 6

T

tables (of data) 7
testes 77
thermoregulation 83
three domain classification 49
thyroid gland 77, 78
thyroxine 78
tissue culture 51
transcription and translation 36
translocation 71
transpiration 71, 72
tRNA 36
trophic levels 97
tuberculosis 55

U

uncertainties 11
units 9
urea 84
urinary system 84

V

vacuoles 12
validity 5
valves 90, 91
variables 5
variation 42
vasoconstriction and dilation 83
vectors
  in disease 55
  in genetic engineering 52
veins 90
viruses 55, 56

W

waist-to-hip ratios 66, 82
Wallace, Alfred Russel 46
water cycle 103
water uptake (plants) 72
white blood cells 58, 59, 89
World Health Organisation
    (WHO) 55

X

X and Y chromosomes 39, 40
xylem 71, 73

Z

zero errors 6
zygotes 32

Index